the practical rock &
water garden

the practical rock &
water garden

A step-by-step guide from planning and construction to plants and planting

Peter Robinson

HERMES
HOUSE

C O N

This edition published by
Hermes House in 2002

© Anness Publishing Limited 2001, 2002

Hermes House is an imprint of
Anness Publishing Limited
Hermes House
88–89 Blackfriars Road
London SE1 8HA

A CIP catalogue record for this book is
available from the British Library.

Publisher Joanna Lorenz
Managing Editor Judith Simons
Executive Editor Caroline Davison
Designer Kathryn Gammon
Editorial Reader Jan Cutler
Production Controller Wendy Lawson

Previously published as
Rock and Water Gardening

1 2 3 4 5 6 7 8 9 10

Page 1: Waterlily (*Nymphaea*).
Page 2: A dramatic waterfall.
Page 3: A cascade falling into a stream.
Page 4: *Persicaria bistorta* 'Superba' (top
right). *Iris foetidus* (bottom right)
Page 5: A drilled rock fountain (top left);
a gushing cascade (top right); a rocky
waterfall (bottom right).

T E N T S

There is a strong affinity between rock and water, and creating a successful partnership between these

INTRODUCTION

two elements is one of the most challenging, but rewarding, tasks in garden design and construction. Rock and water have been used in gardens by various cultures, and these features can be recreated in every type of space, from small city rooftops to large, country gardens.

OPPOSITE: **A seat in an informal garden provides the perfect vantage point from which to view this delightful pool.**

WHY ROCK AND WATER?

OPPOSITE: **Lush, exotic-looking planting along the edge of a cascading watercourse can create an enticingly tropical effect.**

BELOW: **Making a watercourse with slate is one of the most creative challenges in water gardening. Note how the angular strata of the slate pieces are parallel.**

Dig a hole in your garden and you begin a process that can change your life. Make the hole watertight, add water and you have a pool. Shape the excavated soil and use your imagination to add rocks, and a rocky water feature evolves. Add plants, and a water garden is born. As soon as you decide to break away from the stereotype of a pool circumscribed by irregular paving or evenly shaped paving slabs, there are unparalleled opportunities to be creative with natural materials.

THE APPEAL OF ROCK AND WATER

Working with rock and water is an artistic process that does not lend itself to the quick-fix, self-assembly package. An artist knows how important it is to spend time on establishing the initial framework; artists do not take shortcuts or scrimp on costs at this stage. Simplicity is one of the keys to success in a good design, and boldness in the initial design is important. For this reason, explore all possible options in natural materials and be confident with your initial outline. This may mean that a large part of your budget is used

on equipment that allows you to use larger stones. Even apparently inaccessible sites can have large rocks slung in by a road crane, and a small cultivator can be lifted in at the same time to help with excavating and positioning. There are few schemes in which including a few large rocks will not have more impact than using a greater number of smaller rocks, all the same size and shape, and it is not true that larger pieces are appropriate only in large gardens: one large piece of rock in or near a pool in a small courtyard can have great impact.

No matter how small the size of the water feature, it it is important to think about the selection of each rock, how it is presented to its neighbours, the way the faces are positioned, how deeply it is buried and which side is uppermost. If you do not take this trouble, the beauty of each individual rock may not be seen, and a substantial combination of pieces will quickly look unco-ordinated and unnatural. For this reason a gardener may be deterred from attempting a scheme that combines rock and water in favour of a water feature that can be placed in the hands of a landscape contractor or built on a do-it-yourself basis, where the skills required may seem less daunting. The rewards resulting from creating a successful water and rock garden are so great, however, that they more than outweigh any problems that the process may present.

The main essentials to creating a rock and water feature are having an appreciation of the natural landscape and, at a practical level, having some help in lifting the rocks if they are large. Every natural rock pool, stream, river or pool has its own beauty, and each person will interpret these features in a different way. Ideally, the scheme should carry the imprint of your own character, so there is much to be said for playing a direct part in its design. Once the rocks are in position and the water feature is established, it takes a brave person to dismantle the scheme to make adjustments.

It is essential, therefore, that the initial placing is right and that you do not rely on planting to disguise weaknesses. If you are happy with the skeleton of the scheme before any plants are used, you will be doubly satisfied when the plants begin to become established and clothe the rocks.

There is now a greater range of materials and plants available than ever before and nowhere is this variety more apparent than in the availability of natural rocks

and materials for building and refining a water feature. Because of the cost of transportation, the choice of rock used to be determined by the proximity of quarries. Now, most good garden centres offer a good range of rock-garden stone and cobbles, and you can select individual rock pieces for even size and weight. You will find an even better selection of rocks if you are prepared to visit specialist suppliers. Because the rocks are likely to have the greatest influence on the overall character of a water garden, choosing individual rocks can be one of the most exciting parts of the early planning.

Given the importance and long-term impact that the choice and size of rock will have, make this a key decision and allocate it the lion's share of the budget. It

BELOW: **Rigid attention to the choice and placing of hard landscape features is a feature of oriental gardens. The *shishi-odoshi* or Japanese deer scarer provides added interest with its sound and movement.**

is comparatively easy to relocate or replace plants if you are unhappy with their position after the planting has settled in. Moving or changing a rock is not easy, and it is better to postpone a scheme altogether rather than choose the bones of your water garden too hastily.

A well-made water garden is a joy and will give increasing pleasure as the scheme becomes established. Plants can be added, changed, pruned or thinned. Bogs or beds for moisture-lovers can be added, and areas of marginal planting can be established. Specimen trees can be planted to add winter reflection. The planting is, in a sense, the icing on the cake, and it should be the final task that brings the scheme alive.

INFLUENCE OF THE ORIENT

The Chinese and, later, the Japanese were masters of the art of using water and rock. The Chinese garden was strongly linked to the poetic and artistic ethos, and their religion taught the Chinese to revere nature and to regard the garden as a bond with it. The most powerful symbols of nature were mountains and lakes, and this natural contrast was reflected in the garden through the use of rock and water. This contrast echoed the Taoist principle of yin and yang, the unity of opposites, and even in smaller courtyard gardens, a large rock would be included to represent a mountain beside a small pool.

The rocks selected were usually weatherworn limestones, sometimes with quite grotesque shapes, that were dredged out from the bottom of lakes. The rough, towering mountains were more easily represented by the use of eroded rocks, and the holes worn in the rocks over time allowed the light and shadow in the crevices to have maximum effect as a picture. A single rock was used in much the same way as a large statue in Western gardens, and it would be carefully positioned so that it could be admired from every side.

From the Chinese garden sprang the Japanese style, which was greatly influenced by priests returning from China after studying Zen Buddhism. The Japanese shared with the Chinese a veneration for nature, but they refined their gardens with a greater use of symbolism and resorted to the strict placement of ornaments and planting. Unlike the Chinese garden, which was planned as a series of pictures, the Japanese garden was made into one complete whole, with one of a series of disciplined styles predominating.

Instead of copying nature in their gardens, the Japanese strove to capture its essence. Water and rock were equally important, with islands and pools

fed by waterfalls or water rushing through rocks. Waterfalls were greatly admired, and many large landscape gardens were dominated by a carefully sited waterfall. Such features were generally located away from the main house, falling from a valley between two mountains with a background of dense forest. Where there was no water available, a rocky bed would be created to give the appearance of a dried river bed and to represent water.

The symbolism employed in the placing of stones, lanterns and bridges, so important and obvious to the trained Japanese eye, was lost to all but a few gardeners from the West. But even though their significance was not always understood, this did not prevent these gardens from being greatly admired.

OTHER INFLUENCES

Although it might be argued that the oriental influence has had the greatest impact on the use of rock and water in modern garden design, earlier influences from Islam had an equally strong impact on the formal use of water. Early Islamic gardens provided relief and refreshment from the searing heat. Water was formed into long, canal-like features, with nearby pathways and plants forming strict geometrical patterns. This influence spread to southern Spain. Indeed, one of the best-known examples of the use of canals and fountains can be seen at the fortress palace of Alhambra.

This refreshing use of formal water, so well perfected by the Islamic style, was further refined between the 15th and 18th centuries in northern India by the Mogul Emperors. Again there were the traditional canals in symmetrical patterns, but these Indian gardens particularly excelled in exploiting hillside situations to use the consequent water pressure for the most exhilarating fountains and spouts.

The romantic water garden, however, was perfected by the Romans who used water lavishly with statuary and ambitious planting. The gardens of the Renaissance, which centred on Rome, became famous for the noise and movement of water on a grand scale, and fountain design became an art form. Examples can be seen at the Villa d'Este, where ingenious design produced spouting dragons, water organs and the famous pathway of a hundred fountains.

In the latter part of the 15th century, the influence of the Italian Renaissance reached France and just over a century later it burst forth in the form of Le Nôtre's grand designs at Versailles. This set the scene across

Europe where Le Nôtre was imitated by the aristocracy of several countries. This extravagance in water garden design can still be seen in several country estates. Chatsworth, in Derbyshire, is a notable example.

In the mid-18th century, the break from the formal dominance of water in garden design came with a new informal movement in Britain. Compositions involving water used lakes, woodlands and bridges, and gradually the formal use of water receded to the immediate confines of the house. This became known as the Landscape Movement and its more naturalistic approach has had an increasing influence on our smaller gardens using rock and water.

TODAY'S GARDENS

In addition to the influences brought by various cultures to garden design, there is now a greater awareness of the environment than perhaps at any stage in our history and a greater sensitivity to the conservation of wildlife. Just as a reverence for nature was evident in the oriental tradition, the modern rock and water garden has a role to play in conservation. Most informal gardens attract wild creatures, but the combination of rock and water in an informal feature widens the diversity of visiting wildlife.

ABOVE: **This simple bridge, which disappears into vegetation on either side, provides a perfect crossing point. Leave gaps between the cross planks in order to allow the wood to expand when wet.**

The gardens in this chapter use rock and water in a variety of ways, and are designed to help you choose the

ROCK AND WATER IN GARDENS

best feature for your space. General examples of different rock and water features, such as pools and streams, are followed by a plan of a specific garden, which is accompanied by details on the choice of plants and on the important garden structures.

OPPOSITE: **The placement of rocks in this watercourse is superb and enhanced by the mix of plants.**

CHOOSING A STYLE

More and more homeowners are including water in their gardens. If you are planning to introduce water into your garden, it is important to choose a style that suits both your perception of a water garden and the existing features in the main garden. Although water will fit into any size or style of garden, it is particularly suitable for small gardens where the reflection of the sky in the water helps to relieve any feelings of claustrophobia which may be caused by high fences and walls.

When choosing from the many varieties of style it is possible to include, spend some time considering what you want water to do in your garden, and then spend even more time considering what form it should take.

DIFFERENT EFFECTS

The informal water garden will give absolute priority to blending into a natural style, where plants will dominate the overall picture. This style will suit the plantsperson, and offers considerable scope for introducing a lush type of planting which may not be possible in the remainder of the garden. The boundaries of this water garden may well extend into bog areas, and ample space to allow for this natural development should be considered whenever possible.

A formal pool is often the choice for a small garden where there is little or no lawn and the surface is dominated by paving. The formal pool has clearly defined

RIGHT: **This water feature has a grey and yellow theme. The dark slate contrasts well with the edging of the yellow form of creeping Jenny (***Lysimachia nummularia*** 'Aurea').**

OPPOSITE: **A gushing stream edged with rocks and flowers provides a perfect setting for relaxing.**

BELOW: **Here, a flat slab of the block-like rock pieces has been selected to act as the spillstone.**

edges which are generally paved and form geometric shapes like squares, circles and rectangles. Planting is restrained, usually contained in aquatic planting crates and dominated by strong, upright leaves, such as those of irises, which will give a striking contrast to the horizontal expanse of water and the surrounding edges.

Raised pools are similar to formal pools in their suitability for a small space which is surrounded by paving. They are particularly suitable in courtyards or areas surrounded by high fences where they introduce reflected light. They make a good choice for the elderly or disabled as the water can be viewed and touched at close quarters. They are also a good choice if you wish to keep fish. Adding a fountain will also help the fish in heatwaves when oxygen levels are low at night.

Fountains introduce noise, movement and the sparkle of light. They are suitable for formal and informal settings, but are most appropriate in formal ones. Fountains are available in a variety of styles, from large tiered bowls, which spill water from bowl to bowl, to spouts which produce no more than a gentle gurgle in an urn. In addition to the many types of free-standing forms, there are also several informal styles that emerge from ground level through cobbles, millstones or rocks.

Streams and waterfalls bring magic to an informal garden. Even the most modest of slopes is suitable for a stream, and any large expanse of lawn may be relieved by streamside planting and the flow of water. Where there is sufficient gradient, a faster-moving rocky stream will enable you to grow a wider range of plants, such as alpines, in the dry soil near the edge. Creative gardeners will be in their element here with the chance to build waterfalls and rock pools, and fashion different sounds.

ROCK POOLS AND PONDS

The use of rock to form the edges of informal pools is one of the most creative design and construction techniques in water gardening. Every rock, no matter how small, contributes to the overall picture, requiring care in the individual positioning in relation to its neighbour and the other rocks used in the scheme, often extending well beyond the immediate surrounds of the pool. The aim is to create an air of natural informality, rather than an unnatural-looking ribbon of jagged rocks protruding from the surface of the water.

The choice of edge should be given very careful consideration at the planning stage. In small pools in sunny areas, the drop in level during the summer months should be anticipated, and an edge created which prevents an unsightly expanse of liner above the waterline. There is an extensive range of rock types that can be used, including limestone, slate, granite and sandstone. Washed boulders and cobbles have a natural affinity with water and are one of the simplest edges to construct, allowing water levels to vary with the season without exposing man-made liners.

ABOVE RIGHT: **The colour of this Welsh slate is enhanced when it is wet and surrounded by strong foliage colours.**

RIGHT: **An overuse of mortar in the making of retaining walls can soon be softened by covering them with prostrate plants such as broom and ivy.**

OPPOSITE: **In contrast to the angular and sloping formation of a slate watercourse, the strata of weatherworn limestone can be built to create almost horizontal lines.**

A SLATE ROCK POOL

This slate watercourse with its film of glistening water is constructed to run into a rock pool. The pool and rocks dominate a garden where interest is maintained in the winter months by conifers planted among the slate. The main viewing point across the wooden decking is from the living room of the house. The wooden decking overhangs the pool, which makes the watercourse appear to travel under the decking. Timber rounds hold back the soil mound, providing a sheltered niche for a shallow container planted with a delicate, cut-leaved Japanese maple (*Acer palmatum*). A "beach" of Caledonian cobbles links the decking to the rocks. The whole scene is framed with a timber pergola which is clothed in wisteria.

RIGHT: **Decking tiles and a wisteria pergola form a superb frame for a slate watercourse.**

INSET: **The thin film of falling water absorbs large quantities of oxygen, which is a useful bonus for fish like orfe.**

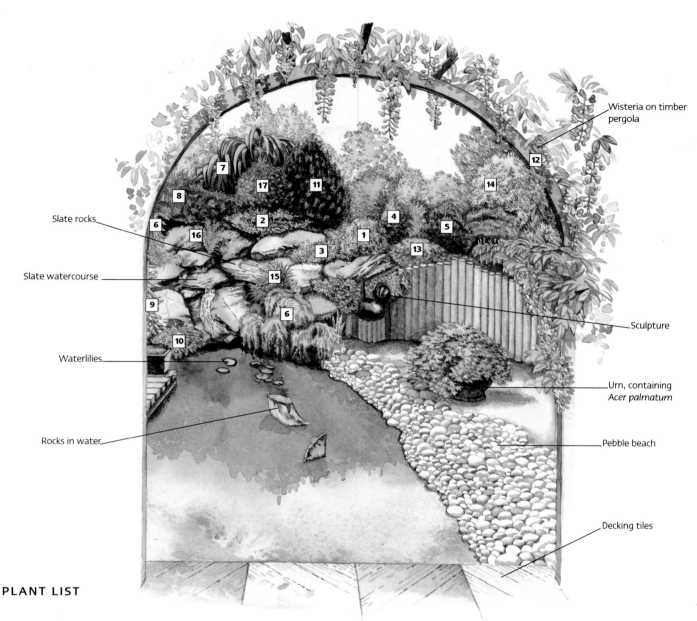

Wisteria on timber pergola

Slate rocks

Slate watercourse

Waterlilies

Rocks in water

Sculpture

Urn, containing *Acer palmatum*

Pebble beach

Decking tiles

PLANT LIST

1 *Rosmarinus officinalis*
2 *Abies koreana* 'Silberlocke'
3 *Helianthemum* 'Rhodanthe Carneum'
4 *Pinus mugo* 'Mops'
5 *Pinus strobus* 'Radiata'
6 *Cedrus deodara* 'Golden Horizon'
7 *Phormium tenax* Purpureum Group
8 *Pinus sylvestris* 'Watereri'
9 *Abies procera* 'Glauca Prostrata'
10 *Cedrus deodara* 'Feelin' Blue'
11 *Pinus parviflora* 'Glauca'
12 *Wisteria sinensis*
13 *Tsuga canadensis* 'Jeddeloh'
14 *Pyrus salicifolia* 'Pendula'
15 *Acorus gramineus*
16 *Dryopteris filix-mas*
17 *Pinus heldreichii* var. *leucodermis*

USEFUL INFORMATION

MATERIALS

• Rock: 12 large pieces of slate for the main watercourse (total weight: 9,000kg/9 tons)
• Washed beach cobbles (1,000kg/1 ton)

PUMP SYSTEM

• Submersible pump under the decking (flow rate of 8,000 litres/2,113 gallons per hour)
• Ultra-violet clarifier under the decking (with two 9 watt u.v. bulbs) from which water is pumped to a biological filter via a 30mm (1¼in) corrugated hose
• Biological filter hidden behind conifers at the top of the watercourse (with three filtration chambers, brushes, profiled foam cartridges and biomedia)
• Spray bar for oxygenation installed above ground

POOL DIMENSIONS

• Area: 4.8 x 2.4m (16 x 8ft)
• Volume of 6,056 litres (1,600 gallons)

RAISED POOLS

Bringing the water surface nearer to eye level and so enhancing the tactile and visual delights of water is a frequently used design method. Whether to draw light into a tiny garden or to add coolness to a shady spot, the proximity of water is especially delightful when it takes the shape of a raised pool. Such pools are ideal in paved areas where a seat can be brought to the side of the pool and the paved surround used as an informal surface to place a refreshing drink. Reflection is a raised pool's particular asset, especially in small gardens with high walls or fences on their boundaries.

There need be no worry about digging holes and having to get rid of excavated soil. Furthermore, the often unforeseen hazards, such as pipework under the soil surface, which are often encountered during excavation, are not a problem with raised pools. If the outdoor space is small or is no more than a paved courtyard, then a raised pool is an excellent solution for incorporating water in the garden.

ABOVE: **In a sloping garden, a raised pool is given extra emphasis by a small, brick and decking surround, which is raised slightly higher than the pool.**

RIGHT: **This elegant raised pool is enhanced by the "peacock tail" effect of the cut sandstone walling pieces which are set into a recess in the wall above.**

LEFT: **Railway sleepers make strong, stable edges for raised and partly raised pools.**

LEFT: **The horizontal lines of this raised brick surround are accentuated by the vertical lines of the planting, which includes iris, rushes and reedmaces.**

A SHADY RAISED POOL

A cool, intimate sitting area surrounds this raised pool where the still, clear water forms the perfect foil for a mixed planting of ferns. Shade is provided by bamboo canes which form spokes from a central hub above the pool and radiate to a hexagon-shaped trellis that echoes the pool's outline. Extensive use has been made of variegated ivies to clothe the trellis and protect the pool from wind as well as to create privacy. To ease any feeling of claustrophobia, circular windows are cut in the trellis to form viewing points of features outside the area or to frame specimen plants in the windows. The shade is too heavy for waterlilies to flower well, but the water remains crystal clear and is broken by drifts of duckweed which are periodically netted off when they cover too much of the surface.

LEFT: **This hexagonal raised pool forms the centrepiece of a shady and sheltered garden retreat, which is surrounded by ivies and "moon windows" that are cut into the lath trellis-work.**

INSET: **The central walling blocks are built without mortar. The gaps between the blocks are then planted with ferns, which surround the column.**

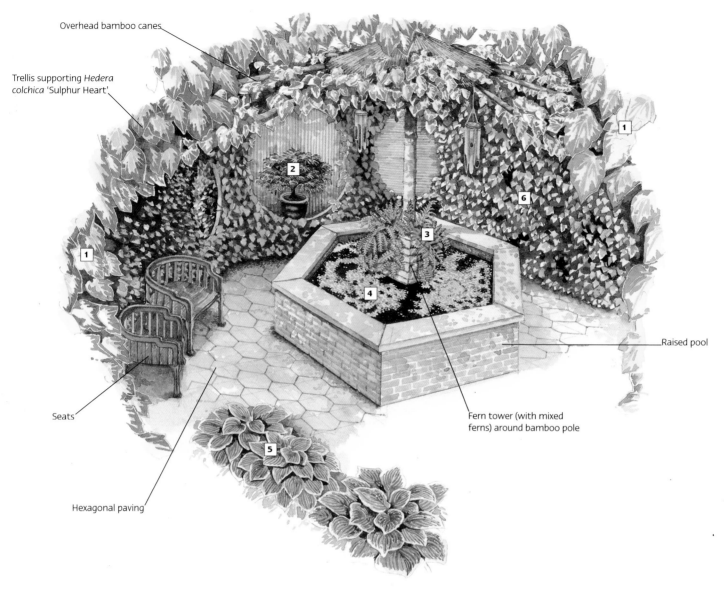

Overhead bamboo canes

Trellis supporting *Hedera colchica* 'Sulphur Heart'

Raised pool

Seats

Fern tower (with mixed ferns) around bamboo pole

Hexagonal paving

PLANT LIST

1 *Hedera colchica* 'Sulphur Heart'
2 *Acer palmatum* var. *dissectum* Dissectum Atropurpureum Group (grown in a container which is framed by a "moon" window)
3 A selection of mixed ferns, including *Asplenium scolopendrium* 'Cristatum', *Blechnum spicant*, *Dryopteris erythrosora*, *D. sieboldii*, *Cystopteris dickieana* and *Polypodium vulgare*
4 *Lemna minor*
5 *Hosta fortunei* var. *aureomarginata*
6 *Hedera helix* 'Glacier'

USEFUL INFORMATION

MATERIALS

- Electric cable: buried under the surrounding paving and drawn through the twin walls of the raised pool to a switchbox on the outside of the twin wall (this allows a neat and hidden supply of electric power for any future pumps or lighting in the pool)
- A length of conduit: this is mortared just under the coping to allow cable to run from any electrical equipment inside the pool to the switchbox on the outside wall

CONSTRUCTION ADVICE

- Raised pools over 45cm (18in) high should be built with double walls on a 45cm- (18in-) wide foundation trench to withstand the pressure exerted by the water
- Wall ties set 1m (3ft) apart between the double walls provide extra strength
- The liner is fixed inside the inner wall and hidden from view by draping it over the inner wall level with the top two courses of brick. The coping is then mortared onto the edge of the liner

WILDLIFE POOLS

One of the undeniable attractions of water is to bring a greater variety of wildlife into the garden. This is increasingly important in urban gardens where many of the birds, mammals and insects, more often associated with the countryside, use a garden pool as a resting point in their busy search for food and water. Garden pools have become a major factor in slowing down the decline of several amphibians, insects and other creatures that can no longer find the right conditions in rural or agricultural environments. No matter how small the pool, leave an area of clear water for a week or two in the summer and, almost miraculously, a chain of life will start. Tiny, nearly microscopic, life appears at first, with the interest growing over subsequent weeks as the pool becomes home to larger and larger invertebrates which arrive on the feet of birds or as eggs hidden away on new plants.

At the top of the food chain, there are several small mammals which are lured to a patch of water in the garden. Hedgehogs, badgers and foxes can often be seen at night, drinking from the pools in gardens, particularly in housing developments that are situated near the countryside. One of the most impressive sights in high summer are the huge dragonflies which dart and hover over the water, looking for shallow water in which to lay their eggs. It is a rich reward for the water gardener to see the freshly emerged ugly larva of a dragonfly turn into a winged beauty in a few hours.

BELOW: **Beneath the striking, pineapple-like tops of the water soldier (*Stratiotes aloides*), the clear water is teeming with life.**

RIGHT: **Astilbes, heather (*Erica*) and honeywort (*Cerinthe*) make a pleasantly informal planting at the side of this cascade and provide shelter for visiting wildlife.**

ABOVE: **A raised decking path provides a good vantage point from which to view the wildlife attracted to this widened section of a shallow stream in a wild garden.**

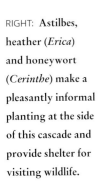

RIGHT: **Common flag iris (*Iris pseudacorus*) and Bowles' golden sedge (*Carex elata* 'Aurea') provide cover as well as a home in which amphibians and birds can hide and feed.**

A TRANQUIL WILDLIFE POOL

The lush informality of this pool makes it an attraction to wildlife. Although similar to an informal decorative pool, it has several design and construction points that are not apparent at first sight. The most important of these is the layer of soil on the pool bottom on top of the liner. This allows the ideal environment for several invertebrates to protect themselves in the mud. There are also several styles of edge to the pool, which allow easy access for amphibians. A small island is left undisturbed to allow rushes and sedges to cover the moist soil and create a safe haven for frogs and toads to bask in the sunshine. Although a compromise is evident in not having exclusively native plants, several of the marginals are indigenous, providing food for insects.

BELOW AND INSET: **Marginals such as sweet galingale (*Cyperus longus*) jostle with giant rhubarb (*Gunnera manicata*) and the umbrella plant (*Darmera peltata*) to provide an excellent home for wildlife.**

Island

Rock

Grass

Bark chipping
path around
edge of pool

PLANT LIST

1 *Iris sibirica*

2 *Gunnera manicata*

3 *Osmunda regalis*

4 *Phalaris arundinacea* var. *picta*
'Feesey'

5 *Cyperus longus*

6 *Iris pseudacorus*

7 *Acorus gramineus*
'Variegatus'

8 *Nymphaea tuberosa*
(white waterlily)

9 *Nymphaea* 'René Gérard'
(pink waterlily)

10 *Menyanthes trifoliata*

11 *Alchemilla mollis*

12 *Astilbe*

13 *Darmera peltata*

14 *Persicaria bistorta* 'Superba'

15 *Mimulus luteus*

USEFUL INFORMATION

MATERIALS

- Bark chippings: on one side of pool. If
  you create a bog garden to one side of
  the wildlife pool, then bark chippings
  are a very good surface for this boggy
  area. Bark chippings act as a mulch and
  help to retain moisture

- Occasional large rock to break up
  the grass edge of the pool

ISLAND CONSTRUCTION

- Islands can be added to the pool after
  construction, but this involves draining
  the pool first. For this reason, it is

advisable to consider the inclusion of
an island during the initial planning
stages

- A flat-topped mound is created during
  the initial contouring of the excavation
  (the top of the mound should be
  finished at about 15cm/6in below the
  anticipated level of water in the pool)

- Turves stacked upside down on the edge
  of the island form a stable soil wall
  (heavy soil is added inside the turf wall)

- Plants in the wet soil soon develop
  a root system to bind the edges of the
  island

BOG GARDENS

A well-planted bog garden can look more natural in an informal setting than a tiny pool with a geometric shape and a ribbon of paving surrounding it. Bog gardens also provide the perfect method of introducing lushness to an otherwise arid landscape. The choice of plants that can be grown in boggy soils is often far more impressive in its diversity than the range of marginal plants available for small pools.

The bog garden is not simply an extension of the shallow water for marginal plants. It is an area of permanently moist soil rather than saturated soil, which allows some of the giants of the plant kingdom to make their impact in an informal garden. Including some plant giants in a patch of bog is a well-known method of making a garden look larger and more interesting. The plants associated with boggy areas are also enhanced enormously if they are reflected in an adjacent pool. However, a small bog garden may be considered a water feature in its own right, even if it is not associated with an adjacent area of clear water. It is certainly one of the least expensive types of water garden.

BELOW: **Candelabra primulas mix with Japanese iris (*Iris ensata*) to form a rich feeding station for insects in early summer.**

ABOVE: **This access bridge links a riot of colour provided by astilbes, iris and primulas along the sides of a stream.**

LEFT: **Bulrushes (*Scirpus*) are perfect bog plants, giving height and form to the plant mix, while the giant Himalayan cowslips (*Primula florindae*) and the variegated figwort (*Scrophularia auriculata* 'Variegata') provide interest in midsummer.**

A SMALL BOG GARDEN

BELOW: **Bog gardens allow a wide range of lush leaf shapes and colours to maintain interest from early spring to autumn.**

INSET: **Access through this small bog garden is provided by log rounds, about 38cm (15in) in diameter and 30cm (12in) deep.**

A bog garden is a valuable water feature in a garden with light soil and little rainfall. Many of the plants are more traditionally used as marginals in shallow water, but, provided the soil is kept wet, most marginals will still flourish without a covering of water over the soil. Such a feature is ideal for the plantsperson who wishes to extend the range of plants that can be grown in an ordinary soil. Access is important to reach the plants as those conditions which encourage ample growth are also ideal for weeds, and deep-rooted weeds should not be allowed to gain a foothold. In this bog garden, access is provided by a stepping stone path of log slices through the centre of the feature. The fresh colours blend nicely and are ideal in a partly shaded site that is viewed regularly from a house window.

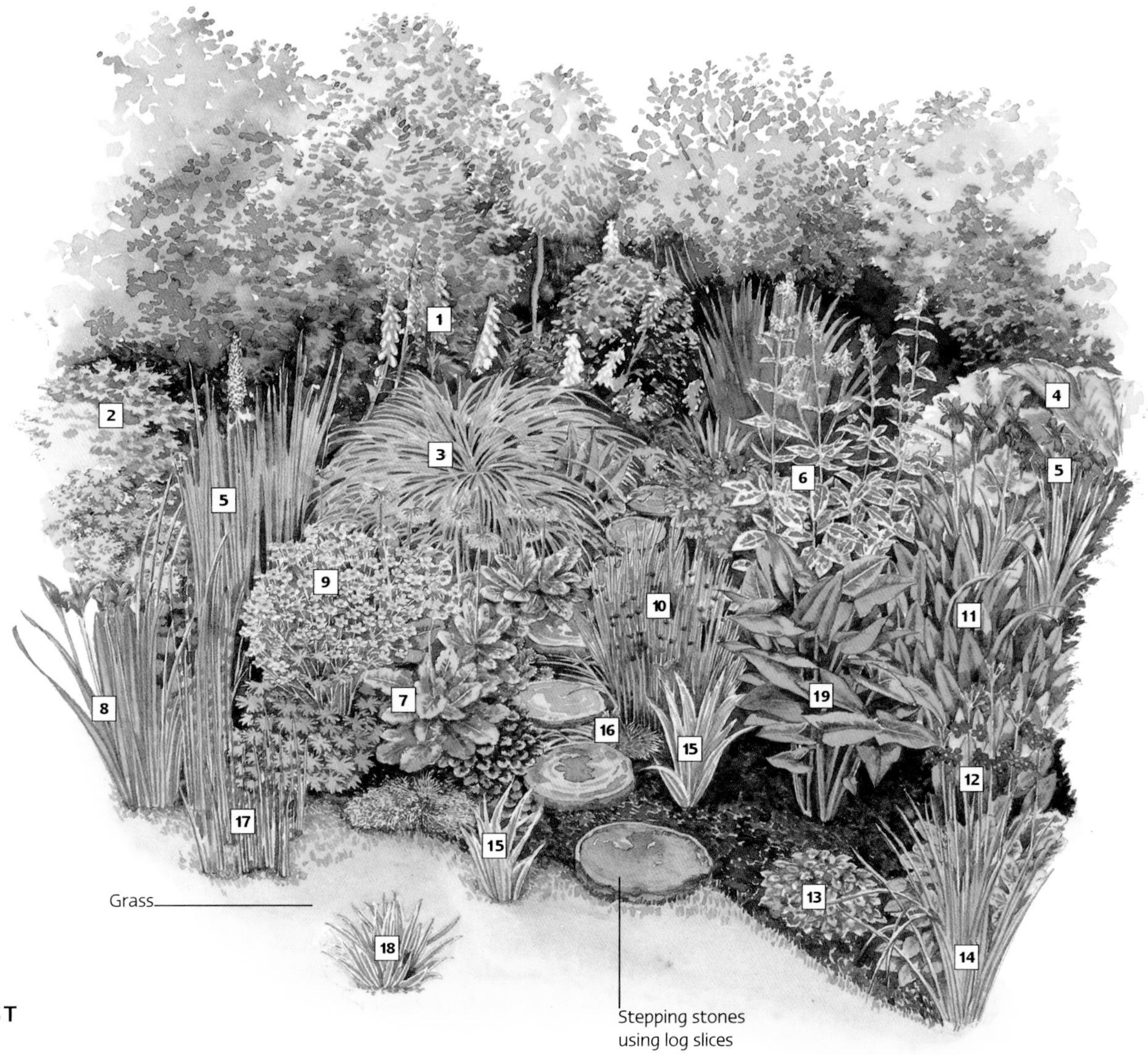

Grass

Stepping stones
using log slices

PLANT LIST

1 *Digitalis ferruginea*
2 *Cornus kousa* 'Snowboy'
3 *Carex elata* 'Aurea'
4 *Gunnera manicata*
5 *Iris sibirica*
6 *Scrophularia auriculata* 'Variegata'
7 *Primula florindae*
8 *Iris ensata*
9 *Ranunculus acris citrinus*
10 *Juncus ensifolius*
11 *Pontederia cordata*
12 *Primula japonica* 'Miller's Crimson'
13 *Epimedium davidii*
14 *Dierama pulcherrimum*
15 *Iris laevigata* 'Variegata'
16 *Viola sororia*
17 *Equisetum ramoissimum*
   var. *japonicum*
18 *Acorus gramineus* 'Variegatus'
19 *Peltandra undulata*

USEFUL INFORMATION

MATERIALS

• Thick bentomat liner: used here to line the bog garden and made from a sodium bentonite geocomposite. Sodium bentonite is a naturally swelling clay which expands to 12–15 times its dry volume when it is fully hydrated. This makes it a very useful sealant when the swell pressure is contained in the form of a clay liner. (Sodium bentonite can also be used to create a watertight seal between a pool and a bog garden.)

• "Rounds" of wood: measuring approximately 38cm (15in) in diameter and 30cm (12in) thick (the rounds of wood should be spaced about 23cm/9in apart and laid onto a mixture of ballast and hardcore for additional stability)

MAINTENANCE

• The bog garden will need to be kept moist for the plants to thrive, so periodically flood with a garden hose during hot, dry weather

GRAVEL GARDENS

A gravel garden may seem, at first, to be incongruous in a garden associated with water. The Japanese were the first to use gravel to simulate water where water was either difficult to include or the aim was to stimulate the imagination. Large rocks were placed singly, and rake markings were created in the gravel to imitate the ripples of water. With the increasing popularity of gravel as a low-maintenance surface in dry areas in Western gardens, features like dried river beds can form either links between water features or schemes in their own right. With the additional benefits of planting, the watery impression can be quite dramatic.

A gravel garden may start as no more than a thin, meandering area, varying slightly in width, which is cut out of an existing lawn. As it is extended, larger plants can be introduced. If a weed blanket or landscape membrane were laid beneath the gravel, it would provide an extremely maintenance-free feature. Gravel gardens are often associated with arid settings, but, by choosing rounded rather than sharp gravel and including smooth boulders, an impression of moisture is much easier to achieve.

ABOVE RIGHT: **Gravel and rock are a good combination in this sun-drenched terrace, which is flanked by lavender.**

RIGHT: **The illusion of water is created in an otherwise arid environment by rocks, gravel and a bridge.**

OPPOSITE: **These steps are made with gravel, timber and slate, and surrounded by a stunning mix of Himalayan poppies, Japanese maples (*Acer japonicum*), primulas and ferns.**

A DRIED RIVER BED

Sometimes the illusion of water can make as satisfying a garden feature as the real thing, particularly where there is insufficient time to devote to maintaining water. Here, a dried river bed has been simulated, with the occasional pocket dug out for the moisture-loving plants. Mixed sizes of cobbles spread over a membrane both suppress weeds and act as a moisture-retaining mulch. The same mulch provides extra frost protection in the winter, allowing ornamental grasses a good start in the spring. The effect has been achieved by starting with a narrow bed at the highest point of the lawn and allowing this to widen as the bed travels down the gentle slope. A simple bridge makes a good crossing point halfway down, further adding to the illusion of water. The taller grasses are planted at the wider, lower section, giving the impression of a boggy zone.

INSET: **Grasses dominate this dried river bed, where the early rust-coloured flowers of** *Calamagrostis* **precede the** *Miscanthus* **which extend interest well into autumn with their flowerheads.**

BELOW: **Lower down, the bed suggests a boggy area where love grass (***Eragrostis***) and other moisture-loving grasses predominate.**

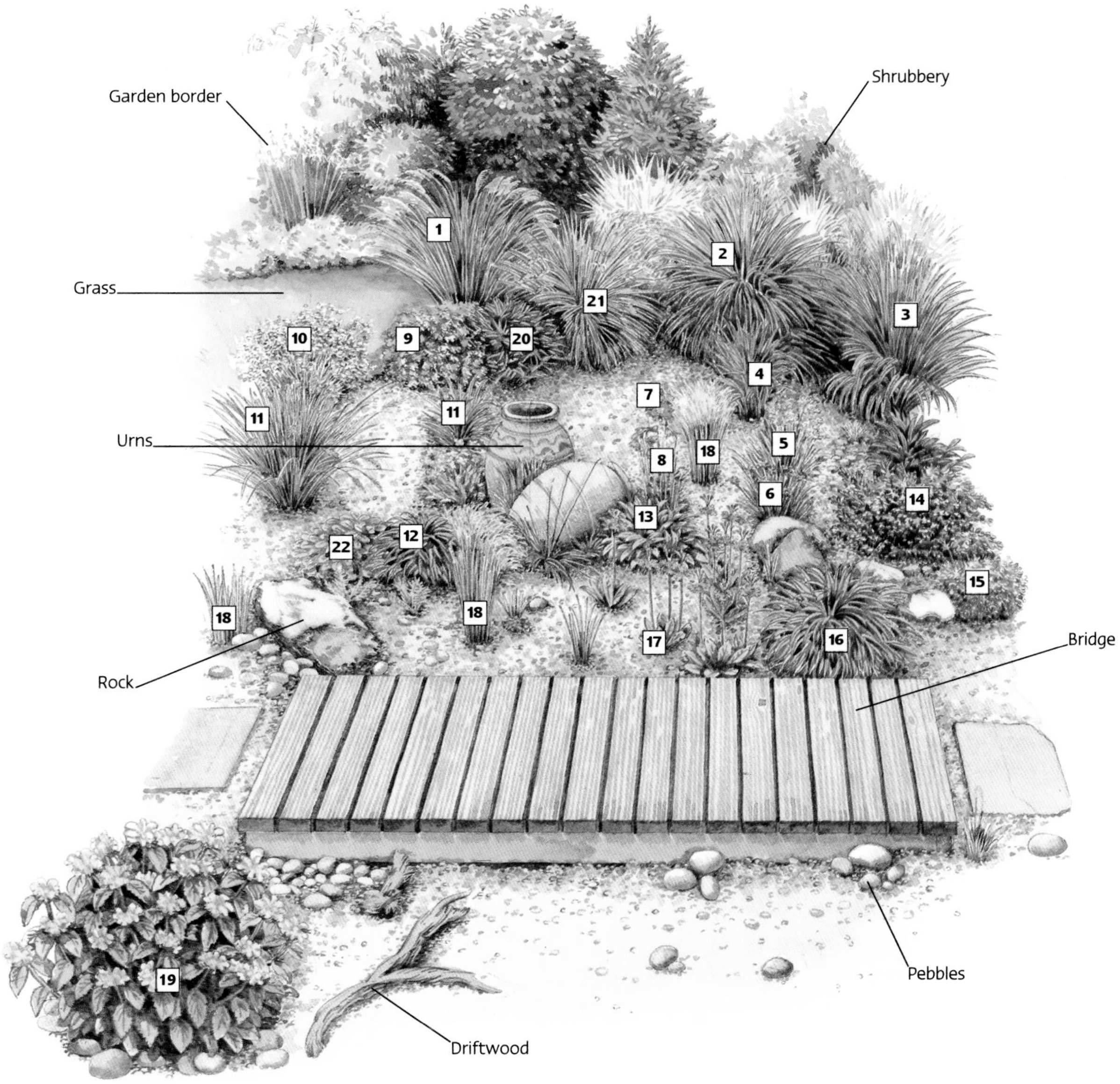
Garden border
Shrubbery
Grass
Urns
Rock
Bridge
Pebbles
Driftwood
1
2
3
4
5
6
7
8
9
10
11
11
12
13
14
15
16
17
18
18
18
19
20
21
22

PLANT LIST

1 *Eragrostis curvula*
2 *Miscanthus sinensis* 'Gracillimus'
3 *Miscanthus sinensis* 'Sarabande'
4 *Miscanthus sinensis* 'Kleine Silberspinne'
5 *Echinacea purpurea* 'White Lustre'
6 *Sisyrinchium californicum*
7 *Campanula carpatica* 'Blaue Clips'
8 *Campanula fragilis*
9 *Oenothera kuntbiana*
10 *Gypsophila paniculata*
11 *Poa labillardieri*
12 *Luzula acuminata*
13 *Luzula sylvatica*
14 *Prostanthera cuneata*
15 *Penstemon pinifolius* 'Wisley Flame'
16 *Luzula sylvatica* 'Aurea'
17 *Primula chungensis*
18 *Stipa tenuissima*
19 *Phlomis russeliana*
20 *Shibataea kumasasa*
21 *Libertia grandiflora*
22 *Viola canina*

USEFUL INFORMATION

MATERIALS

- Heavy duty polythene (polyethylene), such as old fertilizer or compost bags, for lining the planting holes for the vigorous, moisture-loving grasses
- Standard, ultra-violet-stabilized black polythene, 25 mucron (500 gauge) thick: used as a membrane to line the river bed (although it allows no movement of air and water except through planting holes, black polythene is an effective, low-cost means of controlling weeds as well as reducing water loss around new plants)
- Cobbles: these will protect the membrane from being damaged by ultra-violet light (without them it would degrade in approximately three years)

STREAMS AND CASCADES

BELOW: **The sound of a cascade brings life and vibrancy to the garden. It can be made noisier if the water plunges onto a shallow stream bed rather than into a deeper pool.**

The creation of a rocky informal stream epitomizes the most dramatic association of rock and water, and is the supreme challenge to the garden designer and landscaper. A stream brings noise and movement with infinite variations, allowing its impact to be gentle or dramatic. Streams are the ultimate water feature for the imaginative gardener; a small time spent by the side of a stream, listening to the sounds of the cascades and shallow rills, recharges the batteries and brings memories of favourite countryside walks. The home gardener can achieve these heights of creativity with relatively simple projects, particularly if natural streams and boulders have been used as the model.

As with many other products recently manufactured for the growing water-garden market, there are now several preformed stream units to make the construction process easier. Building a stream with cascades can seem daunting to the inexperienced, but the use of these units brings the feature within the scope of the most unskilled gardener. The style and appearance of these units are constantly being improved and now most types of rock are simulated in fibreglass. A more recent innovation is preformed stream units made from simulated cobbles and pebbles. Once the plants have become well established, it is often difficult to tell if a stream has been built using preformed units.

ABOVE: **Elephants' ears (***Bergenia***) are good plants for dry soils at the streamside as they have lush-looking leaves even in drier conditions.**

TOP: **A smooth, ribbon-like cascade falling into a cobble-lined pool creates a more formal effect than a gushing waterfall.**

LEFT: **The pristine clarity of this stream is maintained during summer by the growth of oxygenating plants at the streamsides.**

A CASCADING STREAM

The redevelopment of this garden, which involved the building of a new patio, provided a good opportunity to move an existing rigid pool and create a new stream. The main window of the house looks onto the patio and provides a perfect vantage point for viewing the gurgling stream on hot days. The newly planted surrounds of the stream will take a year or two to soften the rock edges and the rigid pool unit. The limestone rock used in the stream is more difficult to obtain and was originally bought for a rock garden some twenty years ago. The dismantling of old overgrown rock gardens often releases masses of expensive and weatherworn rock which has become increasingly rare and is particularly suitable for making a small stream with a flexible liner.

INSET: **A simple, flat, timber bridge, which is set into the path, accentuates the presence of the stream.**

RIGHT: **It is only a few weeks since the stream was constructed. The initial bareness of the base pool and the surrounding soil will soon be covered by the planting.**

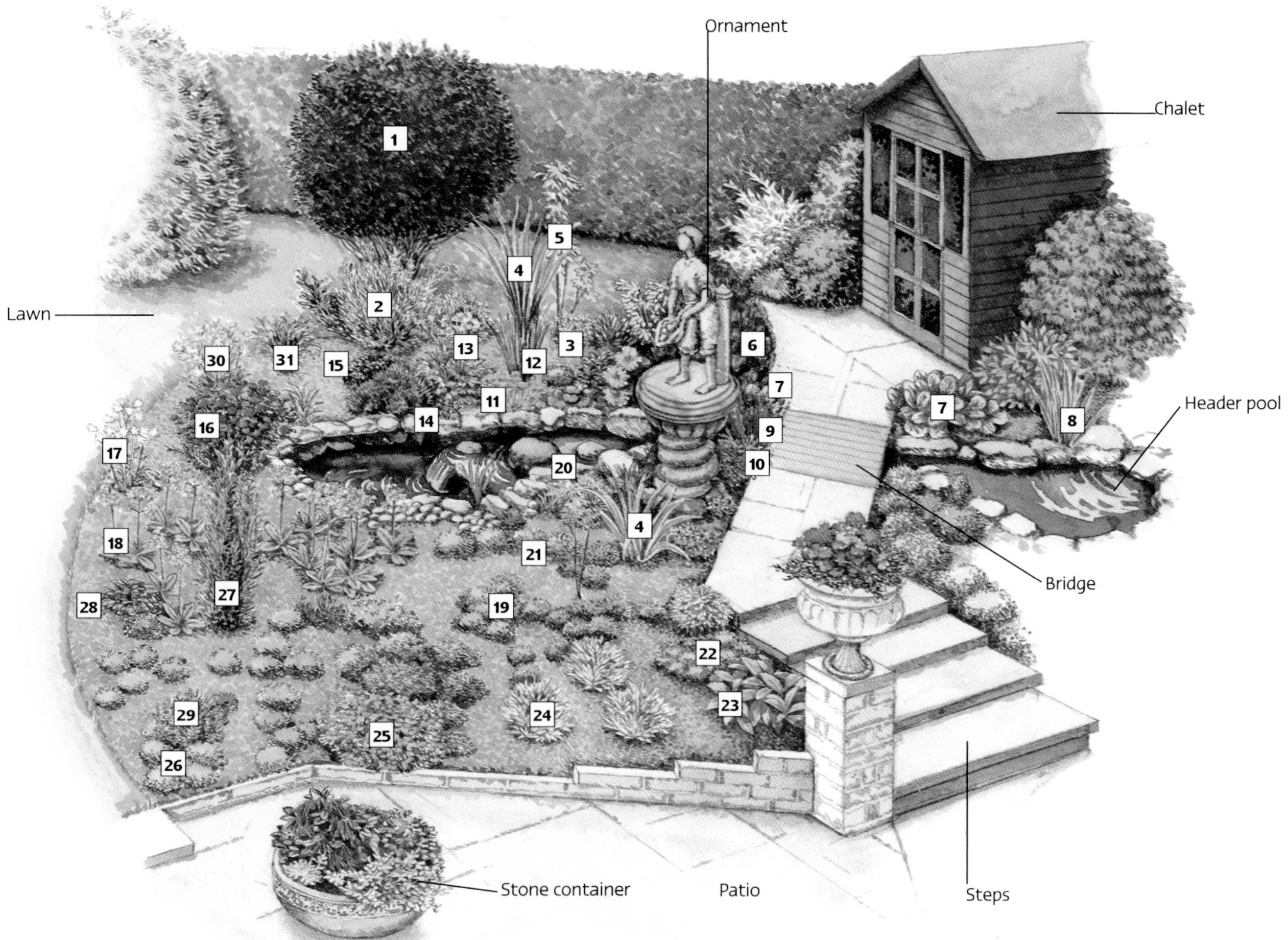

Ornament

Chalet

Lawn

Header pool

Bridge

Stone container

Patio

Steps

PLANT LIST

1 *Berberis thunbergii*
   'Atropurpurea'

2 *Artemisia absinthium*
   'Lambrook Silver'

3 *Brunnera macrophylla*

4 *Phormium tenax*

5 *Acer negundo*
   'Flamingo'

6 *Thuja orientalis*

7 *Bergenia cordifolia*

8 *Iris pseudacorus*
   'Variegata'

9 *Salvia officinalis*
   'East Freesland'

10 *Mimulus*

11 *Sedum*

12 *Iris sibirica*

13 *Astrantia major*

14 *Armeria*

15 *Cistus × skanbergii*

16 *Cistus × argenteus*
   'Peggy Sammons'

17 *Campanula alba*
   'Coronata'

18 *Primula beesiana*

19 *Erica carnea*
   'Springwood Pink'

20 *Dianthus deltoides*

21 *Erica carnea*
   'Springwood White'

22 *Erica carnea*
   'Winter Beauty'

23 *Viburnum davidii*

24 *Convolvulus cneorum*

25 *Helianthemum*
   'Rhodanthe Carneum'

26 *Erica carnea* 'Foxhollow'

27 *Taxus baccata*
   Fastigiata Aurea Group

28 *Fuchsia* 'Tom Thumb'

29 *Origanum laevigatum*
   'Herrenhausen'

30 *Cistus parviflorus*

31 *Olearia nummularifolia*

USEFUL INFORMATION

MATERIALS

- Rocks: 508kg (½ ton) of limestone pieces, each weighing 15–20kg (33–44lbs)

- Black corrugated plastic pipe, 2.5cm (1in) in diameter: used to circulate water to the top of the stream

TIMBER BRIDGE

To make a timber bridge, measuring 1.2m (4ft) long:

- Lengths of decking cross planks, 60 x 15 x 2.5cm/ 24 x 6 x 1in

- Timber joists, 10 x 5cm/ 4 x 2in (length depends on width of stream): placed 50cm (20in) apart onto which the cross planks are screwed at right angles (leaving a gap of 1cm/½in between planks)

- Concrete blocks on either side into which the joists are bedded

TYPE OF PUMP

- Submersible pump for base pool (flow rate of 3,645 litres/963 gallons per hour)

A ROCK STREAM

An informal garden, where water's great attraction to birds is exploited in a stream and pool that almost enters the house, is viewed to the full through a large window, opening on to a small patio edging the pool. The garden is designed and maintained in a relaxed, informal style without too much attention placed upon manicured planting schemes. It is a place to be enjoyed from both inside and out.

The artificial rocks lining the stream are part of fibreglass stream units which have been beautifully disguised to the extent that they are extremely hard to identify among the real weathered rocks. There are shaded nooks and crannies almost hidden along the stream which provide permanent bathing pools for wildlife even when the pump is not operating.

This is a successful example of a design that reflects the owners' love of wildlife and colour.

INSET: **The rocks disguise the preformed stream units perfectly.**

LEFT: **The plant mix is bursting with vigour and seemingly nourished by the pool and stream, which are almost hidden by the lush vegetation.**

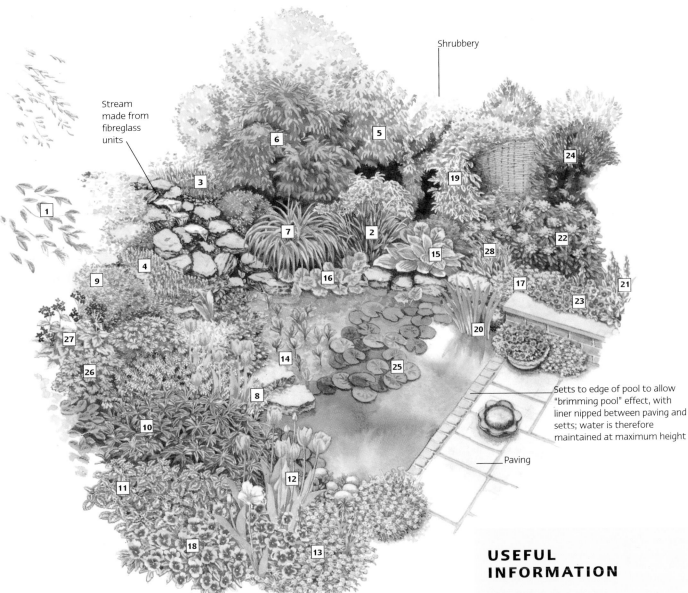

Stream made from fibreglass units

Shrubbery

Setts to edge of pool to allow "brimming pool" effect, with liner nipped between paving and setts; water is therefore maintained at maximum height

Paving

PLANT LIST

1 *Prunus*
2 *Anchusa azurea*
3 *Ajuga reptans*
4 *Geranium* 'Johnson's Blue'
5 *Sambucus serratifolia*
6 *Philadelphus coronarius*
7 *Hemerocallis*
8 *Oenanthe javanica* 'Flamingo'
9 *Erica × darleyensis* 'Silberschmelze'
10 *Cistus ladanifer*
11 *Lamium maculatum*
12 *Tulipa*
13 *Erigeron karvinskianus*
14 *Menyanthes trifoliata*
15 *Hosta fortunei* var. *aureomarginata*

16 *Caltha palustris* var. *palustris*
17 *Erigeron* 'Charity'
18 Pansy (*Viola × wittrockiana*)
19 *Elaeagnus angustifolia*
20 *Iris pseudacorus*
21 *Hyacinthoides non-scripta*
22 *Euphorbia polychroma*
23 *Vinca major*
24 *Prunus lusitanica*
25 *Nymphaea* 'Marliacea Chromatella'
26 *Calluna vulgaris* 'Antony Davis'
27 *Diascia* 'Ruby Field'
28 *Carex pendula*

USEFUL INFORMATION

MATERIALS

- Rock: just over 508kg (½ ton) of 15–20kg (33–44lbs) limestone pieces to edge the pool and stream
- 3 rigid fibreglass stream units: lower unit (1m x 45cm x 15cm/3ft x 18in x 6in); double centre unit (1.2m x 45cm x 15cm/4ft x 18in x 6in)
- 1 rigid fibreglass header pool unit (1m/3ft in diameter, 30cm/12in deep)
- Base pool (3.6m x 1.8m x 60cm/ 12ft x 6ft x 2ft, with a volume of 3,406 litres/900 gallons)

TYPE OF PUMP

- Pump at base of waterfall (flow rate 3,645 litres/963 gallons per hour)

SMALL WATER FEATURES

The trend towards smaller gardens has led to the increasing popularity of small-scale water features, which make little demand on space and which can fit into any style of garden. Many of these are free-standing, such as brimming urns, while others use moving water pumped from reservoirs hidden below ground. Most of these features require little or no maintenance, and are in tune with the lifestyle of the 21st century where there are so many other attractions to place demands on leisure time. The refreshment of water can be introduced at the flick of a switch.

Such features bring small spaces to life by providing a mixture of sound and movement, adding an element of surprise and a setting for interesting plant combinations. What these features have lost in the way of size, they have more than made up for in innovative design, unconventional materials and general appeal. They are often only discovered by visitors after a detailed exploration of the garden or by following the sound of trickling water. With little water exposed, there is much less danger to inquisitive children and, in fact, many water features can be mounted completely out of reach.

BELOW: **Constantly running water, cleverly contrived by a hidden reservoir and a pump, makes this** *tsukubai* **a captivating feature to watch.**

BELOW: The thin film of water constantly rippling from the centre of a millstone never ceases to fascinate.

ABOVE: This terracotta pot, which is being constantly replenished by a spout, is low in maintenance but high in impact.

LEFT: This white waterlily, *Nymphaea odorata* var. *minor*, not only provides flowers, but keeps the water clear with the shade cast by its leaves.

A COBBLE FOUNTAIN

A large garden with an expansive area devoted to lawn can be effectively broken by an informal gravel area, linking patio to grass. Such a design provides the perfect setting to include a cobble fountain among the plants and gravel, especially in the area most used for outdoor living. Gravel areas give great freedom to the planting, both in size of plant and their style. There is a nice mix of hardy and slightly tender plants so that if a severe winter damaged the less hardy specimens, the interest would still be maintained and any gaps made less conspicuous. The paving on the patio area is broken up slightly by replacing some of the paving slabs with the same cobbles used near the fountain. This provides a further link between the garden and the house.

INSET: **The water spout in this cobble fountain is made still more intriguing in the evening when it is illuminated by a spotlight.**

RIGHT: **Used as the mood dictates, the noise and movement of the small cobble fountain brings this corner of the garden to life.**

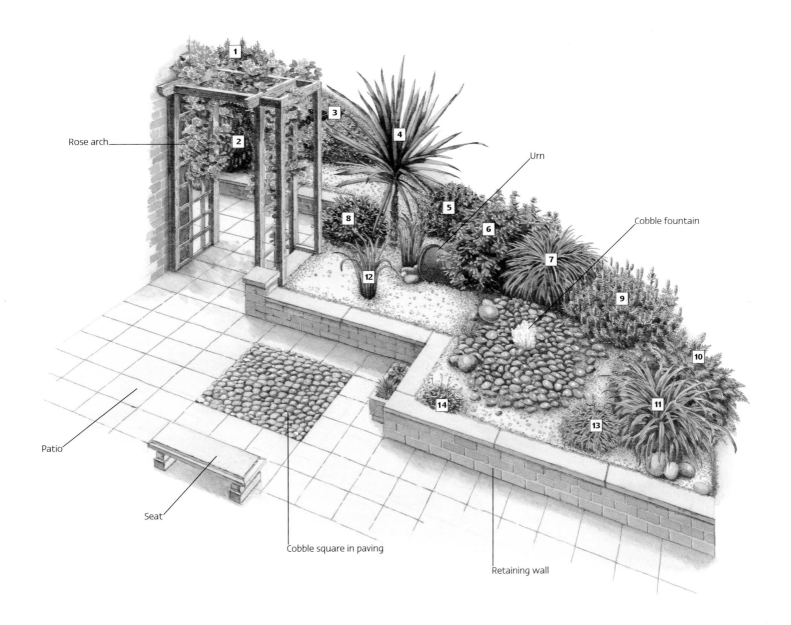

Rose arch

Patio

Seat

Cobble square in paving

Urn

Cobble fountain

Retaining wall

PLANT LIST

1 *Rosmarinus* 'Miss Jessopp's Upright'
2 *Thuja orientalis*
3 *Lonicera nitida* 'Baggesen's Gold'
4 *Cordyline australis*
5 *Rosmarinus* 'Benenden Blue'
6 *Cistus ladanifer*
7 *Miscanthus sinensis* 'Kleine Silberspinne'
8 *Cistus × skanbergii*
9 *Pinus mugo*
10 *Juniperus sabina* 'Tamariscifolia'
11 *Hemerocallis*
12 *Panicum virgatum*
13 *Carex siderosticha*
14 *Armeria maritima*

USEFUL INFORMATION

MATERIALS
- Rounded washed cobbles over the fountain grid
- Pea shingle or gravel: a 2.5cm (1in) deep layer to surround the fountain

LIGHTING
- 20 watt halogen light to illuminate the fountain spout (used below water or above ground) and capable of generating an intense beam of light at extremely low power consumption. The light is supplied with a weather-proof transformer with a 10m (30ft) cable and a 5m (16½ft) cable for the light. The light can be secured in the ground by stakes provided in the kit and there are optional colours for the lens. A yellow light gives the illusion of a flame

TYPE OF PUMP
- Submersible pump in the base of reservoir (flow rate of 1,000 litres/264 gallons per hour)

A BRIMMING URN

INSET: **Caught in the late afternoon sun, the quiet movement of this brimming urn makes a subtle impact in a dry garden.**

BELOW: **The urn makes a good contrast of form to the freedom of design in this grass garden.**

A simple stone seat by a brimming urn forms a lively point of interest in this seaside gravel garden. The gravel groundcover lies on a permeable membrane which prevents the weeds growing through, but, at the same time, allows water to reach the plants. This low-maintenance garden, which is able to survive the rigours of salty winds and low rainfall, is ideal for anyone with little time for gardening. Ornamental grasses dominate the planting, and extra interest in the gravel base is provided by undulating an otherwise flat garden. Odd pieces of driftwood collected from an adjacent beach add a final flourish.

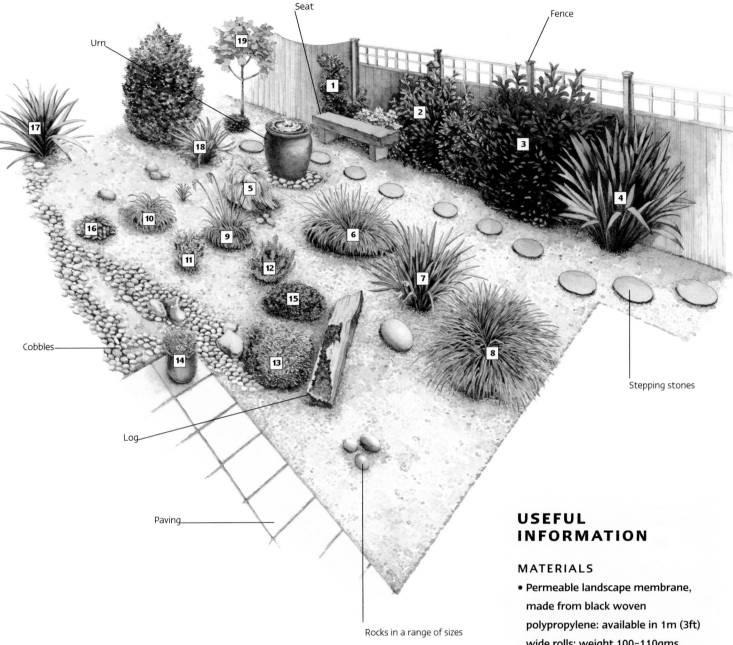

Urn

Seat

Fence

Cobbles

Log

Paving

Stepping stones

Rocks in a range of sizes

USEFUL INFORMATION

MATERIALS

- Permeable landscape membrane, made from black woven polypropylene: available in 1m (3ft) wide rolls; weight 100–110gms per sq. metre (3½oz per sq. yard)
- Urn (1m/3ft high and 45cm/18in at its widest diameter)
- Grades of gravel to cover membrane: 50mm (2in) and over, 40mm (1½in) and 30mm (1in)
- Log and rocks in a range of sizes

TYPE OF PUMP

- Submersible pump in a reservoir beneath the urn (flow rate of 1,560 litres/412 gallons per hour)

PLANT LIST

1 *Choisya ternata*
2 *Elaeagnus × ebbingei*
3 *Photinia × fraseri* 'Red Robin'
4 *Phormium tenax*
5 *Stipa tenuissima*
6 *Helictrotrichon sempervirens*
7 *Iris foetidissima*
8 *Stipa arundinacea*
9 *Stipa gigantea*
10 *Carex oshimensis* 'Evergold'

11 *Teucrium fruticans*
12 *Picea glauca* var. *albertiana*
13 *Helianthemum* 'Wisley Primrose'
14 *Erigeron karvinskianus*
15 *Cryptomeria japonica* 'Spiralis'
16 *Skimmia japonica*
17 *Miscanthus sinensis* 'Variegatus'
18 *Imperata cylindrica* 'Rubra'
19 *Sorbus aria* 'Lutescens'

The finishing touches to a successful rock and water garden can make all the difference to its overall impact.

SPECIAL FEATURES

Many of these features, including lighting and fountains, can be added at a later stage in the construction process. However, it is really best to consider larger features, such as islands and bridges, during the early stages of planning and design.

OPPOSITE: Features such as bridges and large boulders along the length of a stream bring added interest.

DECKING

Wooden decking is one of the best surfaces with which to edge water where there is also a need for an outdoor living area. Unlike most other edges, a substantial overhang can be created to give the illusion that the water runs beneath the decking. Because wood is a natural material, it works well in an informal garden in which straight edges would otherwise look out of place.

Ecologically, a wooden surface has two distinct advantages over a paved surface. First, it allows rainfall to permeate the ground beneath, so that the decking can be built around any existing trees or vegetation, and there is no need to make special provision for extra watering. New plants can be introduced into the decking design by planting them into the soil below and leaving a small aperture, just wide enough for the stem to appear through the surface of the decking. Second, because it is very close to the water, the gap beneath the decking is an excellent home for amphibians, such as toads and frogs. The temperature and humidity in such an area seems to suit them.

From a landscaping point of view, decking offers endless possibilities. New levels, split levels, steps, railings and pergolas are all easier to attach to a structure that is basically a suspended wooden surface.

From a practical point of view, the void underneath the decking can be used to hide equipment and pipes, including ultra-violet clarifiers, biological filters, surface pumps, electrical cables, switches, connectors and transformers. Many of these items can be difficult to hide in a water garden that is dependent on pumps and filtration systems.

The surface of the decking can be made with long wooden planks or individual decking tiles. Both the planks and tiles are available in a range of different woods, but make sure that the surface is ribbed to reduce slip. The decking tiles have the advantage that individual tiles can be lifted for access to any of the equipment stored beneath them. The decking surface is attached to a sturdy wooden framework, which can be constructed to allow greater overlap of the water than any other type of edge.

Although a wooden surface is more sympathetic to an informal, natural design, it can accumulate algae in wet, shady areas, so it should be cleaned regularly with a very stiff brush. Decking is really more suitable for a sun-bleached spot, where there will be less algal growth and where the view will encourage you to sit at the edge of the water.

RIGHT: Decking has limitless applications around water, particularly if there is a change of height, where it can be used for bridges, steps and sitting areas.

OPPOSITE BELOW: Decking planks have been used here to form a raised edge, steps and pathway around a pool with an unusual situation.

FAR LEFT: Decking tiles made with the planks in a diagonal format make an interesting alternative to straight lines of decking and allow for easy access under each tile.

LEFT: The extreme versatility of timber planks is shown here, allowing a restful, sloping curve to be constructed over the top of this lushly planted stream.

FOUNTAINS FOR POOLS

Formal layouts, in which symmetrical balance, clipped hedges and straight edges are prevalent, are the most appropriate settings for fountains, which are more suited to circular or rectangular pools. A regular spray pattern from the fountain jet also enhances this formality. Where hot colours have been used in nearby foliage or flowers, the fountain will have an even more cooling effect. As plants with surface leaves, such as waterlilies, will dislike the constant falling water and associated turbulence, fountain pools tend to be very limited in their planting, confining this to strong erect marginals around the perimeter.

A fountain makes an ideal focal point and if it can be seen from the main viewing area, the droplets of water in the fountain spray will seem to come alive in the sunlight. This effect is enhanced even more if the spray has a plain or dark background. A windy garden is a problem site for a tall fountain or a fountain that relies on a fine spray pattern. Do everything possible to create shelter around the fountain and ensure that the diameter of the base pool exceeds the height of the fountain spray. This will not only create better balance from an architectural point-of-view, but will also provide a sufficiently wide receptacle for drifting spray. On very windy sites the problem can be alleviated by the use of a geyser jet which forms a wide, heavy and frothy jet. This is produced by a special nozzle which introduces air at the sides. A stronger pump is usually required to drive geyser jets, which are quite expensive, but enormous fun.

There are a number of interesting patterns available from the wide range of nozzle designs, and some of the main types are shown here. It is worth visiting a good aquatic centre where these are displayed in pools so that you can assess their suitability for your own garden.

Good maintenance is paramount with fountains, particularly those with fine jets which can become clogged very easily. Keep the water clear of algae and for a fountain pool devoid of plants it will probably be necessary to use algaecides regularly if there is a large surface area exposed to sunshine. In areas of very hard water, add pH adjusters to the water in order to reduce the build-up of lime on the jets, as the frequent topping up required in a fountain pool continually introduces more alkaline water.

OPPOSITE: **There is nothing quite like a fine-spray fountain for catching the light, particularly when it is viewed looking into the light source.**

RIGHT: **If a fountain is required in a waterlily pool, it should have a very fine spray to minimize the disturbance on the surface of the water.**

FAR RIGHT: **Create the simplest of fountains by removing the rose from a fountain head to produce a wide, vertical spout.**

FOUNTAIN SPRAY PATTERNS

Fountains are available in a number of different styles and shapes. The choice of fountain shape depends ultimately on the style of the garden. For example, certain shapes, such as a plume spray, are more suitable for a formal setting.

Plume spray: good for a formal setting

Bell jet: not very good in windy locations

Multi-tier: ideal for underlighting

Single spout: ideal for lighting

Surface rose jet: the simplest spray, often supplied with the pump

Geyser jet: good for windy sites

BRIDGES

When creating routes through a space, two different activities are taking place. One is directional, leading you towards an object or area; the other is spatial, separating one area from another. When these areas are separated by a change of level or by a barrier, such as water, a bridge can provide the route between them.

An attractive bridge not only provides a crossing place but also acts as a strong focal point, and is the true finishing touch to many an informal water composition. A bridge must appear to serve a purpose, and the simpler the design, the more attractive and natural it will appear. Bridges in Oriental water gardens have a much more symbolic function in the garden, and they are often brightly coloured or ornately built. The strong design of an arched bridge that forms a perfect circle with its reflection in the water is not appropriate to the simplicity of the natural landscape

that has become such a feature in western gardens. Regrettably, these arched bridges are often copied in domestic gardens where their steep arches tend to become awkward humps in a path rather than provide a strong reflection. If there is no need for the bridge to be arched, it will be much simpler to construct a straight bridge just above the surface of the water. This will provide a wonderful platform for looking down into the water and give a new viewpoint of the pool margins and their background.

Bridges can be made from a range of materials, including stone, timber, iron and steel. Building a bridge in stone is a skilled operation and should be left to a professional or, at least, a skilled amateur. Indeed, bridges across large expanses of water or big level changes call for specialist manufacture and installation. A simple timber bridge, on the other

BELOW: **Gentle curves and relaxed lines abound in this restful scene. The bridge is curved rather than steeply arched.**

hand, is a much easier affair and can be constructed with minimal building skills. Timber is a versatile construction medium. It is strong and can be cut into shapes to produce designs to suit a wide range of styles. It can be painted to complement or stand out from its surroundings, or it can be left natural, made in heavy sections of hardwood, and allowed to weather. The maximum span for an unsupported timber bridge is 2.4m (8ft); if it is longer than this it will be necessary to build piers in the water.

To bridge a small stream or bog garden, bolt wide timber planks to cross struts fixed firmly into the ground on either side with posts. Safety is always important, so sling stout ropes between these to make handrails, and attach wire netting to the surface to reduce the risk of slipping. At its most basic, rustic sawn timbers would provide a woodland look, but more exotic hardwoods would make this idea perfect for a Japanese-style situation.

Alternative construction materials are iron and steel, which have great strength, enabling large spans to be created. This is often used to support timber in larger bridges. The versatility of metal makes it suitable for both traditional and new designs. Sleek modern forms capitalize on the qualities of steel and wire, which combine visual lightness with great strength.

ABOVE: **Simplicity of design is perfected in this combination of bridge and plants.**

ABOVE LEFT: **A bridge made from larch poles works well in this country garden.**

TOP LEFT: **A bog garden has much more impact viewed from above.**

ISLANDS

RIGHT: **Islands can be a useful refuge for wildlife and can also be made into very attractive structures.**

BELOW: **This modern island design uses a submerged stone surround in order to create a line of reflection from the irises which appear just above the surface of the water.**

An island will add interest to a large, informal pool, and although it is better to incorporate such a feature into the construction from the start, a small island can be added later.

If the position of the island is included in the initial design, the outline of the island can be identified during the excavation. To create a wet island, leave a flat, raised mound just under the surface of the water in the chosen position. When the liner is initially laid over the pool, it should be drawn over the mound, providing a shallow area on which the island can be built. The island should be covered with a thin layer of wet soil, which will be a suitable place for marginal plants or grass. It will also be an ideal safe haven for waterfowl. To prevent the soil from

falling over the sides of the island, rocks should be mortared onto the liner around the edge.

You can also build a dry island for plants that prefer drier soil, such as trees and shrubs. To create a dry island, leave a flat, raised mound when you are digging out the pool. Drape the liner over the hump above the future level of the water, then cut the liner around the shape of the island. Any planting should be allowed to root into this dry soil.

If the island is an afterthought, however, drain the pool and build a retaining wall on the liner, following the outline of the island, until it is level with the water surface. The area inside the wall can then be filled with soil, which should be graded into a gentle mound above the water level.

STEPPING STONES

For narrow stretches of shallow water or streams, stepping stones make the perfect combination of rock and water. You will need to find flat-topped rocks or boulders. These will be heavy, so you will need to enlist some help to move them. Suitable rocks are available from stone merchants and suppliers. In fact, special large cobbles are sold for use as stepping stones or as isolated specimens on a cobble beach. Even if only one or two are used, stepping stones provide a highly pleasing way of continuing a visual link with the other side of a stream. This is best achieved when they marry up to other stepping stones laid into the grass at each side of the water.

Stepping stones are not suitable as a means of crossing water for the elderly, but they do make an excellent aesthetic and functional "prop" if you are creating the type of landscape that is associated with a natural rocky stream. If the water is moving, stepping stones can create ripples in the stream, which will add to the interest and exploit the fascinating properties of moving water.

If stepping stones are to be laid on top of a flexible liner, you will need to protect the liner with some spare scraps of liner or with pieces of black polythene (polyethylene). A wobbly stepping stone would spell disaster, so it is essential to stabilize each rock or boulder by placing it on a nest-like mound of stiff concrete.

Choose the narrowest stretch of water to place either a single stone or an arrangement of stones, because this will not only limit the number of stones that you will have to buy, but it will also look more natural, as boulders are usually held at narrow points, thus creating a dam.

If a stream has been built with one or more waterfalls, the top of a waterfall makes a good point to introduce a stepping stone because the width of the stream will have been narrowed in order to create the waterfall. As well as looking natural, this provides a useful crossing point and a good place to have something to kneel on if you ever need to make adjustments to the fall.

Timber rounds can be used as an alternative to stepping stones in a bog garden, where it will be easier to stabilize them than would be the case in water. It will still be necessary to bed the hardwood trunks on concrete to make sure that they are completely stable. If the timber rounds are thicker than 15cm (6in), then

LEFT: The curving direction of these stepping stones, which meander through a dried river bed, is much more informal and restful than a straight line.

BELOW: This clever mix of flat-topped granite boulders and solid-looking timbers forms an enclosure for the waterlilies as well as an access path.

a hardcore base, rather than a concrete one, will be adequate. To minimize slipping on any growth of algae on the surface of the wood, staple chicken wire to the surface and brush over the surface with a stiff brush to remove any slime.

LIGHTING

Garden lighting adds a new dimension to any outdoor area, but especially when it is used to illuminate moving water at night. Consider the effect of a cobble fountain as its catches the light or an underwater lamp lighting up a waterfall from below. If you like architectural specimen plants, consider underlighting a giant rhubarb (*Gunnera manicata*) or an ornamental rhubarb (*Rheum palmatum*). The effect can be quite stunning.

If you have installed a pump in the pool, it is highly likely that a waterproof connector or switchbox will have been fitted already, so the cost of installation will be minimal. You will need to check if the type of lighting you envisage will be available in both mains and low voltage. There are an increasing number of safety directives limiting the use of mains-powered appliances for outdoor domestic use, and garden lighting is increasingly manufactured in low-voltage systems.

One of the joys of garden lighting is that it can be used to great effect in winter, when there are many silhouettes of trees and shrubs that are perfect for high-lighting. Supplementary lighting provides an opportunity to change completely the direction of the light source that illuminates the garden during the day, and you will find that features take on wholly new identities.

The surface of a pool that is clear of leaves in winter will take on a greater reflective role, and a good way of checking to see if there are suitable outlines that would be reflected by underlighting is to use a flashlight. Use one of the more powerful rechargeable flashlights with an attached plastic bracket so that it will stand up by itself. Place the flashlight under any trees, shrubs or ornaments that are behind the pool when seen from the main viewing window, and then return to the window, leaving the flashlight shining up into the feature. If you are pleased with the result from a strong flashlight, you will be delighted when there is a more permanent spotlight in the same place.

Of course, you cannot try this experiment with underwater features, but there are more obvious places for lighting: directly under a waterfall, for example, so that the light shines up through the rivulets of water, or near a water spout, such as a brimming urn or drilled rock fountain.

Avoid siting a light source so that it shines back into a main viewing area, and always hide the light so that the casings and lenses are not obtrusive in the daytime. If coloured lenses are used, keep these subtle: avoid turning the garden into a multi-coloured fairyland. Amber lenses are soft and will make a water spout resemble a flame, but they tend to bleach the colour from leaves so they are best restricted to non-plant features. When you are using a spotlight to highlight a feature, look out for lenses that will provide a narrow beam of light, which is useful for underlighting waterfalls, and for lenses with a wider beam, which are useful for bathing large trees like weeping willows.

An increasing number of solar-powered garden lights have become available in recent years. These are modestly priced and require no electrical connection. They can be used to mark the edge of an area of water or to highlight the route of a path alongside water, which is especially useful if the garden is used frequently for barbecues or entertaining.

Working out the design can be one of the most exciting stages in the process of creating a water feature. It can be

PLANNING THE DESIGN

very helpful to visit other gardens and to look through books and magazines if you need inspiration for a design that will be suitable for your garden, as well as for ideas on where to site your rock and water feature.

OPPOSITE: **Once you have planned the design of a feature on paper, an understanding of how rocks are arranged in nature can be a great asset.**

INITIAL CHOICES

A rock and water garden does not automatically mean that there will be a small rock garden next to a kidney-shaped pool with a small watercourse running through the rocks. On the contrary, the use of rock with water offers a wide choice of schemes and tends to preclude only those strictly formal designs that are more suitable for gardens with straight lines and symmetrical balance. Including rock with water is generally easier in an informal garden, where there is a sense of freedom in the shapes that are used and where there are slopes, shrubberies, curving borders and plants in groups rather than in rows.

STILL OR MOVING WATER?

The first decision to take, no matter what the size of the garden, will be whether to have still or moving water. Moving water brings life and sound to a garden, and can be either exhilarating or restful. Small, silent electric pumps, which are easy to install and cheap to run, have made it possible for fountains, reservoir features and watercourses to be introduced into the smallest of gardens to create a variety of moods.

The two basic methods of creating moving water are by installing fountains or building watercourses. Watercourses can be formal or informal, while slow-moving streams can be built without the presence of any natural slope. If there is a significant natural slope in your garden it will be difficult to resist the temptation to design a scheme that exploits the noise and glistening movement of waterfalls. In informal settings, the illusion of a natural stream running through the garden can be created and enhanced by streamside marginals and moisture-loving plants.

A flexible liner is so versatile that it is the best choice for creating an imaginative stream or cascade. Few gardens are so level that a stream cannot be incorporated in the scheme; all it requires are space for a base pool or reservoir and an existing garden style into which the stream can be incorporated. Cascades and rocky watercourses need a slope if they are to look natural, and the more room that is available for the water to change direction rather than fall in a straight line, the more successful the finished effect will be.

The expense of materials likely to be invested in a feature with moving water will be more fully rewarded if it can be sited so that it is visible from a much-frequented window. The play of reflected light on waterfalls adds much to the attraction of a watercourse. Keep returning to the window at each stage of the marking-out process, visualizing the angle and direction that the waterfalls will take.

MISTAKES WITH MOVING WATER

If the watercourse is to be an extension of the main pool, the level of water in the pool will drop each time the pump is turned on to charge the watercourse before water returns to the base pool. If the pool is very small and an extensive watercourse is designed to be pumped from it, the pool could be pumped dry. Do not design a watercourse with a larger surface area than the main reservoir pool. If the pool is topped up when the pump is circulating, then there is a risk that there will be too much water in the system and the base pool will flood once the pump is turned off.

Moving water may be introduced later on, and the design of a feature with still water ought to take this future change into account in its initial shape, position and size. A tiny pool, for instance, may not contain a sufficient volume of water to cope with the circulation requirements of a fountain or watercourse. If you plan

RIGHT: **The dominant use and placing of walling stones has created an individual water feature, which makes a powerful statement in what is otherwise an informal garden setting.**

BELOW: **Ambitious stepped cascades require cleaning and the removal of leaves to achieve an even film of falling water.**

ABOVE: **Drifts of moisture-loving plants complete this informal water garden. As summer progresses, day lilies and deep red bistort come into their own.**

OPPOSITE ABOVE: **Waterlilies prefer still water, so bear this in mind when planning the design. Marginal beds create pockets of interest in this garden.**

OPPOSITE BELOW: **A small waterfall brings noise and movement, and increases oxygen levels for fish.**

to add such a feature at a later date, make sure that the pool has an adequate reservoir by increasing the depth, even if it is difficult to enlarge the surface area.

SUNKEN OR RAISED POOLS?

If a still pool is your choice, decide whether it is going to be sunken or raised or partly raised. A sloping site lends itself to a partly raised pool so that it is possible to achieve the necessary level surround, and such an arrangement works well when it is edged with a retaining wall of rock. If the pool is to be sited on a slope that climbs away from the house, cut into the bank rather than making a retaining wall on the lower side of the pool. If you do this, the pool will not be obscured by the mound-like retaining wall and will, instead, be level with the land on the house side of the garden. If, however, the slope falls away from the house, build a retaining wall to make a partially raised pool with the retaining wall on the lower side of the slope. If you do this, the pool will be more visible from the house than if the bank were cut into and the pool partially obscured on the house side.

A raised pool on a flat site tends to be much more appropriate in a formal garden, but small informal pools can be incorporated inside old railway sleepers (ties) with small rocks and alpine plants placed around the water. This is an appropriate solution in small backyards and gardens where excavation would be difficult and where the size of pool is more in keeping with a tiny garden.

A sunken pool will look more appropriate in a larger garden where there is space to surround the water with bog gardens, beds for moisture-loving plants and rock areas. If a sunken pool is edged with rocks, using the same type of rock for outcropping on adjacent areas or for making raised rock gardens will make the pool appear much more integrated within the overall garden.

FISH AND FLORA

If keeping ornamental fish is a priority, it is sensible to consider that filtration may be necessary as the fish grow larger and their numbers increase. Filters require pumps, and pumps require electricity, which will be an additional cost in terms of both the installation of the supply and the running costs, and this may be a factor in your initial plans.

If plants are a priority, allow ample room at the sides of a sunken pool to develop independent boggy areas and ground for moisture-loving plants; the diversity of the planting can be increased over time. The plants associated with a water garden can take up more space than the actual clear water, and beds constructed with flexible liners immediately adjacent to the pool will very quickly appear to be an integral part of the water garden.

OTHER CONSIDERATIONS

There are other factors that will affect your choice of site for the pool. For example, the siting of a feature that needs a pump may be influenced by the installation costs of armoured electric cable. The style of water feature will also have a bearing on its siting. You may want to hear the sound of running water through a window or from a patio. Or, you might like to attract wildlife to the pool, in which case it should be sited as far from the house as possible. You may have a handsome tree that is a prime candidate for reflection in the surface of a pool, while the availability of space around the water's edge for future planting may take precedence.

FIRST QUESTIONS

When you are planning a water feature, these are just some of the questions you will have to consider:

• Do you want moving water?
  - If so, do you want a fountain or watercourse (or both)?
  - Will the main reservoir pool be large enough to cope with the circulation requirements of your fountain or watercourse?

• Do you want still water?
  - Will the pool be sunken, raised or partly raised?
  - Do you want a formal or informal pool?
  - Will you have to make provision for marginal shelves?

• Do you want to keep ornamental fish?
  - If so, you may need to consider filtration, using a biological filter and/or ultra-violet clarifier

• Is growing plants a priority?
  - If so, you will need to allow ample room for independent boggy areas and ground for growing moisture-loving plants.

• Is cost an issue?
  - Remember that introducing a pump, whether for filtration, moving water in a stream or fountain, or lighting will be an extra cost in terms of both the installation and the running costs.

MAKING A PLAN

Once you have decided on the style of water feature, make a rough plan of how you see the garden. This need not be sophisticated, but it should be accurate enough for you to position the pool in relation to existing items such as trees, buildings, walls and slopes. One of the useful aspects of carrying out this exercise is that it will prompt you to start thinking about all sorts of considerations that might not at first have seemed especially important. When you are preparing your plan, make sure that you include all of the following features before you even begin to consider anything exciting like future planting. It might seem laborious, but it will definitely be worth it in the end.

Marking the features identified in the plan below will allow you to see the areas that should be avoided if at all possible – that is, those in shade, those with underground service supplies and those in windy areas – while identifying the desirable areas of the garden: that is, those in sun and those that can be appreciated from the windows of the house. Only when

you have identified all the existing characteristics of your garden will you be in a position to get down to the more creative side of planning.

UTILITIES
Identify and mark the position of all underground services, such as water pipes, gas pipes, electric cables, drains, sewer pipes and manhole covers. If the pool is going to be excavated it is, of course, important that these are avoided. Most of them are deeper than the average depth of an ornamental pool, but do not assume that this is the case in your garden and plan to avoid them if at all possible. If you have no idea where they are, contact the company involved. The utility will have the equipment to trace the route of its pipes if no plan exists.

TREES
The position of trees will affect the siting of a pool due to the shade they cast and their falling leaves. The leaves of some trees, such as yew (*Taxus*), release toxins if they

A TYPICAL DESIGN PLAN

This simple plan shows the underground services, main areas of shade and viewing points. It is invaluable as the first step in the design process.

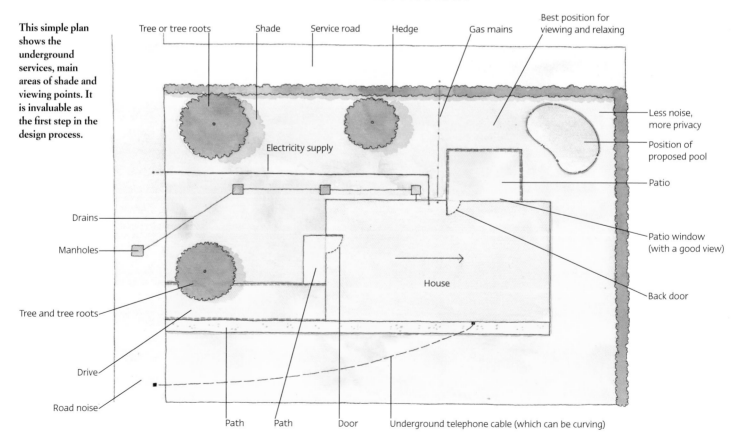

Tree or tree roots · Shade · Service road · Hedge · Gas mains · Best position for viewing and relaxing

Electricity supply

Less noise, more privacy

Position of proposed pool

Patio

Patio window (with a good view)

Back door

Drains

Manholes

Tree and tree roots

Drive

Road noise

House

Path · Path · Door · Underground telephone cable (which can be curving)

accumulate in water, so avoid areas near such trees. Also avoid siting a pool under most conifers because the leaf scales and old needles will drop into the pool almost all year round, particularly after heavy wind, and cause the water's surface to become dirty. The roots of trees can also be a physical obstacle to digging out the soil, and the questing roots of vigorous species, such as poplar (*Populus*) and willow (*Salix*), can damage flexible liners. Although some species of tree produce only light shade, trees such as horse chestnut (*Aesculus hippocastanum*) and sycamore (*Acer*) cast dense shade, and the area under them that is in shade constantly (rather than for a small part of the day) should be marked on the plan.

If there are any items with strong reflective qualities, such as a fine tree, mark them on the plan for consideration when working out the position of the pool.

BOUNDARIES, OUTBUILDINGS AND VIEWING POINTS

Walls and fences as well as outbuildings, such as sheds and garages, should be marked on the plan because they, too, cast shade. They also cause eddies of wind, which gust around the walls on an exposed site. The main ground-floor viewing windows are most important to include on your plan because they will help identify view lines. Doors inevitably mean paths to various points, and in a new garden it is important to establish the route of paths early in the planning.

WIND FUNNELS

Suburban gardens are notorious for having wind funnels between properties and fences. Even if you cannot entirely avoid a wind funnel, you can plant windbreaks or erect trellises in order to filter the wind. Filtered wind, such as occurs in the area behind a hedge or trellis, causes much less damage than eddying wind on the leeward side of a solid barrier. It is amazing that wind strength will be considerably reduced at ground level at a distance of from seven to ten times the height of the semi-permeable barrier on the leeward side of the windbreak. Aquatic plants make sappy growth, which is easily damaged or blown over, and waterlilies detest disturbance to their leaves.

ORIENTATION

It is important that you do not forget to mark the position of the sun in relation to your garden. Most pool plants prefer to be in full sun, and waterlilies will be shy in flowering without it.

ABOVE: **With due care in the design and in their siting, swimming pools can be as ornamental as garden pools, and can break away from the rather traditional rectangular shape.**

LEFT: **A large garden is by no means vital for designing and planting an interesting and attractive pond.**

THE WATER TABLE

There is one very important consideration that should be checked before you make any final decisions about your pool, and this is something that may not be obvious from simply looking at the garden. There may be a problem lurking underground in the form of a high water table.

The water table is the level at which underground water lies in the soil. It is likely to vary from summer to winter, being at its highest in the winter, even rising to within 38–45cm (15–18in) of the surface in some low-lying gardens. Its effect on a pool could mean that the excavation starts to fill with water to the height of the water table in the surrounding land, and, because a sunken pool may well be dug out to 90cm (3ft), this would be a serious problem. It is most likely to be a problem on heavy clay soils on low-lying flat land. It is less likely to be a consideration on light sandy soils or soils on the upper levels of sloping land. There have been some very surprised pool owners, who have woken up to find the liner billowing up to the surface

of the pool because of the water pressure in the surrounding soil. If this happens, placing heavy paving slabs on the liner or pouring concrete into the bottom of the pool is the only solution – short, that is, of rebuilding the whole pool in reinforced concrete.

FINDING THE WATER TABLE

If you are at all uncertain about the level of the water table in your garden, it is a sensible precaution to dig a trial hole on the proposed site. If the trial hole reveals a problem, draining the site is not an easy option and could be very costly. A soak-away or drainage chamber constructed under or near the pool will simply fill with water, so consider other remedies before abandoning the idea of a water garden. If the garden has any slope, consider re-siting the pool on the higher land. If there is no slope, you might prefer to build a pool that is raised slightly above the water table either by elevating the pool sides or by building up the soil level on the

RIGHT: **Before starting work, make sure that a pond made with a flexible liner is not subject to undue pressure from the water table, which will cause it to billow up into the water.**

OPPOSITE ABOVE:

Natural pools, such as wildlife pools, are likely to look best if they are sited at a low point in the garden.

proposed site. Obviously, the latter solution would need to be done sensitively so that the pool does not look like the crater of a volcano. You will probably also have to import large quantities of soil to achieve a natural finish. Raising the walls of the pool is a more suitable solution in a formal garden or in a small garden where the surrounding contours are not so important.

EXPLOITING A HIGH WATER TABLE

You can exploit a high water table by making a natural pool with a gentle, sloping gradient around the sides. This can be done successfully if your garden is on solid clay, which can be compressed into a sunken saucer shape with a heavy hammer. The pummelling will make the clay less susceptible to the seasonal variance in the water table, and, as long as the water level is topped up in periods of prolonged dry weather, it will work reasonably well and cost nothing. Such a pool may be prone to flooding in wet winter weather, but it is possible to overcome this to some extent by a careful choice of planting in the surrounding soil. Such pools are not suitable for fish, however, which can become beached in the surrounding soil in a flood or parched in summer if you forget to top up the pool. As an environment for plants, however, it is second to none, and such a pool will attract a considerable variety of wildlife. Heavy rainfall may cause the water to become cloudy for a while, but this should clear in a few days.

LOW-LYING GROUND

The dream of creating a pool that looks just right in its surroundings inevitably leads gardeners to think about siting an informal or wildlife pool at the lowest point in the garden. If there is no problem with the water table, this is a good choice. There are, however, two minor points to bear in mind. The first is that the lowest point in the garden is invariably a frost pocket, and the cold air that settles there in winter and spring tends to delay the warming up of the water in late spring. Provided your planting does not include early-spring-flowering plants, which will be damaged by frost, such as skunk cabbage (*Lysichiton*), this need be no more than a minor snag. The second point, which is more serious in an area subject to flash rainstorms, is the risk of flooding the pool by water run-off from the surrounding higher ground. Although the flooding may be only temporary after exceptionally heavy rain, the floodwater may contain fertilizers or other garden chemicals. The addition of any chemical to a pool can have serious

HOW TO FIND THE WATER TABLE

It is better to work out the level of the water table in your garden in winter and after a period of heavy rain to assess the highest level that the table is likely to reach. To discover the level of the water table, follow these guidelines:

- Dig a hole about 30–40cm (12–16in) square and to the same depth as the proposed pool
- Leave the hole for a day or two to see if any water seeps in from the sides and, if so, at what level it finally settles

consequences for fish, and even a small amount of fertilizer can cause the water to turn green. Positioning the pool on a slightly elevated part of the garden will do much to minimize these two potential problems, and when the pool has to be drained, the water can be siphoned out to the land, without the need for a pump.

SIZE, DEPTH AND SHAPE

ABOVE: **Small, shallow pools can soon become choked with submerged oxygenators. The depth, rather than the surface area, has more bearing on a healthy balanced pond.**

OPPOSITE BELOW: **The shallowness of this circular pool means that it will need the movement of water, preferably through a filter, to prevent it from going cloudy.**

Restrictions already existing within your garden may give little freedom in determining the size of pool, but if there are few limitations on space, design a pool that is as large as possible. Apart from the greater impact of a large pool, it is an established fact that the larger the volume of water, the easier it is to achieve and maintain clear water. Often it is a lack of confidence that makes gardeners restrict themselves to a small kidney-shaped pool. Costs are, of course, relevant, but the cost of good flexible liners has become more reasonable in the last few years, and a glance at a price list of different-size liners will reveal that doubling the size of the pool does not mean doubling the cost of the liner.

DECIDING ON THE SIZE

Relating the size of pool to the size of garden is crucial. A pool that is too small will be insignificant; if it is too large, your neighbours will think you eccentric. There is no hard-and-fast scale determining the size of pool in relation to the size of garden, and any such scale would, in any case, become hopelessly confusing when it came to defining the boundaries of the water. A pool with sharp, crisp edges is a quite different water feature from a pool where there is planting both in the shallow water and in the boggy and moist ground around its edges. If the latter style is your preference, you will need as much space as possible, and you may find that the lawn becomes a mere grassy path around your water garden.

DECIDING ON THE DEPTH

While there are no definite rules about surface area, there are guidelines to the appropriate minimum depth, both for ease of water management and for the survival of fish in winter, and it can be helpful to understand the ratio between surface area and depth. If you visit an aquatic centre, you will see that preformed units all tend to be about 45cm (18in) deep. This should be regarded as the absolute minimum depth if you are making a pool with sides that are as near vertical as possible and if there are no marginal shelves. Take a closer look at the preformed units, and you will see that most of them have substantial areas of the sides moulded into shallow shelves. It doesn't take much of a mathematician to realize that the water contained in a pool with vertical sides and no marginal shelves will be much greater than the volume of water in a pool with slightly sloping sides and marginal shelves. When it comes to water management, the first pool is substantially easier.

Ease of water management can be defined as the ease with which a stable, self-sustaining ecological balance is created; in layman's terms this means creating clear water. Providing sufficient volume of water in relation to the surface area is the key, and the guideline is to provide a minimum of 378 litres of water to every square metre of water surface (10 gallons of water to every square foot). To achieve this in a pool with marginal shelves and slightly sloping sides, you will need a depth of 60cm (2ft). A depth less than this is an invitation to algae to spread; a depth greater than this is unnecessary in a garden pool of less than 28 square metres (92 square feet), and the water would be too deep for the effective flowering of most types of waterlily. In addition, ornamental fish do not need deeper water in temperate climates. Deeper pools will not cause significant problems, but there is no need to make work for yourself during construction. The main exception to this guideline is in the building of raised concrete pools for large specimens of koi, which is a specialized field of fish-keeping for which the guidelines for ornamental pools do not apply.

DECIDING ON THE SHAPE

The design of the surrounding garden will have a large influence on the shape of the pool. As we are dealing mainly with informal pools, strictly geometric shapes, such as squares, rectangles and circles, are the least appropriate. A kidney shape is the most common for an informal garden pool, and slight variations from this outline will help to give more individuality.

Whatever shape is chosen, bear in mind the practicality of later maintenance, and this means avoiding an excess of shallow inlets or promontories, which will soon succumb to algae and can quickly be completely swamped by the planting. If you have the freedom to make a wildlife pool any shape you want, consider an egg shape. It is strong and simple and has a wider zone, which may even be wide enough for a small island. If a stream or watercourse is envisaged, the shape will look even more natural if the watercourse enters a narrower zone, gradually widening to a more rounded outline.

In addition to the maintenance problems that arise if the outline is too squiggly, there will be considerable wastage if a flexible liner is used because it will have to be cut to fit the complex shapes. Liners can be welded into complex shapes by some suppliers and manufacturers, but this can add substantially to the cost.

The best way to decide on a shape is to lay out a length of string or rope or a garden hose on the proposed site. Some people use sand, but this is not as easy to re-lay if you change your mind. Not only is this process invaluable for deciding on the best site for the pond, but it will also allow you to refine the shape by assessing it from the main viewing points and at eye level, when it takes on a quite different perspective from that shown on the plan. When you are viewing the shape, bear in mind the future planting or any additional beds or rock features around the sides. Leave the string or garden hose in place for at least a day, so that you can observe where shadows fall across it. This exercise is one of the most important tasks in the planning of a new pool, and it is also the simplest to do.

The initial planning stage is almost complete. It is impossible to plot on a plan the placing of individual rocks, but a planting plan could be made at this stage.

Preparing a planting plan at this point may help to ensure that suitable areas are created in and around the pool margins, which may have been overlooked when the position of the marginal shelves was decided. In addition, if the plan is drawn to scale on graph paper you can also see how many plants the pool will accommodate. This is often frustrating, because it can soon become evident that there may not be room for everything, but many of the marginals can be grown in an independent boggy bed at the poolside and it is still not too late to make allowance for this in your final plan.

BELOW: **Decide on the shape of your pool by laying a length of string or rope or even a garden hose on the ground. Play around with the shape and design, viewing it from all angles, until you are satisfied with the result.**

AREAS AND VOLUMES

It is useful, even at the planning stage, to know how to calculate areas and volumes. These statistics will be important when choosing an appropriate size of pump and filter and in determining stocking rates of fish and oxygenating plants. It is also helpful if you need to use a chemical algicide to combat a build-up of algae.

Formal shapes present the least difficulty when it comes to calculating surface area and volume because they are easy to measure. Informal pools are more difficult because their outlines vary, and it is usually easier to base the dimensions on a rectangle or square drawn around the outline. Although the results are approximate, they are adequate for most purposes. When the water feature is such a complex shape that estimating the volume from one outline is not possible, divide the pool into sections, each with its own regularly shaped outline, and add these individual portions together.

CALCULATING SURFACE AREAS AND VOLUMES

Rectangles and squares The surface area can be easily calculated by multiplying the length by the width. The volume is obtained by multiplying the surface area by the depth. Where the depth varies – as in the case of a pool that has marginal shelves all the way around – divide the pool into two transverse sections, each with its own square area, and add the volumes of the two sections together. Remember to use either metric or imperial measurements throughout and do not mix the two. When you are multiplying imperial measurements it is easier if you convert inches into decimal fractions of a foot – 2ft 6in becomes 2.5ft, for example.

Circles Calculating the surface area of a circular pool requires the use of a mathematical constant called pi (π), which is 3.142. First, find the radius of the pool and square this; then multiply the result by pi (3.142). To determine the volume, multiply the surface area by the depth, making two calculations as before if the circle has two levels.

Irregular shapes For simple irregular shapes use the maximum width, length and depth to calculate surface area and volume as above. For more complex shapes divide the pool into approximate squares, rectangles, circles or semicircles and calculate the surface area of each. Add the figures together to calculate the total surface area. Multiply this figure by the depth in order to obtain the volume.

RIGHT: **You can easily work out the volume of a pool that is roughly circular by using a simple formula.**

LEFT: Large informal pool shapes need to be broken down into a series of smaller rectangles or circles in order to work out the volume.

CONVERTING THE VOLUME INTO LITRES OR GALLONS

The formulae for calculating volumes will give a final figure in cubic metres or cubic feet. To convert cubic metres into litres, multiply the figure by 1,000. To convert cubic feet into gallons multiply the figure by 6.25.

The first time you may need to use these measurements will be if you are going to use a flexible liner to make the pool. Remember that the all-important depth of the sides must be added to the length and breadth. A simple calculation of the surface area to give an indication of the cost of the liner would be a very serious underestimate.

If you live in an area where there are local suppliers who retail liners off the shelf, there is much to be said for digging out the hole first then going along to buy the liner. If you can do this, any alterations that you make to the original plan during the digging process, by either slightly enlarging or reducing the pool size, can be taken into account when you buy the flexible liner. If you have already ordered the liner from a mail-order source, you will have to stick rigidly to your original measurements.

HOW TO CALCULATE AREA AND VOLUME

Calculating the right surface area and volume of your pond is vitally important. The following formulae are for common pool shapes:

Calculating surface area
Rectangles and squares
area = length x width

Circles
area = r^2 x pi (r = the radius of pool)

Irregular shapes
area = maximum width x length
(Note: for complex irregular shapes, divide the pool into approximate squares, rectangles, circles or semi-circles and calculate the surface area of each)

Calculating volume of water
volume = surface area x depth
(Note: where the depth varies, such as in a pool with marginal shelves all the way round, divide the pool into two transverse sections, each with its own square area, and add together the volumes of the two sections)

Converting litres and gallons
To convert cubic metres into litres: multiply the figure by 1,000
To convert cubic feet into gallons: multiply the figure by 6.25

Remember to work consistently in either metric or imperial measurements

SAFETY

It is impossible to make a water garden utterly safe, and this may be a major consideration if the safety of small children is a particular concern. Short of fencing the water off completely and having access through a lockable gate, it is perhaps best to postpone building a dangerously deep pool. A design that allows for the introduction of water at a later date is sensible; you could even use the proposed pool area as a sandpit in the short term.

IMPROVING SAFETY

An existing pool can be made safer by making a safety grid that is strong enough to bear the weight of a child and that will sit just under the surface of the water. The grid, which can be made from wood and strong plastic mesh or from the galvanized steel mesh used by builders for reinforcing concrete bases, can be supported in the water by brick piers built from the bottom or on the marginal shelves intended to house aquatic containers of shallow-water plants. Because it is just under the surface of the water it will be quickly covered with algae, which will make it much less conspicuous, and plants can be allowed to grow through the mesh to disguise it further.

BELOW: **This purpose-built, plastic-coated metal grid makes an attractive safety net on a pond surface.**

CHILD-FRIENDLY FEATURES

There are also a number of simple fountain features that are reasonably safe because they do not have an expanse of open water. These include cobble fountains and small fountain spouts that emerge from drilled rocks. These are not only safer features where there are young children in the garden, but they are ideally suited to smaller gardens or where there is limited time for maintaining a more traditional pool. This type of fountain can be taken a stage further by introducing a play element into their design. A cobble fountain can be adapted to allow children to run through the water spout, or a variety of spray patterns, controlled by a simple timing device, can be incorporated into the design. Whether moving or still, water will inevitably fascinate small children, but it must not be allowed to become a source of anxiety for a young family.

Taking care in the design of the edges and margins of a pool can do much to ease any anxiety parents may feel if children are playing near water. If there is a lawn area nearby, boisterous children will often run from the grass towards the water's edge. The slope on this critical area should be gradual, both under and at the side of the water's edge. Many natural pools illustrate this arrangement: the surrounding land forms a shallow saucer, while the water level changes from very shallow to deeper water over a few feet. A man-made pool is much more likely to have a steep edge, unless safety considerations were high on the list of priorities when it was constructed, as this is an easy way of achieving a large volume without taking up too much space. However, a shallow slope towards the edge, as well as making the pool look much more natural and increasing the habitat for marginal plants and wildlife, presents far less danger to children to slip and fall suddenly into deep water. The risk can be reduced still further by creating a barrier of plants, including thick reeds and rushes, on the side of the pool where they are most likely to be playing.

This barrier planting does not need to be all aquatic planting in the shallows. Thick-growing, shrubby, suckering, woody growth soon becomes almost impassable if plants such as dogwood (*Cornus*), shrubby willow (*Salix*), hazel (*Corylus*) and elder (*Sambucus*) are chosen. If you really want a barrier while the children are young, use thorny subjects such as dog rose (*Rosa*

canina), holly (*Ilex*), gorse (*Ulex*) and barberry (*Berberis*). When they are planted thickly, species like these will look fairly natural near water. They can also be removed later when the children are old enough to be safe from any danger.

The choice of surfacing near the water's edge also needs careful consideration, particularly when there are elderly people and small children in the garden. Large, flat slabs of natural sandstone can be very dangerous when they are wet and algal growth forms a thin film on the surface. If paving is used, it is advisable to choose one of the concrete paving slabs that are readily available with non-slip surfaces; they are made in a wide range of sizes and colours. Cobbles, which will slow down children, are so unstable underfoot that they are not an ideal choice and are far more

likely to cause a fall near the water. If access is provided right up to the water's edge, make sure it is stable, and if there is any paving lay it on a mortar base to prevent movement.

ABOVE: **A dome made from plastic pipes and netting acts as heron protection. This could be adapted to increase safety for toddlers.**

LEFT: **A home-made, functional grid, just under the surface of the water and covered by cobbles, reduces the danger for small children until they are old enough for the grid to be removed.**

ELECTRICITY

The possibility of installing electrical accessories in a pool should be considered at the earliest possible stage, even if there are no immediate plans to include any such gadgets. It is so much easier to install cabling before the edges are laid and while there is still disruption from construction than to disturb a maturing water garden.

An electrical supply is normally associated with moving water where the source of circulation is an electric pump. There are, however, other electrical items that can be equally appropriate to a feature with still water, most notably lighting. In addition, an initially small selection of ornamental fish will soon grow and multiply, and a filtration system may have to be installed if you do not intend to reduce the numbers of fish.

There are few pools to which, sooner or later, an electrical connection will not be invaluable, and there are a number of precautions that must be taken to make this potentially lethal partnership safe. Before discussing the safety fittings used in an installation, it would be prudent to employ an electrician not only to fit the pieces together but also to advise you on which items of equipment to buy.

ELECTRICAL EQUIPMENT

The first item of electrical equipment with which you should be familiar is a residual current device (RCD), also known as a contact circuit breaker. Such a device should be considered as a compulsory installation rather than an optional extra to ensure peace of mind. These devices cut off the mains supply within 30

RIGHT: **By introducing electricity to a pool, an exciting new dimension of creative water gardening is made possible with the installation of a dramatic, cascading watercourse.**

milliseconds of the supply being accidentally earthed, quick enough to prevent a fatal electric shock. They can be purchased for indoor or outdoor installation. An indoor switch to pool equipment may seem an unnecessary luxury, but a cable can be taken through a house wall for relatively little extra expense, and the internal switch and RCD can then be controlled from indoors. For something like lighting, which is switched on and off frequently, an internal switch is a boon. For equipment such as filter pumps, which may be running continuously, there is less advantage in having an indoor switch because these would switch off automatically through the RCD if there was a problem.

From the source of the supply protected by an RCD the supply will need cabling to an outdoor connector or switch. Because the route of this cable is likely to cross part of the garden, there is always the risk that it may be cut or damaged when you are cultivating the borders. To prevent this from happening, use special cabling with a thick protective sheathing or armoured coating, and bury it deep enough to ensure that it is unlikely to be exposed during normal gardening activities. As an extra precaution, cover the cable with roofing tiles and lay a marker tape over these to alert any future gardener to the presence of an underground electrical cable.

The buried armoured cable is brought back to the surface at an appropriate point near the pool and connected to an approved waterproof connector or switch. At this connection box or switch the integral cable supplied with the pump or other device is also connected and the circuit is completed.

LOW-VOLTAGE UNITS

An increasing number of electrical accessories, such as pool lighting, are now supplied only as low-voltage units. The current to these accessories is reduced by a transformer to a level of voltage that will not be lethal in the event of a shock. The transformer replaces the RCD used with a mains voltage unit and can be supplied as a waterproofed outdoor fitting or, more commonly, for connecting in a dry airy place inside. Just as the RCD protection is not required, the supply cable to the accessory no longer needs the armoured sheathing, and cheaper low-voltage cable is all that is necessary. It is still prudent to protect this low-voltage cable in a plastic conduit. For some reason it is extremely palatable to mice, which can chew through unprotected cable in no time at all.

ABOVE: **Using three geyser jets, rather than one central jet, helps to blend the mix of formal and informal styles in this arrangement.**

ABOVE LEFT: **Even a shady spot can be brought to life by the movement of a waterfall and an abundance of shade-loving plants.**

LEFT: **This lush mix of leaves and flowers is given added emphasis by the spray of the fountain glistening in the sunshine.**

Water gardening has benefited from a growing investment in the materials suitable for a prolonged life under

MATERIALS AND EQUIPMENT

rigorous conditions. This means that the heavy manual labour involved in building a concrete lining for a pond or watercourse is now a thing of the past. In this chapter, we look at the materials and equipment commonly used for rock and water features.

OPPOSITE: There is a range of rocks available for water and rock gardens, as well as machines to make construction easier.

FLEXIBLE LINERS

With the style, size and site of your scheme worked out, now is the time to decide on the construction materials you will use. Concrete was once used almost exclusively for pool making, but then flexible and preformed liners were developed, and concrete is now no longer the usual choice for domestic pools, especially if they have an informal shape. Flexible liners are the ideal choice for the construction of informal water features. However, choosing a flexible liner has to be done with care. Your supplier will ask what type of liner you would like, and invariably the quality is linked to price.

Flexible liners are available in a variety of materials and thicknesses. Some materials were once manufactured in a choice of colours, but you can usually expect to find only black available now. The liners are sold from rolls of various widths, and, if installations are especially large or involve complicated shapes, they are welded. The most expensive liner is made from butyl and the cheapest from polythene (polyethylene), and in-between the two there is a range of excellent materials which are adequate for most applications.

POLYTHENE

Developed in the 1930s, polythene (polyethylene) was one of the first materials to be used as a flexible pool liner. It is cheap, available in different thicknesses and roll widths, and has a life expectancy of between three and five years. Its main drawback is that it deteriorates in ultra-violet light, which makes it harden and crack. For this reason, it is the least durable of all the flexible liners. Being a little unwieldy to handle, it can be easily torn and it is not easy to repair. Guarantees are seldom given with polythene, and you cannot weld or join one piece to another.

LOW-DENSITY POLYTHENE

In recent years, enormous advances in the manufacture of ordinary polythene (polyethylene) have led to a much-improved product, called low-density polythene, which is still cheaper than most other liners, but without the disadvantages of ordinary polythene. Guarantees are normally given with the two or three grades of manufacture that are available.

RIGHT: **The use of flexible liners allows for much greater freedom when you are working at different levels, as is the case with watercourses.**

TYPES OF FLEXIBLE LINER

Flexible liners are available in a variety of materials, thicknesses and
colours, with varying guarantees according to quality.

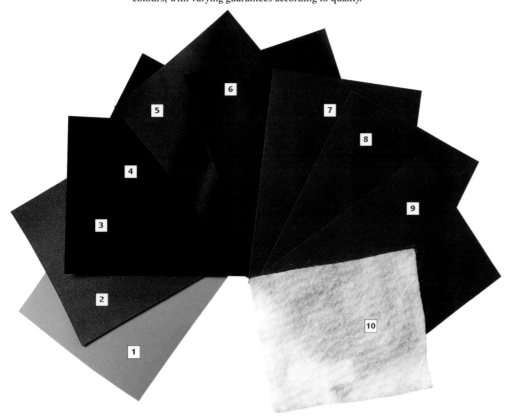

From left to right:

1 Butyl liner

2 Butyl liner

3 Low-density polythene
(polyethylene)

4 Low-density polythene
(polyethylene)

5–9 PVC in different grades

10 Underlay

PVC

About 30 years after the first polythene (polyethylene) liners appeared on the market, PVC liners became available, and these took off dramatically as reasonably priced liners that had overcome the initial difficulties that were experienced with ordinary high-density polythene. It has a minimum life expectancy of between five and 20 years and is available in different thicknesses. Some grades have been reinforced with a nylon mesh, welded between layers of PVC, for extra strength. It can be joined together, and easily repaired. The thicker grades are a little unwieldy to use in awkward shapes, but it is possible to get guarantees for several years.

BUTYL

At the same time as PVC appeared on the market, the real boon to water gardening made its debut in the form of butyl. It still remains the most widely used flexible liner by professional landscapers due to the fact that it has an elasticity that exceeds all other types. Because it is a by-product of rubber, it has the unique property of stretching under the pressure of water, and it will fit more snugly into awkward corners or crevices. It has an almost indefinite life expectancy, with guarantees available for 20 years or more. It is resistant to ultra-violet deterioration and can be repaired with a simple bicycle tyre repair kit. It is very simply extended by heat welding, and portable welding machines are available if welding has to be done on site. It is made in different thicknesses, but note that the thickest grade is very heavy, and you should make sure you have help in moving it about the garden. It is not the cheapest of liners, but it must be considered the best.

UNDERLAYS

Whatever type of liner you choose, it is best protected by an underlay of geotextile membrane, which is virtually impenetrable and, unlike newspaper and carpet, will not rot in wet soil. Soft sand is sometimes recommended as an underlay; this is perfectly acceptable on the pool bottom but is difficult to use on the sides and in any sharp corners, where it can be rubbed off easily. Like the liners, the underlay is available in several thicknesses.

PREFORMED UNITS

If you would like to have a small, formal pool with a symmetrical shape, a preformed pool unit is ideal. Such a pool is relatively easy to install and you will not have to deal with the bulky folds in tight corners which can be a problem with some of the thicker flexible liners. The stronger preformed units are useful for raised or partially raised pools because the walls are strong enough to support the internal water pressure and a more decorative outer wall can be built to disguise the unit.

BELOW: **Preformed units can be used in conjunction with flexible liners to provide a base pool for a watercourse.**

There are two main types of preformed units: rigid and semi-rigid. Rigid units are made of fibreglass or thick reinforced plastic; semi-rigid units are thinner and made from a cheaper plastic, which is moulded into sophisticated shapes under a vacuum process. Both types are better when they are moulded into simple shapes rather than being too fussy, with narrow outlines and several different levels. The regular shapes make it easier to pave around the edges and to disguise the plastic with a slight overhang of

the edge of the paving slabs. Fibreglass units are particularly easy to clean out and they need no more than a wipe over to remove a layer of algae if this becomes a problem.

Both types of preformed unit will have integral marginal shelves, which are positioned at the correct depth and width to support aquatic containers. When the containers are closely packed together and the plants become established, the rather artificial look quickly disappears.

Preformed units are less appropriate for informal pools. They tend to be built into fussy shapes with an excess of shelves, which reduces the volume and makes it more difficult to prevent the water from turning green. Most of the preformed units that are sold have a minimum depth of 45cm (18in), which is important for over-wintering fish and waterlilies during cold winters. A preformed unit that is shallower than this is best used as a small rock pool in a watercourse. This means that there is water moving through it, which will prevent greening as well as rapid fluctuations in temperature.

Although a beginner to water gardening may find a preformed unit tempting because it seems easier to install, such a pool is, in fact, more expensive than a pool of the same size made with the best of the flexible pool liners. In addition, although the units seem huge when they are seen displayed on their sides in a retail centre, they can be disappointingly small when they are dug into the ground.

SOME EXAMPLES OF PREFORMED UNITS

Preformed units are available in a range of different shapes and depths for both pools and for streams.

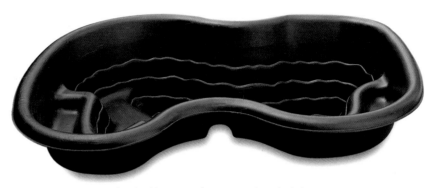

A unit with an even deep zone and ample shelves for marginal plants

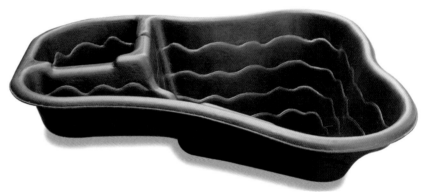

Less digging out is required with this unit which has a deep zone at only one end

A preformed stream unit cast from a gravel bed to give added authenticity to a pebble stream surround

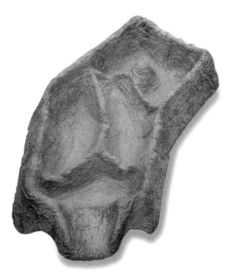

A preformed stream unit with a rock finish and a water basin with a right-hand curve

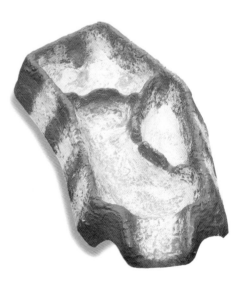

A preformed stream unit with a sandstone rock finish and a water basin with a left-hand curve

BUILDING BLOCKS AND MORTAR

BELOW: **Using bricks and a flexible liner makes for greater stability at pool edges.**

BELOW RIGHT: **Mortar can be used to cement rocks, here behind a flexible liner.**

BOTTOM RIGHT: **There are two grades of reinforcing fibres for adding to concrete or mortar mixes: fine grade (6mm/¼in) for skimming (left), and coarse grade (12mm/½in) for thicker layers.**

Traditional building materials still have an important place in building formal pools or deep rectangular pools for large fish, particularly if the pools are raised. The main change that has occurred in the use of concrete is that instead of moulds being cast inside wooden shuttering (formwork), concrete walling blocks are now used to form the sides and these are then lined with a flexible liner. Alternatively, the walls can be skimmed with mortar, and, when fish pools are constructed, the mortar may be given a final coat of resin.

Concrete is most likely to be used in the domestic rock and water garden in forming the walls of a base pool that has to be vertical to provide room for a greater volume of water and steeper sides for large fish like koi. The walling blocks would prevent the sides of the hole crumbling on a light or sandy soil. A flexible liner would then be used to make the pool watertight and disguise the concrete sides. On heavy, more solid

soils and where the sides could be dug out at a slightly sloping angle, the walling blocks can be dispensed with and the liner simply laid over a sheet of underlay.

Materials based on cement have been used in pool construction since Roman times. They provide a strong, durable, rigid lining that hardens with time due to the constant reaction with water. Concrete pools are ideal for areas prone to vandalism or where flexible liners may wear excessively. Their main weakness is a tendency to leak through hair-line cracks caused by the slightest movement in the surrounding soil. The larger or deeper the pool, the more stresses are placed on the flat surfaces both from underneath and from the sides, particularly in soils like clay that are prone to swelling and contraction.

The use of fibre-reinforced cement, which produces high-performance mortars, has largely overcome these problems and eliminated the construction of thick layers of concrete in situ. The elastic, synthetic,

LEFT: **This excellent mix of hard landscaping materials in the foreground provides a hard-wearing surface from which to view the informal background.**

BELOW: **A small raised pool is an ideal candidate for using reinforced fibres in the mortar.**

reinforcing fibres enable a high proportion of cement to be used, giving a stronger mix but without the risk of cracking that would occur in traditional mixes with a high cement content. The thinner mortar layer allows more movement, and the concrete can be laid on sloping curves on the bottom of a pool without the slumping of wet concrete that occurs with a traditional un-reinforced mix. Despite the relative thinness of the layer of concrete waterproofing, it is very strong, absorbing stresses from the surrounding soil and eliminating the need for a foundation of hardcore or metal reinforcement inside the concrete.

In addition to using reinforced fibre cement to skim the inside of a pool made with building blocks, it is also extremely useful when rocks have to be secured to liners. When waterfalls are built, for example, it is often necessary to use mortar under and behind the rocks to prevent water from seeping behind the fall. In some water garden designs short stretches of stream may need channelling through narrow gullies, and this type of mix can be used to overlap the flexible or rigid liners and to provide a strong, watertight seal.

Mortar is used in several places in rock and water construction, but it does not take the skills of a bricklayer to point between courses of bricks and to watch levels. Fibre reinforcing is an aid to any unskilled gardeners attempting to build certain types of pool.

CLAY LINING

On areas of deep, heavy clay, a near "natural" pool capable of holding water for most of the year can be created by digging out a saucer-shaped pool to a minimum depth of 45cm (18in), thoroughly consolidating the exposed surface with a clay rammer, and adding a 15cm (6 in) layer of soil on top. If you do not have clay soil, then you can either import clay, which can be expensive, or use sodium bentonite clay and bentomat.

SUITABLE SITES

Clay lining is a relatively cheap and easy means of water retention, but it has a number of limitations in size, design and management. Such a clay pool can be constructed only in soil that is as near to clay as possible. Heavy, loamy soils, no matter how much they are consolidated, will not hold water in summer. Clay is generally identifiable by its "putty-like" consistency when wet, and its hard, almost rock-like consistency when dry. The surface becomes slippery when it is wet, but water tends to run off rather than penetrate deeply.

To achieve the compaction necessary to waterproof clay, it is not possible to have a pool with vertical side walls. Gently sloping sides must be contoured, and this means that the pool must be no less than 5–6m (16½–20ft) across in order to achieve the necessary surface-to-depth ratio. If simply left as a small, shallow

BELOW: **Clay lining is ideal for large informal pools, particularly if there is a constant supply of natural water.**

LEFT: **A clay-lined pool is sometimes prone to temporary clouding after periods of heavy rain.**

BELOW: **This metal tamping tool is used to consolidate a clay lining.**

saucer, algae will inevitably accumulate in the warm water, and the drop in level in small pools in summer will be very noticeable. Not only does the clay absorb water, but water is also lost through both evaporation and transpiration from any aerial leaves. Bear in mind that the exposed clay will dry out extremely fast during excavation, and the surface must be covered at once with sacking or polythene (polyethylene).

The roots of plants such as waterlilies and some vigorous marginals will also penetrate the submerged clay and spread very rapidly. Extreme care is therefore needed in the choice of planting if the pool is not to become overgrown. Subterranean creatures like worms and moles may also burrow through the clay and damage the waterproofing.

Despite these drawbacks, puddled clay pools have their uses, particularly in rural areas where there is plenty of space and where they make ideal wildlife pools.

BENTONITE CLAY AND BENTOMAT

A recent development that refines the basic clay-lining method and improves its water-holding capacity is the use of an imported clay called bentonite. This is a mineral clay that absorbs water, swelling to 10 to 15 times its volume when wet, and that has strong bonding qualities. It has been used extensively by engineers to waterproof rivers and canals. The name is derived from Fort Benton, Montana, where it was discovered as a volcanic ash, and it is sold loose, under a variety of tradenames, in 50kg (110lb) bags.

When the bentonite is dispersed loose, difficulties can be experienced in achieving an even cover, but this problem has been overcome by impregnating a textile quilt with bentonite. The textile, known as bentomat, is draped over the pool mould in overlapping strips, 3.6m (12ft) wide. The mat, although very heavy, is much easier to use than the loose product and is rolled out over the excavation, rather like a flexible liner. When this layer is covered with soil and watered in, it becomes a sticky, impervious gel, which should be covered with a further layer of soil, 30cm (12in) thick. However, some calcareous soils affect the bentonite, reducing its ability to swell. It must also not be allowed to dry out once used because the calcium particles present in the mix of sodium and calcium, which shrink as they dry, are unable to swell again. If the bentonite is applied in powder form, rather than laid in textile form, the recommended rate of application is 10kg per square metre (22lb per square yard).

If fish are to be introduced to the pool, you will need an ample depth of pool and an adequate covering of soil to stop chemicals leaching from the bentonite.

PUMPS

ABOVE: **Electric submersible pumps bring tiny water features to life.**

If you are contemplating a moving water feature, such as a fountain or watercourse, you will need a pump. The great majority of pumps now sold are submersible models, which require no more than a connection point near the pool. With the exception of some more recently introduced solar-powered pumps, all pumps run on electricity, either on mains (utility) voltage or on reduced low voltage through a transformer. When you are buying a pump, make sure that it has enough cable to reach a suitable connection near the pool. Low-voltage pumps are restricted in their output and

are suitable only for small fountains or waterfalls. They are supplied with a transformer, which should be housed under cover close to the mains power socket. Because the cable from the transformer to the pump connector does not pose a threat to life if it is accidentally severed, it can be hidden under the soil or paving. Mains voltage, on the other hand, must be protected in strong casing and buried to a depth of 60cm (2ft).

TYPES OF PUMP

Most submersible pumps come with a flow adjuster and a T-piece connector, which can be fitted easily to the pump's outlet. Once the size of the flexible delivery pipe from the outlet is known, an adapter can be selected to fit over the outlet socket to couple up with the bore of the delivery pipe. The T-piece connector allows the pump to circulate water in two directions, to a waterfall and to a fountain, at the same time. In this case, it is advisable to fit a flow adjuster to each pipe fitted to the T-piece in order to balance the different flow requirements. Delivery pipes are fitted to connectors by galvanized hose clips.

There are two basic types of submersible pump. A standard pump will operate a waterfall or fountain with a strainer on the intake to sieve solid debris. The other sort of pump can handle solids, and is necessary if there is also a biological filter in the pool. These filters need to run almost continually in summer, so the pump should be designed for continuous running.

Before choosing a pump, you should also consider whether its main purpose is to drive a fountain or a waterfall. If these features are ambitious projects, the pump for a waterfall will need to be capable of handling a great volume of water, while a pump for a fountain will need to create greater pressure than volume.

The other main type of pump is called a surface-running or external pump. This is situated above the water in a well-ventilated housing chamber. It is mainly used by fish-keepers because its running costs and capacity for handling large volumes of water makes it more suitable than a submersible pump in a fish tank. For the purposes of making watercourses through rocks, submersible pumps are adequate and easier to install.

Another innovation in pump design has emerged in the limited introduction of solar-powered pumps. As with any solar-powered device, the siting is important in terms of receiving adequate levels of sunlight, and at present these pumps are suitable only for running small fountains.

SITING A PUMP

The type of feature will determine the position of a pump. Although the natural place for a fountain is in the centre of a pool, this makes it difficult to reach the pump to make any adjustments or clean the strainer. In a small pool this may not be a problem, but in a larger pool the fountain can be supported remotely from the pump, which should be located at the pool side for easy adjustment.

Pumps should be sited at the base of a waterfall rather than at the opposite end of the pool because this increases the efficiency of the pump by reducing the friction loss in the delivery pipe. It also reduces strong currents, allowing the water to remain as still as possible, conditions which are appreciated by waterlilies.

In general, pumps should be sited just above the bottom of the pool on a shallow plinth in order to reduce the amount of sludge sucked into the strainer. If the pump is used in winter, raise it even higher so that it does not disturb the warmer water there.

Unlike a pump that is used solely for a waterfall, a filter pump needs to draw water from the maximum area and not allow localized pockets of undisturbed water to build up. The shape of the pool will influence this, and it usually means that in a long pool the pump is sited at the opposite end to the return pipe from the filter.

When locating a surface or external filter, above-water biological filters need to be placed at the highest point in the circulation system. They can be disguised by dwarf and prostrate conifers or hidden under raised decking. If disguising the filter is difficult, install a bottom filter, where a network of perforated pipes connected to the pump's inlet draws the water though the filter medium.

CHECKLIST FOR BUYING A PUMP

When you are selecting a pump, consult a specialist and be prepared to answer the following questions:

- What will the pump be used for?
- What will be the bore of the delivery pipe?
- If you are going to have a filter, check the wattage of the pump and find out if it is designed for continuous running. Some modern pump designs are far superior to those of older pumps, and minimize the running costs
- If you are planning a waterfall, what is the height of the header pool above the reservoir pool and what distance will the water need to travel?
- If you are planning a waterfall, what width of water will be required to form a curtain over the stones? (As an approximate guide, allow for an output of 227 litres/60 gallons an hour for every 2.5cm (1in) of width of the waterfall stone at a height of 1m/3ft above the bottom pool.)
- What is the capacity of the base pool? This is particularly important if you are introducing filtration or for waterfall pumps, which should not change the water too quickly. The flow rate per hour of the pump should not exceed the volume of water in the pool
- What style of fountain do you have in mind and what height do you want the spray to reach? A foaming geyser jet fountain, for example, will need a stronger pump so that the suction of air through the venturi valves in the geyser provides the frothy effect

TYPES OF SUBMERSIBLE PUMP

Modern submersible pumps have an enormous range of outputs. Check the running costs if the pump is to be used continuously. The pumps shown here represent a typical range.

Remove control unit and receiver

18,000 litres (4,755 gallons) per hour

5,000 litres (1,321 gallons) per hour

1,200 litres (317 gallons) per hour

FILTERS

BELOW: **Although well planted, small pools that are heavily stocked with fish will need filtration for optimum fish health.**

OPPOSITE: **The number of fish that can be kept in a pond depends on its size.**

As soon as a pump is introduced to a water garden there is an opportunity to incorporate a biological filter. These are not essential in a well-balanced pool, but if the pool is well stocked with fish there is a real advantage to having supplementary filtration.

BIOLOGICAL FILTERS

A biological filter is most commonly operated by a pump that delivers water from the pool through the biological filter, which is placed above water level at the poolside. Some filters can be fitted under the water,

and these rely on the pump sucking the water through the filter medium rather than pushing it through an above-pool filter.

Biological filters work by converting the harmful nitrites that result from fish waste and rotting organic matter into useful nitrates as well as by cleaning the water of algae and debris. These large biological filters are housed in black tanks and can be extremely unsightly, so that hiding them should be a priority. They need to be large because they house a variety of materials that both filter mechanically and biologically.

In order to maximize the surface area inside the filter, where the beneficial bacteria will grow and purify the water, filter media are available in various shapes and configurations, including foam, baked clay granules, lava rock, cut pieces of plastic pipe and carbon-coated polypropylene ribbon. To achieve maximum filtration, water enters through a spray bar, which distributes the water over the layers and blocks of the different filter media, then it is returned, usually through a low-level pipe, to the pool. An overflow system is provided in case the system clogs up in heavily polluted water. Bacteria take several weeks to become effective and the filter must be kept on continuously.

ULTRA-VIOLET CLARIFIERS

These specialist filters, which are electrically powered, are extremely effective in controlling the single-celled green algae, and they operate in conjunction with a biological filter. They work by forcing the freely dispersed algae to congregate in bunches which means that the biological filter can collect them more easily later in the circulating system. Water passing through the filter is exposed to ultra-violet light from bulbs in the clarifier, causing the algae to clump together. They should be positioned so that the water passes through the clarifier before reaching the biological filter.

A BIOLOGICAL FILTER

A typical biological filter in which the water runs vertically through the chambers of biomedia.

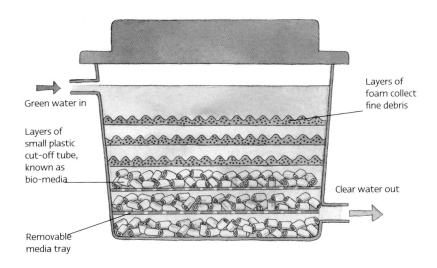

Green water in

Layers of small plastic cut-off tube, known as bio-media

Removable media tray

Layers of foam collect fine debris

Clear water out

A DIFFERENT TYPE OF BIOLOGICAL FILTER

This biological filter contains a mix of ingredients and vertical chambers, each with a different role in the filtration process.

AN ULTRA-VIOLET CLARIFIER

This detail of an ultra-violet clarifier shows the intake and output ports.

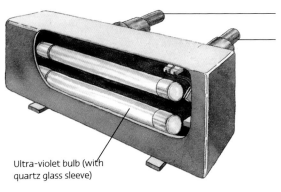

Green water in

Clear water out (the algae are now bunched together, making them easier to collect in a biological filter)

Ultra-violet bulb (with quartz glass sleeve)

PIPEWORK AND VALVES

There is a range of pipes and valves, mostly made from plastic, with which you will need to be familiar when building a rock and water feature. As time goes on, you will find it easier to use pipes, valves and garden hoses together.

PIPES

The delivery pipes for watercourses are usually flexible, unlike the rigid pipes that are used for small fountains. The flexible pipes come in a range of diameters, from about 10mm (½in) to 50mm (2in), and the bore required relates to the length of pipe and the role the water plays in the watercourse. As there is considerable friction loss in the pipe over a long distance, the rate of flow from the pump is reduced. It is therefore always sensible to err towards selecting a larger size if you are not sure, because there are no hard-and-fast rules when it comes to specifying which diameter should be used for a given length. Most pipes are now made in corrugated black plastic, which has largely superseded the clear plastic pipe that is also used for the purpose. The corrugations make the pipe strong yet flexible enough to curve around tight corners.

DELIVERY PIPES

Flexible corrugated delivery pipes are made from PVC, and are available in a number of different diameters.

30mm (1¼in) in diameter

25mm (1in) in diameter

20mm (¾in) in diameter

10mm (½in) in diameter

FOUNTAIN PIPES

Rigid fountain pipes of different diameters and lengths with a sleeve connection piece for additional length, if required.

10cm (4in) in diameter

20cm (8in) in diameter

ABOVE: **Fountains for pools require a rigid extension pipe.**

ABOVE RIGHT: **Watercourses need flexible piping to deliver water from the base pool to the top of the cascade.**

VALVES

You are only likely to come across two types of valves. The more common is a flow-adjusting valve, which is very useful on a watercourse. Although the pump may have such a valve fitted to the outlet, this is inconvenient to adjust when the pump is submerged. By fitting a separate valve in the pipe, you will have complete control.

The second valve, the non-return (shut-off) valve, is less commonly used and seldom necessary. It would be necessary on a suction pipe fitted to a surface-running (external) pump if the pump were not capable of priming itself after being turned off. A non-return valve might also be used in a watercourse where the end of the delivery pipe enters the header pool below the water level. Unless a non-return valve is fitted into the pipe, the water would siphon back from the header pool into the base pool every time the pump was turned off.

VALVES

Valves, such as the flow-adjusting valve shown below, are used to alter the rate of flow in a system.

Flow-adjusting valve or flow-adjuster
for altering the rate of flow

OTHER EQUIPMENT

Other pipes are used to connect delivery pipes of different diameters and to change the direction of flow in the system.

Galvanized hose or jubilee clip with hose
protector inside clip

Hose reduction junction pipe to connect
flexible pipes of different diameters

T-piece junction pipe to connect pipes
and change direction

BUYING ROCK

The edge around the water has the greatest impact on the overall effect of a water feature in the garden as a whole. Completely surround a pool with hard paving and the water is immediately separated from the planting and the pool becomes more artificial. In designing and building an informal pool that makes use of rock, you are immediately suggesting a more natural feature that requires sympathetic handling of all the finishing touches. Substituting pieces of rock for a paved edge is not the solution if the rocks are simply positioned on the liner above the water level, where they will look entirely unnatural. Position the rocks so that they appear to emerge from the water; they will look even more natural if the same rocks are used in the surrounding area.

BELOW: **The choice and arrangement of these large rocks and pebbles is in total harmony with the planting.**

The use of rock near to the pool is the key to success in blending rock and water. On a sloping site there is ample opportunity to use rocks in retaining banks and terraces, but even on a relatively flat site some types of rock will look perfectly natural if the rock used is the type that would naturally form a type of flatbed outcrop.

Before you finally decide how the rocks will be used, you must first choose the type of rock you would like to use, and then find out whether it is available and how much you will need.

RELIABLE SOURCES

Begin by visiting a good garden centre, where the rocks are likely to be displayed in large wooden boxes. The rocks will be of a fairly even size and weight so that customers can lift them out of the box to inspect them. If only two or three are needed, they can be put on a cart and transported home in the boot (trunk) of a car. Each of these rocks is likely to weigh 25–50kg (56lb–1cwt), so buying individual rocks will be a practical option only for small-scale schemes, where there are several smaller sizes mixed in the selection.

It is sometimes possible to construct a scheme by building it up little by little, adding outcrops at later stages, but if an ambitious scheme is envisaged from the very beginning, you need to organize bulk deliveries from the garden centre. As a rough guide, if you are building a small rock garden allow 2 tonnes (2 tons) for every 4.5 square metres (15 square feet) of rock area. This is not a hard-and-fast rule, because no two rock gardens are the same, and flatbed outcrop rock areas require fewer rocks than a terraced rock area on a slope. Remember, too, that a garden centre is likely to carry only a limited range of rocks in fairly small sizes. If the selection available does not satisfy your needs, your next point of call will be a landscape supplier, which you may also see advertised in your local directory under stone merchants or suppliers.

The selection here will not only be more extensive but it is also likely that when you visit the supplier, you will see the rocks displayed in bays in loose heaps. There will also be a wide variety of sizes available. Prices here will be quoted by the tonne (ton), and the supplier will deliver direct to your home. This source is infinitely superior to the garden centre because there

LEFT: **Where wide spillstones are needed in a watercourse, take ample time to select a thin piece of rock at the suppliers to ensure success at this critical point in the construction.**

is so much more variety in size, and it is this that will ultimately produce a more natural-looking rock feature. If you are building the rock feature by hand, you must stipulate a maximum weight. If you have some mechanical help, check with the hire contractor on the lifting capacity of the machine.

For ambitious features, for which a minimum of a full lorry load of rock is required, it is worth visiting a stone quarry. One of the joys of a stone quarry is being able to inspect old pieces that have been left lying about so that the cut surfaces will have weathered. There is also the chance that the pieces are lying on the ground for closer inspection (unlike the stone suppliers, where they are heaped into mounds), and it is worth talking to the quarry staff about the stones you find to explain why you like them and what type of stone you would like to form the majority of the load.

The haulage contractor is another key link in the chain, because careless tipping of the rock from the truck can result in several broken pieces. Try to be on hand when rocks are delivered, not only to explain where the rocks should be unloaded but also to explain to the driver how gently you want this precious cargo to be handled.

TYPES OF ROCK

For the best results, try to use rocks that are found in your local area so that the feature will blend in smoothly with its surroundings. There is a wide range of rocks to choose from, most of which can be bought mail-order.

SANDSTONE AND LIMESTONE

These are sedimentary rocks, formed in layers under the pressure of water above. They have numerous horizontal strata lines, which have weaknesses in them, causing them to split along the lines. These weaknesses can be exploited in rock-garden building, particularly if the natural rock formation has numerous vertical fissures as well. The quarried rocks produced from these formations, known as "freestones", are ideal because they have strong, natural sides. When one rock is placed on top of another, linking these fissures both horizontally and vertically becomes an essential part of the art.

Sandstone One of the best and most widely available rocks is sandstone. Depending on its source, the colour can vary from a light yellowish-grey to a dark reddish-brown. Although a strong rock, it weathers quickly, and the strata patterns look more interesting with time. It is porous, which can be both an advantage or disadvantage when used with water. Its porosity could be an advantage in wet areas with mild winters, where moss and algae quickly form on the surface, making it look mature in a short time. When used with ferns and moisture-loving plants in a shady place, the rock surface almost disappears in a very short time, becoming carpeted with a thick mossy growth.

Some sandstones are so soft in structure that the porosity can lead to problems in severe winters when the wet rock freezes and ice particles form within the rock strata. This causes the rock to split and break up over time, so it is worth checking with local suppliers or landscapers on a source of harder sandstone.

If sandstone is to be used to form a watercourse, check that it has a harder consistency and has had time to weather. It would, for example, be disconcerting to create a waterfall with large pieces of freshly quarried stone. The stones under and at the sides of the waterfall might turn a dark brownish-green within a week or two, while the surrounding stones, positioned away from the water, might remain a much lighter colour for several years. Although the lighter stones will gradually darken and blend in, it will look very unnatural at first.

York stone is another form of sandstone. It is quarried in Yorkshire and has varying degrees of hardness. Some of the best natural paving materials are produced from York stone because it not only resists wear, but is easily cut into thin layers, making it ideal for paving slabs.

There are several reddish sandstones, such as Monmouth and Cheshire reds, that are harder than many sandstones. Millstone grit is a good choice for a harder sandstone that shows the strata well. In the United States, two popular sandstones are flagstone and bluestone.

Welsh granite chippings

Sandstone chippings

Blue slate

Scottish quartz chippings

Limestone This became popular in the early days of rock gardening when the weatherworn, irregular shapes so common on the rocky limestone pavements of northwest Britain supplied the domestic market. Overquarrying spoilt this natural resource, and this type of stone can no longer be removed. There are, however, many old rock gardens, and these still supply the enthusiast who is looking for a special shape. Flatter, less weathered pieces are still quarried in bulk in Britain, mainly from Derbyshire, Wales, the Mendips, the Scottish Lowlands and central Ireland. The harder limestones suitable for rock garden building are carboniferous limestones, and they are mainly grey in colour. The exceptions to the grey colour are Mendip limestone, which is bluish or golden, and the Cotswold and Purbeck rocks, which are creamy, sometimes almost yellow.

The grey limestones are not quite as porous as sandstone, but they can leach a minimal amount of lime, making them unsuitable for placing near acid-loving plants. If they are in contact with the water in small pools in a hard-water area, the small amount of leached limestone will exacerbate the alkalinity of the water.

Marble, another form of limestone, is created when limestone is exposed to very high temperatures. It is too expensive to be used in rock gardens other than for cobbles and pebbles on a small scale.

GRANITE

This superb rock is very hard, fine-grained and non-porous. If it has surfaced in the form of glacial boulders, which have become rounded and smooth, it is ideal for placing alongside streams or in boggy meadows. Granite rocks lack the crevices that the alpine enthusiast seeks, but for a watercourse the rounded boulders are worth seeking out. Scottish quarzite, along with mica and feldspar, is an ingredient of many of the granite deposits found in Scotland. When crushed, it releases chippings which make valuable hard-wearing top-dressings.

SLATE

This very hard, angular stone comes in shades of grey, green and purple, often marbled with sinewy whitish streaks. During its formation, shale was squeezed so hard that the flaky mineral mica recrystallized at right angles to the pressure. This means that the rock splits easily into thin sheets, and these can be exploited when placed with a slight tilt on a watercourse. Devon rustic stone, a colourful slate, is very hard-wearing and readily available in block-sized pieces that are easy to handle.

Welsh green granite

Snowdonian slate

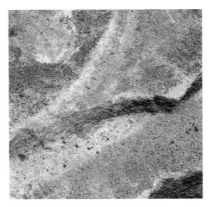

York stone

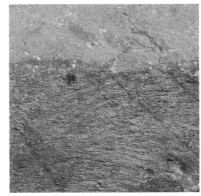

Devon rustic stone

Snowdonian plum slate

White marble cobbles

Red marble pebbles

Snowdonian blue slate chippings

ALTERNATIVE EDGINGS

As well as the vast selection of rocks and boulders that can be used to build a rock and water feature, there is also an array of alternatives you may wish to consider. You may, in fact, like to use a combination of different edgings, such as rocks, cobbles and grass edging, around the same pool or water feature.

COBBLES

If a rock edge to a pool is either inappropriate or too ambitious, rounded, river- or sea-washed cobbles can be used to make an informal edge. To look natural, they will need to emerge from a shallow gradient under the water, which means that they would not be appropriate for an edge with marginal shelves or steep sides. Cobbles blend well with other edging materials, so use them in association with these on just a part of the edge. Remember that a pool edged completely with a shallow, saucer-like gradient of cobbles will need to be much larger in surface area than a pool with steeper sides to achieve the same volume of water. There is also a greater risk of algae, such as blanketweed, forming in the warm, shallow water over the cobbles.

The popularity of cobble surfaces in modern land-scaping has resulted in an increasing variety of types of cobble in various colours and sizes becoming available. It is worth visiting a good landscape supplier to see the selection available because achieving a natural "beach" effect is the main aim. Keep the general colour range the same and avoid introducing too many colours from cobbles sourced from different areas. It is not necessary to pay the premium for white cobbles, which are intended for more dramatic or formal landscape settings.

Washed, bagged cobbles can be expensive if they are used for a large area, and it is worth finding out about supplies from a local gravel quarry, which would be much cheaper. Quarried cobbles may need washing and will almost certainly have to be checked for split cobbles before they are spread on a flexible liner. Split cobbles have very sharp edges and could easily cut a liner. Large areas of beach could also be covered with a layer of 10–20mm (½–¾in) river-washed, rounded gravel, which is available in loose loads or bags, and this would be a suitable base for the larger mixed sizes of beach cobble.

RIGHT: **A grass edge looks natural, but will require more maintenance and some foundation support if it is subject to heavy wear.**

FAR RIGHT: **Irregular paving makes a good pool edge for both straight and curving outlines.**

In addition to the decorative nature of an area of cobbled edge, this zone will also act as a corridor for amphibians, enabling them to gain easy access to and departure from the water. You will also find that birds will be attracted very quickly to the shallow water to bathe and drink.

GRASS EDGES

An edge of grass can look the most natural of all edges, but there are several precautions to take if they are not to become muddy, unkempt banks. First, because an area of grass provides a stable place on which to stand at the very edge of the water, it is likely to become worn and compacted quite quickly. This compaction can lead to crumbling sides under the liner on light sandy soils, and any grass growing below the waterline becomes impossible to mow.

The other drawback that is associated with grass sides to pools is the problem of grass clippings flying into the water when the grass is cut. This becomes a management problem, which can be resolved only by the type of grasscutter used. There are a number of lawnmowers that are effective at gathering the cut grass in a box or a bag.

PAVING

Even in informal designs, there are occasions where a part of the pool edge will look quite natural when it is edged with paving, particularly if a path leads to the paved edge across a lawn or through a border. How well the paving is integrated into an informal design for water will depend on how much of the edge is paved, and the type of paving used. It is only when the entire edge is paved that the pool begins to lose its informality and its relationship with the immediate surrounds of the garden.

For informal shapes, the irregular style sometimes known as "crazy paving" tends to be the most suitable choice because the cut pieces of natural stone allow a curved edge to be created more easily than is possible with square or rectangular paving stones. There are also several colours available in the stones that are used for crazy paving, and some colours will blend better with the rock used elsewhere in the water garden. Many edges of crazy paving are spoiled by bad laying, particularly in the pointing of the mortar where it is used too liberally. A good area of crazy paving will have a balanced mix of sizes, the pieces will be laid flat and firm, and the pointing will not dominate.

ABOVE: **This pool edge uses timber rounds, which are sunk into a thin, shallow trench and then secured with concrete.**

LEFT: **This cobble "beach" edge uses cobbles of mixed sizes, which makes the finished effect look much more natural.**

There are several alternatives to irregular paving in both natural stone and simulated stone slabs. The main requirements for a paved edge are that it should be level, as non-slip and natural looking as possible, and the colour should blend rather than make a vivid contrast.

Building your rock and water feature is where the design and planning is put into practice. In this chapter, the

CONSTRUCTING ROCK AND WATER GARDENS

practical step-by-step sequences are accompanied by a list of the materials and equipment that you will need. The vast majority of the projects require little in the way of do-it-yourself skills, but specific building skills are identified where necessary.

OPPOSITE: **This unbroken curtain of water shows what can be achieved through the careful attention to surfaces and levels.**

INITIAL EXCAVATION

Firstly, you will not need a plug for drainage in the bottom of your proposed pool. The pool is not going to be drained regularly like a bath, and there is always a danger that the plug may not be 100 per cent water-tight. Plugs are necessary only in pools for keeping fish such as specimen koi, where regular cleaning out is necessary.

When you are digging out a new pool in a lawn or an area of rough turf there are three distinct layers to be removed, each one having a different function later. The top layer of turf should be removed to no deeper

than about 5cm (2in), and, if space is available in the garden, the turves should be stacked in a neat pile. Arrange them upside down, and after a few months they will have rotted down to produce a superb fibrous loam, which is ideal for potting aquatic plants.

The next layer, the topsoil, is about 30–38cm (12–15in) deep and it, too, could be valuable depending on the soil type. If it is heavy clay it will have few uses; keep a small supply for helping to seal minor leaks in a replenishing system. Similarly, at the other end of the scale a sandy soil is of little value as future

RIGHT: **This new pool is made with a flexible liner and is at the stage of being filled with water. It is important to pay particular attention to levels so that the liner is not exposed above the water line. This is a good time to plant the oxygenators before it becomes so deep that waders are required.**

FAR LEFT: **When you are digging out a new pool in a lawn, you will need to remove a layer of turf first.**

LEFT: **When you are excavating a new pool or stream, remember to keep some of the excavated soil to build up the contours along the edges.**

compost or top-dressing. If the soil is a nice friable loam, however, it is worth its weight in gold and should be either used to top-dress the borders or stacked, like the turves, for future use. Finally, the bottom layer or subsoil, which is generally a different colour from the topsoil, should be kept only if you have plans to change any garden contours later on, when it should be stored separately from the topsoil. If you do not plan to use the subsoil, dispose of it; do not add it to your borders or beds elsewhere in the garden.

If a rock and water feature is envisaged, hang on to every barrowful of soil, topsoil and subsoil, until the scheme has been created. The subsoil can be placed at the bottom of a gently contoured mound and the topsoil returned on top of it. If this mound is made near the pool it could make a perfect start for a raised watercourse. The main thing is to stop the mound from looking too contrived, particularly on a flat site, by keeping the proportions and gradient as natural looking as possible. The height of the mound should be no more than one-fifth of its width, and it should have gently sloping sides. Small, steep, circular mounds covered with rocks positioned at various angles will look completely unnatural. They look even worse if the water spouts from the top of the mound rather like an erupting volcano.

SOIL PROFILE

A typical soil profile usually consists of three main elements: an upper layer of dark, fertile topsoil; a middle layer of lighter, infertile subsoil; and a lower layer of bedrock, which ranges from a few to hundreds of yards deep.

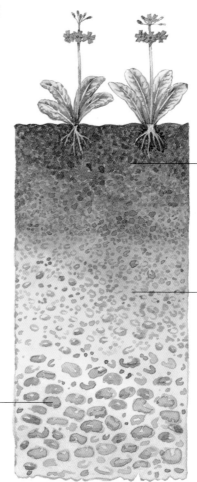

topsoil is the dark layer of soil that contains organic material

subsoil is usually lighter in colour and contains little or no organic nutrients

bedrock is usually below the level of cultivation

POSITIONING ROCKS

A good, natural-looking arrangement of rocks in the surrounding area is one of the most important aspects of construction, which can make or break the success of a pool or other rock and water feature. Without this attention to detail in the choice and position of materials in the surrounding area, a successful feature can be spoilt.

When you have chosen a design for the scheme and selected the type of rock to use, the actual positioning of the rock should be undertaken with as much care as any aspect of the excavation. The elements that will be in the background are as important as the pool itself, and it is easy to become preoccupied with the mechanics of the pool and fail to capitalize on the qualities that give water its appeal.

First of all, you will need to decide whether this is a job you can do yourself or whether you will require help. The size of the rocks will make the decision for you, but there is much to be said for having help, even if you feel that you can manhandle the rocks yourself. Placing rocks involves a great deal of moving to and fro, as you step back some distance from each one to view its effect from a distance. You cannot possibly assess whether the rock is sitting correctly when you are working on top of it. The slightest adjustment in the angle at which it is placed or the depth to which it is buried will have a profound effect on its success, and if there is someone to help make these fine adjustments, it will save a lot of walking about to check from various angles.

MOVING ROCKS

A sack trolley is invaluable for moving heavy rocks around the garden and into place.

1 Roll the rock onto the trolley platform so that the weight is pivoted over the wheels when it is being moved.

2 Pull the handles back in order to manoeuvre the heavy rock more easily.

CREATING ROCK FORMATIONS

You may need outside help to move larger pieces of rock into place, but if you are moving rock yourself, there are certain principles for positioning and grouping rocks that will ensure you achieve a natural-looking formation, largely by taking into account such factors as the shape of the rock as well as the strata that run through rock.

1 Where the slope is steeper, choose blocky rocks rather than flat ones.

2 In groups of three, a cluster of rocks with tops parallel to each other have greater impact and naturalness.

3 When positioning angular rocks, aim to keep the top of the rocks parallel to each other.

4 By burying a large part of the rock, an outcrop looks more natural than if it is sitting on the surface.

Once the first rock is in position, all the other rocks must relate to it so that it looks natural, and as the number of rocks increases, constant checking is ever more important. If the rocks look menacingly heavy, try every possible means to get a small excavator as well as a skilled driver on the site. Skilled drivers who know how to cradle the rocks in slings beforehand so that they can be lowered gently into place are worth their weight in gold.

POSITIONING ROCKS ON A FLAT SITE

A feature on a steep slope will need ample supplies of rock to make terracing, but avoid using too much rock on a flatter site. Remember that you are trying to achieve a setting for water, rather than a collection of rocks, and water works best if it is not overly dominated by the rock. Outcropping with clusters of rocks is a successful way of using rock on flat sites. Even though the positioning of adjacent rocks in a cluster will need careful placement, this care will result in a more successful scheme than single rocks of the same size scattered evenly around. Where single rocks are used, they should be big. Indeed, large, rounded boulders that appear to have been deposited centuries ago look superb, particularly alongside a stream.

POSITIONING ROCKS ON A SLOPING SITE

For more ambitious landscaping schemes that include a slope, flat-topped rocks that suggest the strata of natural rock formations work well. Having placed the first stone at the bottom of a slope, line up the faces of any adjoining rocks so that they are at the same level and face the stones in the same direction. As you build up the slope, keep the same distribution of rock faces and their tops, and it is for this reason that flat-topped rocks work much better. Angular pieces, with points sticking in the air and no suggestion of natural strata, can easily look a complete mess and spoil the water garden rather than providing an appropriate setting for it.

Imagine a wall of outcropping strata and attempt to simulate this. When you are positioning a rock, cut into the base of the slope so that the rock tilts slightly backwards into the slope. Pack soil around the back of the rock so that no more than two-thirds of the rock is exposed. If the slope is steep and the rock face needs to be terrace-like, the front faces of the rocks in the next layer should be set slightly back from the rocks beneath them, but still follow the all-important near-horizontal and vertical strata that were established by the very first stone at the bottom of the slope.

CONSTRUCTING EDGES

Choosing a successful co-ordination of the materials to make the edge of a pool is helped by visiting a supplier with a wide range of materials. The construction can then be approached with the confidence that not only will the colours and textures work well, but other rocks for waterfalls and streams would make a suitable combination. Whatever material is chosen, the rule in pool construction is to hide the gap of liner at the surface around the pool which becomes even more conspicuous in the summer with increased evaporation.

ABOVE: **This is a well-chosen and carefully positioned mix of boulders and rocks; the boulders can also be used as a crossing point.**

Rock edging The rocks around a pool should be partially submerged to achieve a natural effect. The rocks will also need to be supported on a foundation slab. The liner is passed over the slab and the rock bedded into a layer of stiff mortar or concrete. Ensure the liner finishes above the level of the water at the side of the pool.

Cobble edging The first essential in introducing naturalness to a cobble edge is to arrange the sizes so that the main body of cobbles increases in diameter from below the waterline into the drier margins. To prevent the cobbles from rolling to the pool bottom, a concrete support should be constructed at the edge of the pool.

Grass edging An edge of grass is very natural-looking and very suitable for a wildlife pool. However, the edge of the pool will become worn fairly quickly, which can cause the sides to crumble. This can be avoided by underpinning the turf with a small foundation.

Timber edging An alternative method of taking grass to the water's edge is to construct a vertical timber wall, which will extend from below the waterline to just below the level of the grass. The timber wall looks most attractive if it is made with timber rounds, 5–8cm (2–3in) in diameter, which are placed tightly side by side to form a palisade-like barrier. Proprietary lengths of "log roll" could also be used instead of complete rounds, and these are already joined together by galvanized wire strands. For both these systems to be made stable enough to prevent any crumbling into the pool, a small trench, about 15cm (6in) deep and 10–15cm (4–6in) wide, must be dug out at the pool edge. A concrete support should be added in front of this trench. The pool liner is then run over the concrete support and into the trench before finishing above the waterline beyond the trench. A mix of stiff mortar is placed on the liner and the timbers bedded into the stiff mortar before it hardens. Make sure that the timber rounds are straight and tight together because they cannot be moved once the mortar sets. After a day or two, when the mortar will have set hard, soil can be backfilled behind the timber edge and the liner can be wedged upright so it is held above the waterline. Turf can then be laid right up to the timber edge on the fresh soil, which is now supported at the water's edge.

Paved edging Prepare the area to be paved by scraping away some topsoil. If the subsoil is not firm, remove this too and replace it with 8–10cm (3–4in) of hardcore. Top this with about 5cm (2in) of damp sand, which must be raked and levelled, then cover with the underlay and liner. Begin by placing the perimeter pieces along the edge of the water, checking that they fit well together and that they overlap the water by 2.5–5cm (1–2in). Use the largest of the pieces to give extra stability, with the straight edge overlapping the water. If you are laying on a curved edge, however, the shortest side might have to be used over the water to give a gentle angle for the curve. Mix some mortar on a nearby hard surface or board, then lay the first stones onto dabs of mortar trowelled onto the liner. Press the slab down onto the mortar dabs and bed it firmly before laying the adjacent slabs. Check the slabs are level with a spirit level. To adjust the height, tap with a club hammer over a block of wood. The gaps between the slabs must be filled with a fairly wet mortar mix to hold each slab in place. They should be laid on a slight slope to reduce run-off from any adjacent paving or grass.

ROCK EDGING

A rock used as a pool edge is best partially submerged with a foundation slab under the liner.

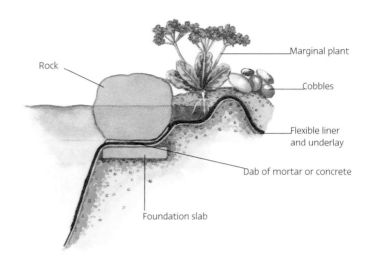

Rock · Marginal plant · Cobbles · Flexible liner and underlay · Dab of mortar or concrete · Foundation slab

GRASS EDGING

A grass edge is subject to heavy wear and tear.
It should be supported by a natural stone walling block which is placed on a deep foundation of stiff mortar or concrete.

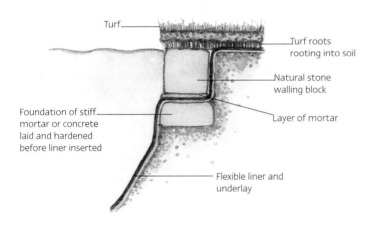

Turf · Turf roots rooting into soil · Natural stone walling block · Foundation of stiff mortar or concrete laid and hardened before liner inserted · Layer of mortar · Flexible liner and underlay

COBBLE EDGING

To prevent cobbles from rolling into the deeper zone of the pond, a shallow shelf should be made with the kerb under the flexible liner in order to give extra stability.

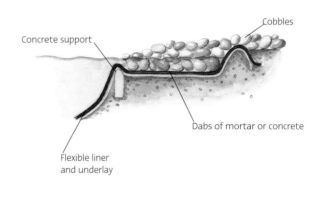

Concrete support · Cobbles · Flexible liner and underlay · Dabs of mortar or concrete

TIMBER EDGING

Log roll or individual timber rounds placed side by side make a good edge when mortared into a thin trench just under the level of the water. Turf edging can then run up to the timber edging.

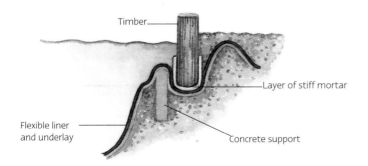

Timber · Flexible liner and underlay · Layer of stiff mortar · Concrete support

PAVED EDGING

When using a paving slab to provide an edge, ensure that there is a small overlap above the water, and mortar the slab onto the liner above a foundation of hardcore.

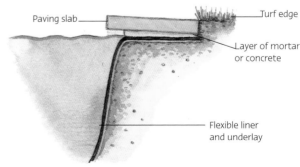

Paving slab · Turf edge · Layer of mortar or concrete · Flexible liner and underlay

MAKING A POOL
with a flexible liner

YOU WILL NEED

- Garden hose, rope or sand
- Spade
- Polythene (polyethylene) sheet
- Rake
- Spirit level
- Straight-edged piece of wood
- Sand or underlay
- Flexible liner
- Bricks or heavy stones
- Large scissors
- Paving for pool surround
- Ready-mix mortar
- Mortaring trowel

The versatility of flexible liners has made them the most popular of materials for a variety of applications. They provide the greatest scope for pool design, and can be used on their own for informal pools on heavy soils or for formal pools where crisper definition and better stability around the edges are needed. They can also be used with concrete or walling blocks to secure the sides of an excavation. Liners are now so widely obtainable that you can dig out the pool and make a multitude of last-minute adjustments to the shape and depth before buying.

CALCULATING THE SIZE OF LINER

The most common mistake in calculating the size of liner is to forget to allow for the depth of the sides and for a slight overlap. Aquatic centres supply liners from rolls, and you may gain a slight increase in size free of charge when the liner is cut. Liners bought by mail order are usually the exact size, so it is vital that your measurements are correct.

To calculate the size of the liner, measure a rectangle that encloses the shape of the pool. After measuring the maximum length and breadth, measure the depth of the pool and add twice that measurement to each dimension.

The measurements for length and width represent the bare minimum of liner required. It is prudent to add about 30cm (12in) to each measurement to provide a small overlap of 15cm (6in) on each side. For brimming or reflective pools, where the surface of the water has to be level with the surrounding edge, it will be necessary to add a little more than the width of the paving or bricks that will edge the pool to provide enough liner to extend beneath and behind this edging. The end of the liner will finish by being held vertically behind the edging material.

One rectangle of liner can be used for a variety of pool shapes, including designs with narrow waists to make a crossing point

to add interest, for example. Where the wastage would be excessive for very narrow sections, smaller joining pieces of some types of liner can be welded together at specialist suppliers or taped together on site using proprietary waterproof joining tapes. Large creases in the corners of rectangular pools or sharp curves in informal shapes are inevitable, but they can be made to look less conspicuous if the liner is carefully folded before filling the pool. A covering of algae and submerged planting will eventually disguise the fold almost entirely.

If there is ample surplus liner, features such as bog gardens can be made around the sides. When a kidney-shaped pool is created, a small bog area can be achieved using the corner piece of a rectangular liner. Instead of cutting off the surplus liner, place soil on the liner and prevent it from spreading into the water of the main pool by a small submerged retaining wall of inverted turves, rocks or walling stones.

1 Mark out the shape of your pond with a piece of rope or garden hose or by sprinkling sand. If the pond is to be sited in a lawn, remove the turf by stripping off the grass to a depth of 5cm (2in) in squares of 30cm (12in) and stack upside-down in another part of the garden for later use.

2 Dig out the hole to a depth of 23cm (9in), angling the sides of the hole slightly inwards. By digging the sides at this slight angle there is less future risk of damage by expanding ice in severe winters and the sides are less likely to subside or crumble. The soil from the top 23cm (9in)

can be stored on a polythene (polyethylene) sheet nearby if it is likely to be used for any new contouring of the surrounds later. Rake the base of the hole to a rough level finish after the first layer of soil has been removed and mark with sand the position of any marginal shelves around the sides of the hole. These shelves should be 30cm (12in) wide and be positioned where you anticipate having the shallow water plants. The inner or deeper zone, avoiding the marginal shelf outlines, can now be dug out to the full depth of the pond, i.e. a further 23cm (9in) if the pond is to be 45cm (18in)

deep or a further 38cm (15in) if the pond is to be 60cm (24in) deep. The soil from this deeper zone will be subsoil and can also be used later if it is placed underneath any fresh topsoil. It should not become mixed with the freshly excavated topsoil. If you do not envisage using this subsoil later, then remove it from the site.

3 Rake the bottom of the pond to achieve a level surface. A spirit level on a straight-edged piece of wood supported by a vertical piece of wood will show levels. Smooth over the entire surface by raking the bottom to remove any sharp stones. Go over the sides with your hands, removing any protruding roots or sharp-edged objects, gently firming the surface by patting. Line the pool with about 1cm (½in) of damp sand – it should stick to the sides if they slope slightly. If the soil is stony, drape a piece of underlay across the hole and the shelves, leaving an overlap around the pool of about 30cm (12in). Lay the flexible liner over the sand or underlay.

4 Place temporary weights, such as bricks or heavy stones, on the edges of the liner so that it is not blown back into the pool. Before the water is poured in, check that there is ample liner above the edge of the pool all the way round. Fill the pool with water to within a few centimetres (inches) of the finished level so that any adjustments to the level of the sides can be made by adding or removing soil behind the liner.

5 The bricks or stones temporarily holding the edges of the liner can be removed. Build any edging before the water is filled to the final level. Never trim the surplus liner until you are completely sure that the water level and edging are satisfactory. This pool is to have a paved edge, so cut away the surplus liner and underlay, leaving an overlap around the edge of about 15cm (6in) to be covered by the paving.

6 Bed the paving on mortar, covering the edge of the liner. The paving should overlap the edge of the pool by about 3cm (1in). Finish off by pointing the joints with mortar using the mortaring trowel.

MAKING AN INFORMAL ROCK POOL

RIGHT: **Creeping thyme is a perfect carpeting plant for the dry soil where the pool edge is watertight.**

BELOW: **This is a good example of a rock edge, softened perfectly with *Caltha polypetala*.**

This informal pool uses the soil that was removed when the hole for the pool was excavated together with some pieces of rock in order to form the pool edge. The marginal plants grow in the wet soil behind the rocks, as do moisture-lovers further away from the water. Where the rock edge is made watertight, alpines can also be grown. The excavation process is the same as for an informal pool except that the marginal shelf is much wider to provide sufficient width for the rocks and for soil behind the rocks in which to plant marginals.

1 Mark out the shape of your pond with a length of rope or garden hose or by sprinkling sand. Stand back and view the shape from all angles to check that you are happy with the finished result.

2 Dig out the hole to a depth of 23–30cm (9–12in), angling the sides of the hole slightly inwards. By digging the sides at this slight angle there is less future risk of damage by expanding ice in severe winters and the sides are less likely to subside or crumble.

3 Rake the base of the hole to a rough level finish after the first layer of soil has been removed and mark with sand the position of any marginal shelves around the sides of the hole. These shelves should be 45cm (18in) wide and be positioned where you anticipate having the shallow water plants.

4 The inner or deeper zone, avoiding the marginal shelf outlines, can now be dug out to the full depth of the pond, i.e. a further 38cm (15in) for a 60cm (24in) deep pond. The soil from this deeper zone will be subsoil and can also be used later if positioned underneath any fresh topsoil. It should not become mixed with the freshly excavated topsoil. If you do not plan to use this subsoil later, then remove it from the site. Rake the

YOU WILL NEED

- Garden hose, rope or sand
- Spade
- Rake
- Spirit level
- Straight-edged piece of wood
- Underlay
- Flexible liner

- Bricks or heavy stones
- Rocks
- Ready-mixed mortar
- Cobbles
- Mortaring trowel
- Marginal and moisture-loving plants

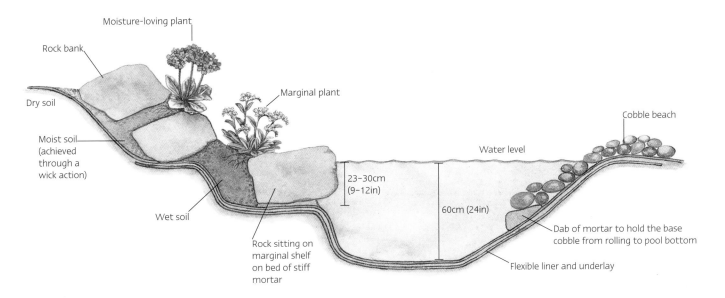

Moisture-loving plant

Rock bank

Dry soil

Moist soil (achieved through a wick action)

Marginal plant

Cobble beach

Water level

23–30cm (9–12in)

60cm (24in)

Wet soil

Rock sitting on marginal shelf on bed of stiff mortar

Dab of mortar to hold the base cobble from rolling to pool bottom

Flexible liner and underlay

bottom of the pond to achieve a level surface. A spirit level on a straight-edged piece of wood rested on the bottom will show levels.

5 Smooth over the surface of the pond by raking the bottom in order to remove any sharp stones or protruding surfaces. Go over the sides with your hands, removing any roots or sharp-edged objects. Gently firm the surface by patting.

6 Drape the underlay across the hole and the marginal shelves, leaving an overlap around the pool of about 30cm (12in).

7 If the flexible liner is small enough and help is available, it is much easier to unfold the liner away from the pool and then lift it in by the four corners. Take care not to disturb the underlay as the liner is lowered into place. Unfold a larger liner according to the supplier's directions.

8 Place weights, such as bricks or heavy stones, around the edges of the liner so that the wind does not blow the edges into the pool.

9 Lay the rocks on the liner on the inside edge of the marginal shelf, providing extra rigidity and protection for the liner with a bed of stiff mortar.

10 Once you are satisfied that the rocks are secure along the marginal shelves, backfill soil between the rocks and the edge of the flexible liner, making sure that the liner edge is always kept above the future water level.

11 The pool will look more natural if it is not completely surrounded by rocks and if a portion of the edge is made into a cobble beach. If you decide to include a cobble beach as part of the edging, there are a few points to bear in mind. To achieve a natural-looking effect, choose cobbles in a good range of sizes. Arrange the cobbles so that the main body of cobbles increases in diameter from below the waterline into the drier margins of the pond. In order to prevent the cobbles from rolling to the bottom of the pool, place a dab of stiff mortar on the flexible liner below the waterline, as is shown here. Alternatively, you can dig a small trench along the side of the pool and fill it with concrete to provide a support at the edge of the pool and lay the flexible liner over this (see page 107). Cut off any surplus liner around the pool.

12 Plant the marginals plants in the soil pockets between the rocks and fill the pond with water.

MAKING A WILDLIFE POOL

Having a large pool in order to attract a host of wildlife fascinates many people. The location of the pool is obviously one of the primary considerations. Siting the pool too close to the house will do nothing to encourage shy wildlife to approach the pool. If you are lucky enough to have a large garden, then you can easily situate a wildlife pool at the bottom of the garden, perhaps shielded from the house by shrubs or trees. This will make any wildlife feel more secure, and you will soon find that a range of insects, birds, amphibians and small mammals will become regular visitors.

ABOVE LEFT: **The first priority in a wildlife pool is to create a small, shallow beach on part of the edge.**

ABOVE RIGHT: **This large informal pool will be a real magnet to wildlife in hot, arid weather.**

RIGHT: **The beach edge totally surrounds this wildlife pool with its pockets of informal foliage and colour.**

1 Mark out the shape of the pool with a piece of rope or garden hose or by sprinkling sand. Choose a site close to some cover to encourage creatures to the edge.

2 Knock in pegs, approximately 2.5cm (1in) in diameter and 15cm (6in) long, at 1.8m (6ft) intervals and 15cm (6in) outside the outline. This will help you to establish an even level for the pond, which is a useful technique when you are working over a large area.

3 Fix one peg as the datum point for the finished water level of the pool. Using the spirit level and a straight-edged piece of wood, knock in the pegs so that the tops are level.

4 Any variations in level around the outline will become obvious once the pegs are level, allowing you to make adjustments to the surrounding soil.

5 Dig out the hole just inside the pegs to a depth of 75cm (30in) in a saucer shape, making the gradient on the sides shallow enough to retain soil without it slumping to the centre of the pool. Store the excavated soil on a polythene (polyethylene) sheet nearby as some of this soil will be required later.

YOU WILL NEED

- Garden hose, rope or sand
- Pegs, about 2.5cm (1in) in diameter and 15cm (6in) long
- Spirit level
- Straight-edged piece of wood
- Hammer
- Spade
- Large polythene (polyethylene) sheet
- Rake

- Underlay
- Flexible liner
- Bricks or heavy stones
- Washed, rounded cobbles
- Ready-mix mortar
- Flat rocks
- Plants (including bunches of oxygenators, deep-water aquatics and marginals)

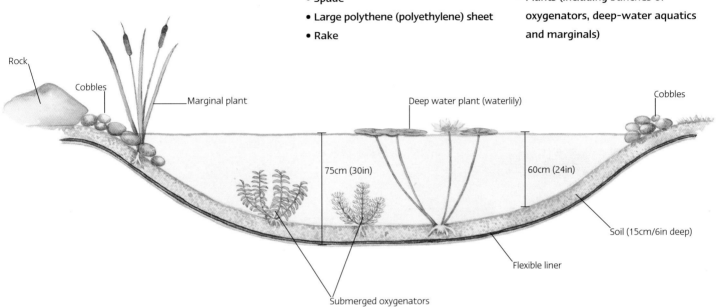

Rock

Cobbles

Marginal plant

Deep water plant (waterlily)

Cobbles

75cm (30in)

60cm (24in)

Soil (15cm/6in deep)

Flexible liner

Submerged oxygenators

6 Rake the surface of the excavation to remove any sharp stones and exposed roots.

7 Drape the underlay across the hole, leaving an overlap of 8–15cm (3–6in) around the edge.

8 If the liner is large and heavy, follow the supplier's instructions on unfolding. This may involve placing the folded liner in the centre or at the end of the hole before unrolling a loose drape across the excavation. Make any adjustments to the liner by enlisting help to lift the four corners. Take care not to disturb the underlay as the liner is lifted and lowered into place.

9 Place weights, such as bricks or heavy stones, around the edge of the liner to prevent the wind blowing the edges into the pool.

10 Spread some of the topsoil removed earlier to a depth of 15cm (6in) over the liner.

11 At various points around the edge, create an edging of cobbles, ensuring that they will sit above and below the future water level. A dab of stiff mortar on the liner below the waterline into which the lower cobbles are bedded will stop the cobbles rolling

into the pond. Place large, flat rocks around the waterline for amphibians to hide beneath.

12 Before filling the pool, check that there is enough liner above the level pegs all the way around the pool outline. If the pool is large and it will be difficult to reach the centre, plant bunches of submerged oxygenators in the soil.

13 Pour in the water gently so as not to disturb the fresh, dry soil. Place a tile or flat rock just under the end of the garden hose to spread the flow as it trickles in.

14 As the water level rises, other plants can be put into the layer of soil just before the water reaches them.

15 Complete filling to within a few inches of the finished level so that any final adjustments to the sides can be made by adding or removing soil behind the edge of the liner. Remove the bricks holding the liner in place, along with the pegs. Finish the edges.

16 The water will be cloudy after filling. This is caused by fine soil particles escaping from the saturated soil. This will settle in a week or two, and should not be cured by a water change.

MAKING A BOG AREA
with an independent liner

Most informal water gardens would look incomplete without the companion plants in the moist or wet soil near the water. Such an area not only increases the variety of plants, but also makes the pool appear more natural. The wide range of species that can be grown in these conditions is one of the many bonuses of having an informal pool. Using a liner to create a bog garden is one of the simplest and cheapest ways of creating a permanently moist environment that will allow these plants to achieve their potential.

An independent bog garden is much more satisfactory than one that has been created by extending the liner that is used

for the pool. Plants in a bog garden tend to have lush foliage and as a result make high demands on soil moisture. Where the bog garden is linked to the pool, the wick effect of moisture from the pool to the bog will lead to a fall in the water level, which can be considerable in hot, sunny weather. A separate bog garden can be managed independently of the pool, and it is also possible to add fertilizers to the soil in the bog garden without any danger of upsetting the balance of the chemistry in the pool water. The siting and design can be so organized that the bog garden appears to be a natural extension or a separate feature.

Because the waterproofing material used to line the bog garden is completely covered with soil and is pierced at the bottom, there is no need to use expensive, ultra-violet-resistant liners. Heavy-duty polythene (polyethylene) of the kind sold by builders' merchants is perfectly adequate. The liner must be pierced so that the wet soil drains slowly or it will become completely stagnant and anaerobic, but this slow seepage of water through the bottom means that a whole range of moisture-loving plants that would not survive in a saturated soil can be grown as well as several marginals that will thrive in the damp conditions.

YOU WILL NEED

- String or sand
- Spade
- Polythene (polyethylene) sheets
- Rake
- Bricks or stones
- Garden fork
- Flexible plastic pipe, 2.5cm (1in) in diameter
- Small electric drill
- Wooden bung
- Screw
- Pea shingle or gravel
- Timber to tamp the backfill
- Garden hose and connector fitting
- 1 elbow joint
- Rigid plastic pipe, 2.5cm (1in) in diameter

1 Mark out a suitable shape with string or sand, then dig a hole about 40cm (16in) deep with slightly sloping sides to minimize crumbling on light sandy soils. Store the topsoil you have removed on a polythene (polyethylene) sheet nearby because you will use it later to fill the hole. Rake the sides and the bottom of the hole smooth.

2 Drape a sheet of polythene (polyethylene) into the hole and mould it roughly into the outline. Use bricks or stones to hold the sheet of polythene in place around the edges so that it does not blow away.

3 Use a garden fork to pierce the liner in one or two places to allow water to seep slowly away from the bog. On a light sandy soil in areas of low rainfall, only one or two piercings will be necessary. If the surrounding soil is heavy clay, then you will need to pierce every metre (3ft).

4 Pierce a flexible plastic pipe at 15cm (6in) intervals with small holes. As these tend to become blocked easily, use a small drill to ensure the holes are large enough.

5 Insert a bung into one end of the pipe. This can be made from a piece of old broom handle. Secure the bung by drilling a screw through the pipe into the bung.

6 Spread pea shingle or gravel across the bottom of the hole to a depth of 5cm (2in). Lay the flexible pipe across the shingle so that it protrudes slightly above ground. Spread a further layer of pea shingle, 5cm (2in) thick, across the pipe and rake level.

7 Replace the topsoil, which has been stored at the side of the hole, until it reaches the original soil level, and tamp it down to consolidate it. Any surplus liner sticking out of the ground can be trimmed off and the surplus soil disposed of.

8 Attach a garden hose with a hose-connector fitting to the plastic pipe sticking out of the ground. Plant up the bed and nourish the planting by watering the bog area until the water appears on the surface. Disconnect the hose and connect the flexible pipe by an elbow joint to a rigid, upright section of pipe and use this to top up the bed every week in dry weather.

MAKING A DRIED RIVER BED

Gravel gardens are becoming increasingly popular, and are more convincing if they have a definite theme, such as a dried river bed. This is simple to construct in that it places no demands on levels and waterproofing, yet, when successfully designed, it has a distinctly watery theme. It helps if the width of the river bed varies from one end to the other, and, if there is a slight slope in the garden, this looks even more effective with the narrow origin of the river bed at the top of the slope. On a totally flat site, introduce a slight curve to simulate the meandering line which a river would take on low-lying, flat land. It can look most appropriate in a long or narrow garden where the viewing point from the house allows the length of the river bed to be framed in a downstairs window.

As with all gravel gardens, there is a greater freedom in the planting arrangements compared with having to work within the disciplined confines of a border.

Access to individual plants or plant groups is possible from all sides, and even after heavy rain you will not encounter the associated problems of picking up mud or compacting the wet soil by walking on it.

BELOW: **The origin of this dried river bed appears from a thick shrub border and is sparsely planted, initially with a selection of drought-loving plants.**

INSET: **As the bed becomes wider in the lower section, moisture-loving grasses are introduced and allowed to grow through an old bottomless boat for a further watery effect.**

YOU WILL NEED

- Garden hose, rope or sand
- Spade
- Rake
- Landscape membrane
- Large scissors

- Squares of polythene (polyethylene)
- Small pea gravel or shingle
- Rounded pebbles or cobbles

- Planting compost (soil mix)
- Plants (including moisture-lovers)
- Watering can
- Large boulders

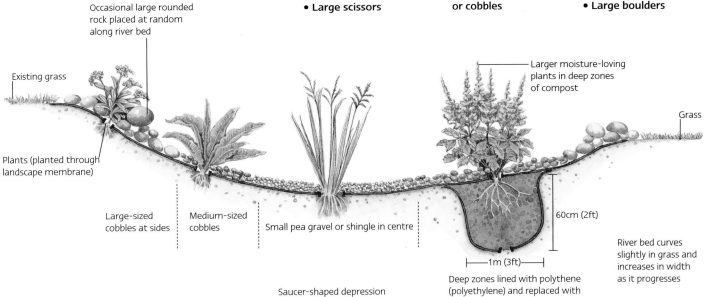

Occasional large rounded rock placed at random along river bed

Existing grass

Plants (planted through landscape membrane)

Large-sized cobbles at sides

Medium-sized cobbles

Small pea gravel or shingle in centre

Saucer-shaped depression no deeper than 15–23cm (6–9in)

Larger moisture-loving plants in deep zones of compost

Grass

60cm (2ft)

1m (3ft)

Deep zones lined with polythene (polyethylene) and replaced with humus-rich compost (soil mix) after digging out

River bed curves slightly in grass and increases in width as it progresses

1 Mark out the shape of the bed with a thin line of sand or with a length of rope or garden hose laid on the ground. View the shape from all angles, particularly from any upstairs windows.

2 If the proposed site is on existing turf, remove the turf to a depth of 2.5cm (1in), and stack somewhere inconspicuous for later use or remove from the site.

3 Create a shallow, evenly sloped, saucer-shaped depression across the width of the river bed along its length. The depth of the base of the saucer need be no more than 15–23cm (6–9in), depending on the width of the bed. Rake smooth and remove any sharp objects.

4 If moisture-loving plants are to be included in the bed, mark their positions and dig out large planting holes, about 60cm (2ft) deep and 1m (3ft) in diameter.

5 Line the whole river bed with a landscape membrane, which allows moisture through, but prevents the growth of weeds. These materials are often sold in 1m- (3ft-) wide rolls.

6 If planting holes have been dug out beforehand, cut out holes in the membrane above the planting positions and line the holes with squares of polythene (polyethylene), piercing the base with a hole.

7 Cover the whole area of the river bed with small pea gravel or shingle and 2-3 grades of rounded pebbles or cobbles, using the larger sizes on the outside and the smaller sizes in the centre.

8 Plant into the bed where desired by scraping back the cobbles and cutting a cross in the membrane. Fold back the flaps of cut membrane and remove enough soil from underneath to allow the plant roots to be spread out in the planting hole with supplementary planting compost (soil mix).

9 Water the new plants thoroughly before covering the compost (soil mix) with the folds of membrane. Push back the pebbles over the planting position.

10 For the moisture-loving plants in the specially dug larger planting holes, place some of the removed turf from the earlier preparation of the river bed in the bottom of the holes before inserting the planting compost (soil mix). The turf helps to retain more compost in the planting holes before any surplus can seep out through the hole pierced earlier in the polythene (polyethylene) lining.

11 Add larger boulders onto the river bed to add interest between the plants.

INSTALLING A PREFORMED UNIT

If you choose a preformed unit, do not be tempted to skimp on the preparation of the hole and make sure that the sides and base are evenly supported. The larger units are extremely heavy when full of water and are subject to enormous strain if they are not properly supported. This can result in hairline cracks forming in even the thicker fibreglass units. Greater care is necessary with the plastic preformed units because their sides are less rigid and can bend in any uneven pressure of water and soil.

YOU WILL NEED

- Preformed pool unit
- Bricks
- Canes and a garden hose, rope or string
- Spade
- Rake
- 2 pieces of straight-edged wood: one long enough to straddle the sides of the pool unit and the other slightly shorter
- than the length of the pool in order to check the level at the bottom of the hole
- Tape measure
- Spirit level
- Knife or secateurs (pruners)
- Soft sand
- Timber for tamping the backfill
- Suitable edging material such as paving slabs to create an informal edge

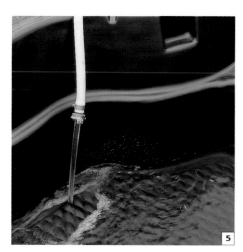

3 You will need some help to place the unit in the hole and press it down firmly onto the raked surface so that an impression is made of the shape of the base. Lift out the unit, then dig out from 5–8cm (2–3in) outside the impression that has been left by the unit's base. When the depth of the pool plus an extra 5–8cm (2–3in) for a layer of soft sand has been reached, lay a plank of wood across the width of the hole and check that the hole is the right depth with a tape measure. Use a spirit level to make sure that the base of the hole is level.

4 Cut away any tree roots that may have been exposed and rake over the bottom to remove stones and any other objects with a sharp edge. Check the sides for sharp edges with your hands, gently patting firm any loose soil. Firm the base evenly before spreading a layer of soft sand, 5cm (2in) deep, across the bottom. Again, get help to lower the unit carefully into place. Make sure that the unit is sitting level by placing the spirit level on a straight-edged piece of wood across the sides; check the level in all directions.

5 Gently add water to the unit to a depth of 10cm (4in) and fill between the sides of the unit and the sides of the hole with sand or sifted soil to a depth of 10cm (4in) from the bottom, so that it is equal to the level of the water in the pool. Use a flat-bottomed piece of timber – a cut-down broom handle, for example – to firm this backfilled sand or soil into place.

6 Repeat the process of adding 10cm (4in) of water to the pool and 10cm (4in) of sand or soil outside, making sure that no air pockets are left as you backfill around the pool. Use your spirit level to check that the unit is still perfectly level after each addition of water and sand. When the pool is nearly full, the weight of the water will keep it quite stable. The edging can then be put in place. Crazy paving makes an excellent choice for informal edges, covering the rim of the pool and just overlapping the water.

1 To mark out a symmetrically shaped preformed pool, invert the unit onto the proposed site and use sand to mark around the edge of the rim. An irregularly shaped unit should be stood upright on the proposed site and temporarily supported by bricks to prevent it from falling over. The outline can then be marked by pushing canes from the rim into the soil directly beneath, at intervals of about 1m (3ft). A garden hose, rope or string can then be placed around the canes to mark the outline on the ground.

2 Skim off the turf in 30cm (12in) squares and stack them where they can rot down. Excavate the soil down to the level of the first marginal shelf, working from 5–8cm (2–3in) outside the outline. Lightly rake and level the dug surface.

CREATING A CLAY-LINED POOL

BELOW: **Large informal pools are ideal candidates for lining with clay. This pool will be attractive to wildlife. A small, thatched summer-house provides a perfect vantage point from which to view visiting creatures.**

The introduction of flexible liners has meant that clay, like concrete, is no longer a common method of pool construction. It can, however, be a good proposition if there is already heavy clay on site or if it can be bought cheaply from a local source. Making a clay-lined pool is not a viable economic undertaking for a small pool if the clay has to be imported from some distance away. It is not completely waterproof, and the very slow absorption of water through its sides makes it more appropriate for large pools and wildlife pools in rural areas.

Few garden soils are composed entirely of clay and in order to check whether the soil in your garden contains sufficient clay to make a puddled pool, there are two simple tests. The first and easiest is to roll a sample between the palms. If it falls to pieces it is unsuitable. It should stay tacky when moist and stain the skin as it rolls.

A more accurate test requires placing a sifted sample in a jar of water to which a teaspoon of salt is added. Shake it vigorously and leave it for a day or two. It will settle into bands of sand, silt and clay from the bottom upwards. If it is suitable for pool making, at least two-thirds of the sample should be clay, which forms the top layer.

The process of clay puddling means lining a hole with a thick, compacted layer of clay, preferably in several thin layers. It should be at least 15–25cm (6–10in) thick, so work out the area of the base and sides first to find out the quantity you need.

If you do not have a ready supply of natural clay or cannot obtain it locally, you can instead use sodium bentonite clay and bentomat matting, which is much easier to install and will generally achieve better results.

YOU WILL NEED

- String, sand or canes
- Spade
- Rolls of bentomat matting
- Bag of sodium bentonite crystals
- Plants (including oxygenating plants and marginals)
- Garden hose
- Tile or stone slab

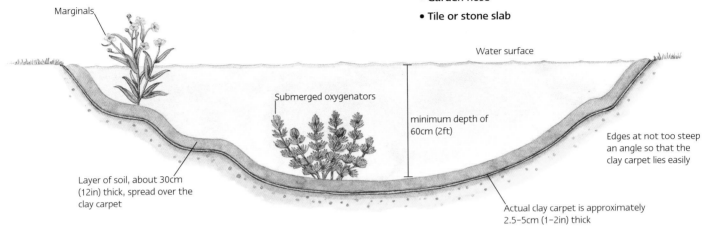

Marginals

Water surface

Submerged oxygenators

minimum depth of
60cm (2ft)

Edges at not too steep
an angle so that the
clay carpet lies easily

Layer of soil, about 30cm
(12in) thick, spread over the
clay carpet

Actual clay carpet is approximately
2.5–5cm (1–2in) thick

RIGHT: This natural
pool in a shaded site,
with its inky black
water, is lined with
clay. This allows the
moisture-loving
plants greater freedom
around the edge,
which is kept moist.

LEFT: Tree roots can
be a menace in clay-
lined pools where
there is a very low
water table. Here, the
water table is fed by a
spring, keeping the
water table high and
allowing ample water
for the tree roots.

1 Mark out the position of the pool on the ground with string or sand or with a series of canes.

2 Excavate a saucer-shaped depression to a minimum of 60cm (2ft) at the deepest point. Avoid creating steep sides to the hole. Save the topsoil for replacing on the clay carpet later.

3 Roll the bentomat over the excavation and over the edges. Overlap any additional strips by about 15cm (6in), sprinkling loose bentonite crystals between and over the joints to strengthen the seal.

4 Cover the bentomat with a 30cm (12in) layer of soil, avoiding soil which contains heavy levels of fertilizer.

5 Suitable marginals and oxygenating plants can be planted directly into the soil. Avoid using very vigorous marginals, such as *Typha*, *Sparganium* and *Schoenoplectus*, and instead choose less vigorous types – *Caltha*, *Veronica* and *Myosotis*, for example.

6 Add water by resting the end of the garden hose on a tile or stone slab and letting the water in slowly. This prevents the freshly installed soil from being dislodged. The fine particles of debris, silt and clay may take several days or weeks to settle on the bottom, but the water will then begin to clear.

MAKING A CONCRETE POOL

RIGHT: **A shallow pool, which acts as a base pool for a fountain, is made from concrete blocks skimmed on the inside with a waterproof mortar.**

BELOW: **A concrete block wall provides strength and water-proofing inside the dry wall surround of this pool, which is disguised by the natural walling stones.**

Before the widespread use of flexible liners, concrete was the only material used for ornamental pool construction. It often involved complicated shuttering (formwork) to make a framework into which fresh concrete was poured. Although modern materials have largely superseded concrete in pool construction, there are still situations in which concrete pools are more suitable, such as places where soil conditions are too unstable for sunken pools with flexible liners. Concrete is also good for raised pools, which need strong side walls to withstand water pressure. Fish-keepers also use concrete pools, as the rigid vertical side walls necessary for pools with large specimen fish are more suited to concrete construction. Instead of using wooden shuttering and pouring wet concrete into the moulds, most concrete pools are now made using concrete walling blocks to make the rigid framework and this is then skimmed with fibreglass mortar to make it watertight.

YOU WILL NEED

- String and canes
- Spade
- Concrete mix for walling block foundations
- Spirit level
- Straight-edged piece of wood
- Rake
- Soft sand

- Reinforcing fibres
- Ready-mix mortar
- Plasterer's trowel
- Concrete walling blocks
- Hardcore
- Paving slabs as surround
- Paint brush
- Black waterproof sealant

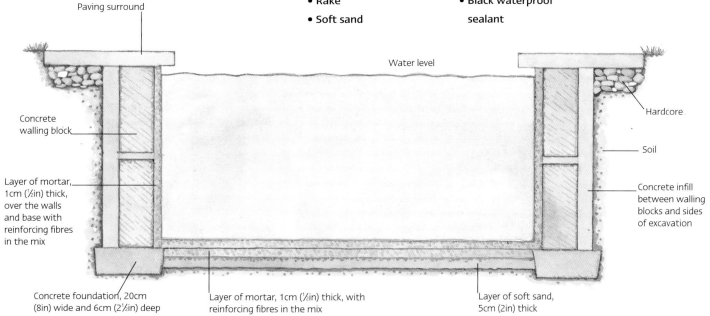

Paving surround

Concrete walling block

Layer of mortar, 1cm (½in) thick, over the walls and base with reinforcing fibres in the mix

Concrete foundation, 20cm (8in) wide and 6cm (2½in) deep

Layer of mortar, 1cm (½in) thick, with reinforcing fibres in the mix

Water level

Hardcore

Soil

Concrete infill between walling blocks and sides of excavation

Layer of soft sand, 5cm (2in) thick

1 Mark out the outline of the pool with string and canes, making a nick in the soil along the outline.

2 Dig out the area to a depth of 75cm (30in). If you are keeping the soil, do not mix topsoil and subsoil.

3 Dig a 20cm- (8in-) wide trench to a depth of 6cm (2½in) around the inside of the base of the excavation for the concrete wall foundations. Pour in the concrete mix and level the top of the foundation. Check that the foundations are level using a spirit level on a piece of wood, and leave to dry for 24 hours.

4 Dig out about 6cm (2½in) soil from the base of the pool and rake to remove any stones. Spread and rake, then level and firm a 5cm (2in) layer of soft sand so that it is just below the top of the wall foundation.

5 As the base of the pool is well supported by the soil beneath the sand, all that is necessary is to skim the sand with a 1cm (½in) layer of fibre-reinforced mortar with a plasterer's trowel, overlapping the concrete foundations by 5cm (2in).

6 After a minimum of 24 hours, concrete walling blocks are then mortared onto the foundations and the levels checked with a spirit level. After the mortar has set, give added strength to the walls by filling in the gap between the soil wall and the walling blocks with a stiff concrete mix. Fill in the inside of the blocks if these have been made with internal cavities.

7 Allow a further 48 hours for the whole structure to set thoroughly. Dampen the whole surface of the internal structure, including the base, before covering with a 1cm (½in) layer of fibre-reinforced mortar. To give the corners added strength, make a rounded cornice edge where the walls meet each other and the base.

8 Replace the top 10cm (4in) of soil with hardcore to help form a secure base immediately around the pool. Mortar the paving edge onto the walls of the pool and the hardcore base. Place the paving surround so that it overlaps the inside wall of the pool by 2.5–5cm (1–2in).

9 Allow the internal walls to dry for a further 48 hours, then paint them with a black waterproof sealant. This will also prevent any impurities from the mortar from seeping into the water.

BUILDING AN ORNAMENTAL POOL
for fish

Specialist fish-keepers tend to prefer raised pools if possible, particularly collectors of large specimen koi. Apart from being able to see them easily, it is useful to have vertical side walls both below and slightly above the water surface to prevent them leaping out onto the surrounding paving. The practicalities of pool hygiene and management for large fish call for more attention to the design and construction than the average pool.

For the ornamental garden pool a good compromise can be found in building a more traditional sunken pool and adding filtration. The more formal designs have the advantage of paved edges which, provided they have a slight overhang above the water surface, will help to stop the fish's tendency to jump out. An external filter can be more difficult to disguise in a formal pool and one of the more aesthetic ways of hiding a large external filter is to build a raised waterfall alongside the pool where the filter can be positioned above the pond level. The black box-like filter can then be disguised by the planting around and behind the waterfall. Where external filtration is not possible there are large internal pond filters which can be used, although they are not as easy to clean and maintain as an external filter.

RIGHT: **The quantity of fish in this small pool is dependent on the extra oxygen supplied by a waterfall and a hidden filtration system which prevents the water becoming toxic.**

YOU WILL NEED

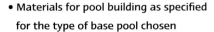

- Materials for pool building as specified
  for the type of base pool chosen
- Materials for stream building as specified
  for the type of stream chosen
- Biological filter
- Ultra-violet clarifier
- Submersible filter pump
- Flexible delivery pipe and hacksaw
  for cutting to appropriate lengths
- Galvanized hose clips
- Magnet attachment to reduce blanketweed
- Flat rock to disguise end of pipe

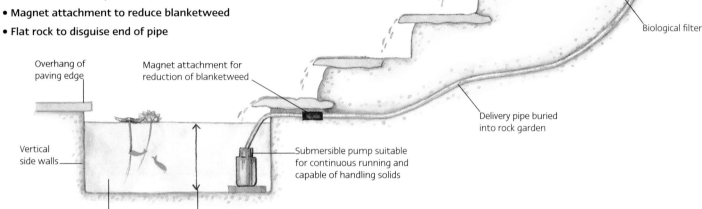

Outlet from ultra-violet clarifier into biological filter

Delivery pipe enters ultra-violet clarifier before entering biological filter

Conifers to disguise the filter

Outlet into waterfall from biological filter

Biological filter

Overhang of paving edge

Magnet attachment for reduction of blanketweed

Delivery pipe buried into rock garden

Vertical side walls

Submersible pump suitable for continuous running and capable of handling solids

Pond

Ideal minimum depth of 60–75cm (24–30in)

1 Following the instructions given previously, build a pool, either from concrete or with a flexible liner, which has an adequate volume for a collection of ornamental fish. A preformed unit pool could also act as a fish pool although the size may limit the numbers that can be kept. The three necessities for making a pool suitable for fish are a minimum depth of 60–75cm (24–30in), no shallow sloping sides, such as beaches, where larger fish may flip out, and an overhang of 2.5–5cm (1–2in) if any paved edge is used.

2 Follow the instructions for making a stream with rigid stream units or a flexible liner.

3 The following steps show how to set up a filtration system in a pool for fish. The two main ingredients for a fish pool are a biological filter and an ultra-violet clarifier, which need a mains electricity supply. Work out the volume of the pool, and consult a dealer regarding the size of filter and clarifier you will need. There are various designs for the interior of a biological filter and several filter mediums may be used. The dealer will supply the most suitable filter medium for your needs.

4 Position the filter behind or to the side of the top stream section or header pool so that the outlet from the filter will be piped into the stream. Place the

filter, which measures about 60cm (24in) wide and 60cm (24in) deep, slightly higher than the top of the stream and in a position that allows the planting to hide it.

5 The filter pump should be suitable for continuous running and for handling solids. If it is too small, the filtration will be inadequate; if it is too large, it will change the water too often. The volume of the pool should not pass through the filter more than once an hour.

6 Hide the delivery pipe from the pump in the soil alongside the stream and connect it to the ultra-violet clarifier at the top of the stream with a galvanized hose clip. Use another short length of pipe to connect the outlet of the clarifier to the inlet of the biological filter with hose clips. Fix the magnet attachment to the pipe where it runs under the first fall above the pond.

7 Finally, connect a short length of pipe from the outlet of the filter to the header pool or top stream section, disguising the end of the pipe with a flat rock where it enters the stream. Fill the base pool with water and turn on the system. Run it continuously for a few weeks to allow the bacteria to grow on the media and begin to work. Once the system is working after a few weeks, keep the pump operating as the beneficial bacteria will die if water is not passing through for any length of time.

BUILDING A RAISED POOL

YOU WILL NEED

- String, rope, pegs or sand
- Preformed pool unit
- Spade
- Rake
- Gravel
- Railway sleepers (ties)
- Builder's square
- Electric saw
- Sand and sieved soil
- Galvanized steel brackets
- Screws and screwdriver
- Nails and hammer
- Polythene (polyethylene) sheet
- Spirit level
- Straight-edged piece of wood
- Timber for tamping the backfill
- Small rocks
- Creeping and mat-forming alpines
- Alpine grit

Raised pools are easier to empty than sunken pools, and they suffer from fewer problems, such as leaves and other plant debris blowing in. They require very little excavation and are an ideal solution on sloping sites. Substantial surrounds, such as twin walls, are necessary when a raised pool is made with a flexible liner in order to withstand the internal water pressure, and this makes them more costly to build than sunken pools; if they are built with brick or walling stone, some degree of bricklaying skill will be necessary.

A simple raised pool can be made by installing a rigid preformed unit and surrounding it with a raised edge of several courses of old railway sleepers (ties), secured with brackets. Alternatively, a rigid unit can be raised above the ground according to the height and type of rock edging.

INITIAL PREPARATION

Mark the outline of the shape that the raised wall of railway sleepers (ties) will occupy. Check that the preformed unit will fit inside the outline. Clear the turf and other plants from the ground beneath the position of the pool and rake the soil level. Spread a layer of gravel, 5cm (2in) deep, over the marked-out area. This will prevent the bottom course of sleepers from sitting on wet soil.

1 After marking out and preparing a level site, lay the first course of sleepers to the shape required. For a simple rectangle, which will hold a variety of preformed shapes, you will need to cut down half of the sleepers to form the two shorter sides and use a builder's square to check that a true right angle is formed by the sleepers on the short side. A square surround with sides that are the same length will save considerable cutting. Whenever possible, butt a freshly cut edge to the inside of a neighbouring sleeper so that it is not exposed.

2 As the courses are placed on top of each other, place the next course of sleepers (ties) in a different pattern. Extra rigidity in the construction is then provided by bonding the joints. Continue adding courses until the correct level of the preformed unit is reached. If this is not the exact height of the preform, add another sleeper so that the wall is higher than the pool.

3 When sufficient height is reached (in this case the height of four sleepers/ties), spread a 5cm (2in) layer of sand inside the surround to act as a base for the preform. This will make any final levelling of the rigid unit much easier.

4 Make the structure more rigid by screwing a galvanized steel bracket inside the corners of the surround to connect each sleeper (tie) to the next.

5 Extra rigidity will be given by driving in galvanized nails, 15cm (6in) long, from one course of sleepers (ties) to the next. Knock the nails in at an angle on the inside edge of the surround so that they are not seen later.

6 Line the inside of the raised bed with a sheet of cheap polythene (polyethylene) secured to the sleepers (ties) by nails. This helps to prevent small mammals like mice from creeping inside the gaps between the sleepers and making nests in the soil or sand.

7 Enlist help to lift the pool inside the sleepers (ties) and check that the sides are level. Keep the sides of the pool just lower than the top of the sleeper wall.

8 Add sieved soil between the pool rim and the sleepers (ties). Firm this with a ramming tool like a sawn-off broom handle and then level the backfilled soil around the rim. The area between the edge of the pool and the sleepers can now be landscaped with small rocks and a selection of alpine plants, top-dressed with alpine grit.

5

6

7

8

BUILDING A SEMI-RAISED POOL

For a pool that is not installed completely above ground level, a good compromise is to bury only the deeper zone of the preformed pool unit below ground level, leaving the marginal shelves above ground. This will protect fish and plants from any sudden changes in temperature. Informal walls of rock can be used to surround the bed, the aim being to make the final arrangement look as natural as possible.

YOU WILL NEED

- String, rope, pegs or sand
- Preformed pool unit
- Spade
- Sheet of polythene (polyethylene)
- Rake
- Sand
- Gravel
- Railway sleepers (ties)
- Builder's square
- Electric saw
- Sieved soil
- Galvanized steel brackets
- Screws and screwdriver
- Nails and hammer
- Spirit level
- Straight-edged piece of wood
- Timber for tamping the backfill
- Large and small rocks
- Alpines and alpine grit

1 Mark the position of the pool and the shape of the unit on the ground. Clear the ground of turf and other materials. Rake the exposed soil to produce a shallow tilth. Lift the preformed unit onto the soil and press it down to mark the position of the deeper zone. The imprint in the soil should be enhanced by spreading a narrow line of sand around the deeper zone so that the area to be dug out has a clear outline.

2 Put the unit to one side and dig a hole with slightly sloping sides, 5cm (2in) wider than the imprint and 5cm (2in) deeper than the deep zone. Place the soil from the hole on a sheet of polythene (polyethylene).

3 After reaching the final depth, rake the bottom level and add an even layer of soft sand, 5cm (2in) deep, over the base. Lift the unit back into the hole and check that it is level in all directions. If necessary, lift out the unit and add or take away sand from the base, checking the levels each time. When you are happy with the level, add some sand as backfilling around the sides.

4 Build a retaining wall of railway sleepers (ties), as described in the previous project. The wall should be slightly higher than the top of the pool unit and positioned just outside it. You will need to add and firm soil between the sleeper wall and the sides of the pool unit. Continue to add 8–10cm (3–4in) of water to the unit to keep it stable as you build up the soil infill inside the sleeper wall, which should be slightly higher than the top of the pool. The level will sink slightly as the soil settles.

5 While building the surround, check that the pool remains perfectly level. Arrange the rocks on the soil surround, using any flat, thin pieces of rock to disguise and overlap the pool edge. Plant with alpines, and top-dress with alpine grit to conserve moisture. Water in the plants, then bale out the shallow water from the unit to remove any soil. Fill the pool to the full depth and plant with containerized marginals and submerged plants (see inset to main picture).

4

5

BUILDING A STREAM
with a flexible liner

YOU WILL NEED

- Marking pegs, string, rope or sand
- Spade
- Rake
- Soft sand
- Underlay and flexible liner
- Corrugated delivery pipe
- Large, flat-sided spillstone
- Ready-mixed mortar
- Mortaring trowel
- Rocks
- Submersible pump
- Hose connectors
- Flow-regulating valve
- Cobbles

This stream has been constructed using one sheet of flexible liner because there are no sharp changes of direction. The size of liner is calculated by placing a tape measure loosely along the proposed line of the stream and adding extra length for the height and number of vertical falls. Additional length should also be anticipated in the overlap into the base pool, and the folds made in the liner. Finally, in measuring the length, allow additional liner for the depth of the header pool. The width should be measured as the maximum width of the stream, even if this is for only one section. The header pool is likely to be the widest part of the watercourse and by adding twice the depth of this pool to its width, you will be able to measure the exact width of liner needed and buy it in one sheet.

It can be difficult to assess accurately the size of pump required to use with a stream, and advice should be sought from the supplier. It is always better to err on the side of over capacity rather than buy a pump that has to work hard to maintain the volume of water over the waterfalls.

Check that the diameter of the delivery pipe is suitable for the outlet of the pump. To feed a reasonable length of stream – say 4m (13ft) – the pipe should be preferably 2.5cm (1in) in diameter.

1 Mark out the route of the watercourse with pegs and string or rope or by sprinkling sand. Decide on the position of the waterfalls because the stream will have to narrow to waists at these falls. A stream with falls is a series of narrow, level pools at different heights. By making these pools level, water is retained in each section when the pump is turned on. If the sections slope towards the base pool, the stream would dry up as soon as the pump is switched off.

2 Begin to excavate at the edge of the existing base pool which is made with a preformed unit. This is the point where suitable stones will form the outlet into the pool. The gradient of the slope and the size of the rocks will govern the height of the waterfalls. Dig out and rake a flat-bottomed trench, 23cm (9in) deep, from the base pool to the point where there will be a waterfall from the header pool. This is excavated at the top of the stream. Line the trench with a 2.5cm (1in) covering of soft sand, then the underlay and liner can be unrolled into the excavation. Allow the liner to rest on the marginal shelf and unroll it along the

stream to just beyond the outlet waterfall. Ensure the liner and underlay are placed correctly over the excavation, and that there will be enough to overlap the sides of the stream once it is pressed into the contours. Bury the delivery pipe beside the stream; it should reach from the bottom of the base pool to beyond the header pool.

3 Select a large stone with flat sides as the spillstone for the outlet waterfall into the base pool. The stone should be placed on a stiff dab of mortar on top of the stream liner and positioned so that it overhangs the side of the base pool.

4 Place rocks along the stream edge on top of the liner, ensuring that they are higher than the top of the spillstone into the base pool. Soil can later be placed between the liner and the rocks for creeping marginals in the wet soil (see inset).

5 At the top of the stream, place a stone in the centre of the liner, over which the water will flow from the header pool into the stream. To prevent the water seeping under this spillstone, fold the liner behind the stone and place smaller rocks behind and to the sides.

6 As the supporting walls for the waterfall are built up, mortar these into place behind and around the spillstone, ensuring that the small pleat in the liner is hidden between rocks and covered with mortar. Make sure that the side stones flanking the spillstone finish at a higher level so that the water is channelled over the spillstone.

7 Bring the end of the delivery pipe to the surface above the rocks behind the header pool. Use a flat stone to conceal the pipe where it enters the header pool. Keep the end of the pipe above the waterline in case it siphons the water back into the base pool when the pump is turned off.

8 Fill the base pool with water, attach the pump and valve to the pipe, and turn on to test the flow of water. Add some soil around the rocks beside the stream and plant a mixture of moisture-lovers and alpines. Disguise the folds of the liner on the stream bottom with rounded cobbles.

BUILDING A STREAM
with rigid units

YOU WILL NEED

- Plastic dustbin (trash can)
- Length of corrugated flexible pipe
- Roof tiles
- Submersible pump
- 2 bricks or a piece of broken paving
- Timber for tamping the backfill
- Galvanized metal mesh
- Cobbles
- Preformed stream units
- Small stakes or pegs and tape measure
- Spade
- Soft sand
- Spirit level
- Straight-edged piece of wood
- Bucket
- Flow-adjusting valve

You may prefer to use rigid, preformed stream units instead of a flexible liner to build a stream. These eliminate the need for mortar and require very little skill to install. Installation is much quicker than with liners, largely because you do not have to wait for mortar to harden, and the units can be easily removed if necessary.

The strongest stream units are those made from fibreglass. They are resistant to ultra-violet light and strong enough to withstand a certain amount of movement in the soil mound. The vacuum-formed plastic types have a limited life expectancy and are much more easily damaged. Most types are available in a variety of finishes, such as pebbledash or textured rock.

Because streams are best created with a header pool at the water's point of origin in the system, check that you can also get a suitable pool in the same finish as the stream units. These pools must contain sufficient water to ensure that when the pump is not running there is no surge of water when the flow is turned on.

Unlike streams made with a flexible liner, there is no moist edge in the soil immediately surrounding the units, and this dry soil is not suitable for marginal and moisture-loving plants. There are, however, several creeping plants, such as *Acaena*, *Arenaria* and *Erigeron*, that will grow in these dry conditions and quickly disguise the rather artificial edges of the units.

1 This stream runs into a submerged reservoir rather than a pool, so dig a plastic dustbin (trash can) into the ground where the stream ends. Mound up the spoil from the excavation and some extra soil in a gentle slope along the route of the proposed stream. Bury a length of flexible pipe, which forms the delivery pipe from the pump, along the length of the stream to reappear above the surface at the top of the stream. Here, the pipe was taken through a low wall when it was constructed. Protect the pipe by covering it with roof tiles before replacing the soil. Use a pipe with a minimum diameter of 2.5cm (1in) if the distance from the reservoir to the top of the stream is more than 3m (10ft).

2 Place the pump on a piece of broken paving at the bottom of the reservoir to keep the pump intake just above any sludge which might accumulate at the bottom of the reservoir. Connect the pump cable to the nearby connection point and connect the plastic pipe to the pump outlet. Measure the

length of the stream between the reservoir and the top and select the required number of stream sections. There are different lengths available so buy the sections first before marking out the stream outline.

3 Backfill the soil and firm around the rim of the reservoir before placing a piece of galvanized metal mesh over the top. Place a few cobbles on the mesh to hold it in place until the preformed units are finally installed.

4 Lay the stream units down roughly on the ground to design a route. Vary the direction as much as possible; it is much easier to do this with preformed units than with flexible liners. Mark out their positions with small stakes or pegs.

5 Remove the units and, starting at the bottom, dig a shallow trench for the units and line it with a layer of soft sand. Press the first two sections firmly into a level position with the outlet of the bottom section projecting over the reservoir by 7–10cm (3–4in). As the units are designed to hold a thin film of shallow water when they are level, pour in some water to check the final level and flow over the rim.

6 The stream units are designed to overlap one another and produce a gentle cascade even with a small pump. This flow is achieved with the bucket and will be increased when the pump is turned on.

7 Once the final section has been installed at the top of the stream, add some water to check the position and levels. Backfill the soil around the sides in order to blend the edges of the units into the mound. To disguise the side of the top stream section, mound cobbles on top of the wall and around the stream source. Use more cobbles to blend the sections into the surrounding mound of soil.

8 To adjust the flow of water over the cobbles, insert a plastic flow-adjusting valve into the flexible pipe at a convenient point near the top of the stream. Fill the reservoir, then turn on the pump to check that the stream is flowing satisfactorily. Finish arranging cobbles over the metal grid.

BUILDING A MEANDERING STREAM
for a flat site

BELOW: **Meandering streams look effective with cobble edges that are interspersed with larger boulders and occasionally planted.**

BOTTOM RIGHT: **A gentle stream can support an array of lush vegetation.**

In complete contrast with rocky, fast-moving streams, a flexible liner can be used to create a stream where there is hardly any slope at all. This style of stream is an ideal addition if there is an existing base pool in a heavily planted garden, and the stream is used to break up part of the lawn to create additional interest. A stream of this style can also be created without an existing pool or the need to build one: the stream can appear to run through the garden without beginning or ending. The stream does not have to be dominated by rocks; it can have softer, more rounded stones and boulders along its course, looking as if they have been deposited along an old river bed. If it is to be effective and not dependent on having a pump running continuously, a man-made stream is nothing more than a very narrow pool that is designed to overflow at a given point as soon as the pump introduces more water.

In such a scheme the header pool does not have to be a conspicuous affair; it is simply a means of providing the illusion of natural water entering the garden. This may be a small spring, a culvert appearing from the bottom of a wall or a boggy area with a log or stone disguising the end of the delivery pipe. The main essential in creating a natural-looking scheme is to devise a meandering route that widens in parts and follows as closely as possible the direction that water would take naturally on a flat site.

Before you begin, check the level of the garden, because even a relatively flat site will have a slope, no matter how inconspicuous. If the highest point can be identified, try to plan a scheme that has this as the source of the stream. This will not only avoid the difficulty of building the stream against a slope but also do away with the need to make slight changes in the levels.

YOU WILL NEED

- String, canes or garden hose
- Pegs, about 2.5cm (1in) in diameter and 15cm (6in) long
- Hammer
- Straight-edged piece of wood and spirit level

- Spade
- Polythene (polyethylene) sheet
- Rake
- Underlay and flexible liner
- Thin, flat stone
- Ready-mixed mortar
- Mortaring trowel

- Cobbles or river gravel
- Corrugated plastic pipe, measuring 1–2.5cm (½–1in) in diameter
- Roof tiles
- Rounded boulders
- Submersible pump
- Flow-adjusting valve

Flat rocks bordering the line of the stream: (7–10cm (3–4in) thick

Marginal plant

Grass surround

Cobbles lying on stream bottom

Water level

Marginal

Depth of shelves along streamside: 23cm (9in)

Underlay

Depth of excavation for liner: 38cm (15in)

Soil backfilled into excavated profile

Stream depth at base of saucer: 15cm (6in)

Flexible liner

1 When you have chosen the source, mark out the route of the stream with string, canes or a garden hose, working back from any existing pool.

2 Knock in the pegs about a metre (yard) apart along the route of the stream. Place a length of straight-edged wood and a spirit level on the pegs to identify any slight depressions or rises in the ground so that the surrounding soil can be adjusted if necessary. As long as the outlet point from the stream into the base pool is lower than the pool sides, there will be a flow when the pump is turned on. If this point is established first, then you can ensure that all other edges are higher than it.

3 If the route of the stream is through a lawn, remove the turf and stack it in a convenient place to rot down for later use. Leave the pegs identifying the level in place.

4 Dig out the soil from the stream to a depth of 38cm (15in) in the centre and if the stream is wider than 60cm (2ft), then create shallow marginal shelves, 23cm (9in) deep, along the sides. Stack the soil on a polythene (polyethylene) sheet because it will be needed after the liner is inserted. Rake the bottom of the stream and the shelves to make them level, removing any sharp stones.

5 Place underlay along the length of the stream before draping the single length of liner into the stream contours. Use rocks to hold down the sides of

the liner to stop them blowing about in the wind. To create a spill point and prevent the erosion of soil from the stream into the base pool, secure a thin, flat stone on the liner with a dab of mortar at the point where the stream enters the base pool.

6 Take some soil from the nearby heap of topsoil and put it on the liner to form a shallow saucer shape inside the excavation. The soil will help protect a cheap liner from ultra-violet light and provide a medium in which suitable plants can grow. Top-dress the soil with rounded cobbles or washed river gravel to help prevent it from being washed away when the stream is running.

7 Bury a corrugated plastic delivery pipe along the side of the stream so that it runs from the base pool to the source of the stream. Protect the pipe by covering it with roof tiles before replacing the soil.

8 Position a few rounded boulders on the liner at the source of the stream to simulate a small spring.

9 Install a pump in the base pool and connect the outlet to the plastic delivery pipe. As the water will only trickle through this stream, a flow adjuster should be fitted to the delivery pipe to regulate the flow. Fill the pool with water and turn on the pump to check that the stream is running satisfactorily. Place a few boulders along the stream edge and plant the marginals.

INSTALLING A BRIMMING URN

YOU WILL NEED

- Underlay and a piece of old carpet
- Spare pieces of flexible liner
- Bricks or decorative walling blocks
- Ready-mix mortar or brick or stone adhesive
- Galvanized metal grid or mesh
- Wire cutters
- Plastic-coated wire
- Submersible pump
- Urn
- Electric drill with a suitable bit
- Water-tank coupler or waterproof sealant with rigid delivery pipe
- Flexible delivery pipe or plastic pipe
- Hose clip
- Copper pipe, 10mm (½in) in diameter
- Cobbles and stones

Reservoir features, which can be used to create focal points in the garden, require minimal maintenance, and the relatively simple construction techniques involved can be applied to a range of features, including large urns. As with a drilled rock fountain, where the water trickles, rather than gurgles, from the top, the brimming urn can be an attractive proposition to the garden owner who wants to introduce the movement of water without any noise. In more formal types of garden, too, an urn can be used to make a stronger statement than other smaller fountain features.

Most urns are made of terracotta, and you must check that your urn will be frost resistant if it is to remain outside all winter. If there is the slightest doubt about its frost-hardiness, the urn should be painted with one of the proprietary water sealing paints that are recommended for outdoor use for sealing brick walls or other absorbent surfaces.

If you are using a brand new urn, paint it as soon as you obtain it, because terracotta is likely to be completely dry at this stage. If you are converting an existing urn that has been outside in a moist climate for some time or has been used to contain plants, dry it as much as you can before painting. If you do not, the moisture will be locked into the terracotta and could cause it to crack if there are any severe fluctuations in temperature. Apply three coats of paint both inside and out, allowing each coat ample time to dry thoroughly before applying the next. One advantage of the sealant on the outside surface is that the water will flow much more evenly than on the raw terracotta. The water flow is also helped if the rim is level, so if you are buying a new one, choose a suitably rimmed style.

The urn can be sited as a free-standing feature in a border or on paving or gravel. Or, it may form a strong focal point in the centre of an existing pool. If it is to be free-standing, the method of installation is the same as for installing a millstone fountain, except for the details given opposite for inserting the delivery pipe into the urn. The steps on the opposite page describe how an urn can be installed in a raised flowerbed or soil border.

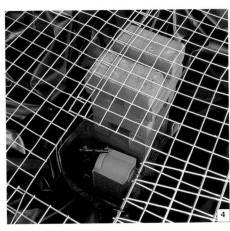

1 A good site for a brimming urn is in a small garden where there is a paved or concrete base which would be difficult to break up in order to sink a reservoir. This pool will create an adequately sized reservoir which will not require frequent topping up. Remove the plants from the centre of the bed, but leave some of the perennials to soften the edges. Remove most of the soil.

2 Place a square of old carpet or underlay at the bottom of the hole to protect the liner. Drape the liner in the hole and build up a pier of bricks in the centre until it is level with the top of the bed. Bond the bricks together for extra strength with ready-mix mortar or a brick or stone adhesive.

3 Place a sheet of galvanized metal grid over the hole. The sheet should be large enough to be supported by the sides of the hole and the brick pier in the centre. Cut a square in the grid large enough for the pump to pass through and secure with plastic-coated wire to form a hinge.

4 Place the pump in the bottom of the reservoir by passing it through the small access square next to the brick pier.

5 Drill a hole in the bottom of the urn large enough to accept a 10mm (½in) water-tank coupler. If it is not possible to obtain a water-tank coupler, a rigid delivery pipe from the pump can be passed through the base hole, made to the same size as the pipe, and sealed with silicon sealant. The advantage of the coupler is that the pipework can be dismantled at any time without breaking the watertight seal. Connect enough flexible pipe to the coupler to reach the outlet of the pump and secure with a hose clip.

6 Connect a 10mm (½in) rigid copper pipe to the coupler on the inside of the urn. Cut the length of copper pipe so that the top is just below the rim of the urn.

7 Pass the loose end of the pipe through the brick pier and connect it to the outlet of the pump. Fill the urn and reservoir with water and check the fountain spout.

8 Place a permeable membrane, such as underlay, over the grid. Cover with cobbles and stones.

MAKING A COBBLE FOUNTAIN

YOU WILL NEED

- Plastic dustbin (trash can)
- Spade
- Soft sand
- Spirit level
- Hand trowel
- Timber for tamping the backfill
- Rake
- Cloth
- 2 bricks or a piece of broken paving
- Submersible pump
- Rigid delivery pipe with flow adjuster
- Tape measure
- Sheet of polythene (polyethylene)
- Scissors
- Galvanized metal mesh in two grades, both larger than the diameter of the dustbin
- Wire cutters
- Cobbles

1 Choose a small, level site near a window in an area of paving or in front of a border so that the fountain will provide a good focal point. The cobbles can be arranged in any shape or extend as far as you wish, but the area for the fountain need be no more than a circle with the diameter of a plastic dustbin (trash can). Mark out the diameter of the bin and dig out a hole slightly wider and deeper than its dimensions. Place a shallow layer of sand at the bottom of the hole.

2 Put the dustbin (trash can) in the hole to ensure that the rim is just level with the surrounding soil. Check that the sides are level by placing a spirit level across the top of the dustbin. If any corrections are necessary, lift out the bin and make adjustments to the bottom of the hole.

3 Backfill the gap between the bin and the sides of the hole with soil and ram firm with a piece of timber. Mound the surrounding soil slightly to make an even saucer shape and rake to remove any stones. Remove any soil that may have fallen into the bin, and wipe out the inside with a cloth.

4 Place two bricks at the bottom of the dustbin (trash can) to act as a plinth for the pump. This prevents the intake of any debris that accumulates at the base of the bin.

5 Check that the length of rigid plastic pipe used for the fountain spout from the pump will be 5–8cm (2–3in) higher than the sides of the dustbin (trash can).

6 Place the polythene (polyethylene) sheet over the bin (can) and surrounding area and cut out a hole slightly wider than the fountain pipe. Fill the bin with water.

This is one of the most popular of moving water features for small gardens because it is safe, easy to maintain and will fit into any size or style of garden.

A cobblestone fountain consists simply of water falling through a spout onto cobbles arranged around it, bringing movement and a gentle or turbulent sound. Such a feature is ideal for a patio, where it can be seen from indoors, and it also makes an ideal subject for garden lighting. An amber lens on a small low-voltage spotlight hidden by a nearby rock, for example, makes the water spout resemble the flames of a fire, providing an excuse for endless daydreaming.

The water level in the reservoir should be checked regularly if the fountain is used in hot, sunny weather. Water will evaporate from the cobbles in wind and sun, and if the pump is allowed to run dry the motor will be badly damaged. As a precaution, when using the fountain intermittently, pour 2 gallons of water into the reservoir before you turn it on.

7 Lay the polythene (polyethylene) sheet over the dustbin (trash can), with the fountain pipe protruding from the hole.

8 Place a piece of galvanized mesh large enough to rest on the rim of the bin over the hole and the delivery pipe from the pump.

9 Place a smaller mesh on top of the larger mesh in order to catch any small cobbles used for the surface of the fountain. The small mesh would not be strong enough on its own to support the weight of large wet cobbles.

10 Hide the surface of the polythene (polyethylene) and mesh with a layer of cobbles. Check that the height of the spout is working satisfactorily. When you are satisfied with the fountain, finish arranging the cobbles. Add some plants, ensuring that they are integrated into their surroundings. Make the connection from the pump cable to a convenient waterproof switch so that the pump can be controlled easily.

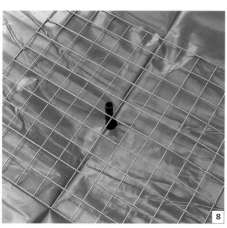

5

6

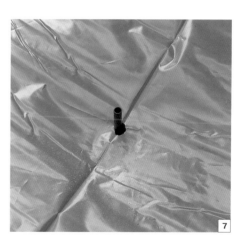

7

8

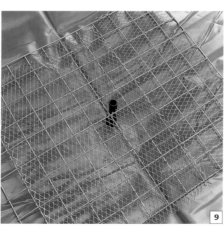

9

10

INSTALLING A MILLSTONE FOUNTAIN

YOU WILL NEED

- Spade
- Reservoir tank
- Soft sand
- Spirit level
- Timber for tamping the backfill
- 2 bricks or a piece of broken paving
- Submersible pump
- Rigid plastic delivery pipe
- Reservoir lid
- Fibreglass millstone
- Length of log roll, 1m (3ft) long and 30cm (12in) high
- Large cobbles

The simple cobble fountain can be easily adapted to make similar reservoir features, such as a millstone fountain. This allows the pumped water to emerge from the centre of a millstone and ripple over the surface before falling over the sides into a reservoir below.

The millstone is better suited to a traditional setting than a cobble fountain, which is versatile enough for use in both modern and older-style gardens. If the water outlet from the stone centre is carefully controlled, it can be a much quieter affair than the cobble fountain, as the water spreads evenly before rippling over the surface of the stone. Select a level spot where the fountain will make a good focal point.

The size and weight of the millstone will affect the method of construction because a plastic dustbin (trash can), which can be used as a reservoir for a cobble fountain, will not be strong enough or large enough to support a heavy stone. A fibreglass millstone, however, can be used with a plastic dustbin. If you choose a heavy millstone, then you will have to support it on piers inside the reservoir. There are several ways of achieving access to the pump, but the simplest is to make a reservoir under the millstone with a wider diameter. An access point can then be created between the edge of the millstone and the edge of the reservoir.

The fibreglass millstone fountain shown here is available in kit form from most good garden centres.

1 Dig out a hole slightly deeper and wider than the reservoir tank and line the base with soft sand.

2 Place a spirit level across the rim of the tank to check that it is level in the hole. Backfill and firm the gap between the tank and the soil with soil or sand so that the tank fits rigidly in the hole. Check the level again after backfilling.

3 Place the pump in the reservoir with a short length of rigid plastic pipe, 10mm (½in) in diameter, attached to the delivery outlet of the pump. This pipe is normally supplied with the kit, but if one is not supplied it needs to be approximately 45–60cm (18–24in) long. This can be cut to the exact size required with a hacksaw.

4 Fill the reservoir with water to within 2.5–5cm (1–2in) of the rim.

5 Place the reservoir lid firmly on top of the rim. This has a central hole that will fit over the delivery pipe.

6 Place the millstone centrally on top of the reservoir lid. The delivery pipe should not protrude from the central hole but should be just below the surface of the millstone.

7 Top up the reservoir with water until the water seeps through into the reservoir lid which acts as a base for the millstone.

8 Turn on the pump so that there is just enough flow for the water to gently ripple over the sides. If the flow needs adjusting, lift off the millstone and adjust the pump's flow regulator.

9 Position a retaining wall of flexible wood log-roll above and below the millstone, especially if it has been sited, as here, on a sloping site.

10 Add layers of decorative, washed river cobbles to disguise any of the reservoir rim that is showing. It is also advisable to add some planting as well as more cobbles in order to integrate the feature into the surrounding garden.

MAKING A DRILLED ROCK FOUNTAIN

The rock fountain is an adaptation of the cobble and millstone fountains. It uses a piece of rock as the centrepiece, and the fountain spout issues from a hole drilled in the rock. Modern power drills can cut through almost every type of stone, so there is no restriction on the type of rock; it is worth looking around good landscape suppliers for suitable pieces. Although sandstone is one of the easiest rocks to drill, the softer the stone, the more likely it is to break up after severe frosts, particularly if the rock is wet before a frost. Talk to your supplier about the suitability of individual pieces, because sandstones vary widely from region to region and even from quarries in the same region.

One of the advantages of the rock fountain is that it allows the gardener to introduce a certain amount of individuality to the feature. Each rock fountain is unique, unlike the millstone and cobble fountains, which have become so popular that self-assembly kits are available and simulated millstones are being produced in fibreglass.

Rather as the Chinese introduce a particular rock or arrangement of rocks into their gardens, this style of fountain can bring a sculptural element to the garden, and it will make a superb focal point. The higher and more slender the rock that is selected, the greater will be its dramatic impact, and some pieces of slate are ideal for this type of feature. The fountain will work best if the outlet delivers volume rather than water under pressure. Many sculptures and ornaments that have been adapted as fountains are spoilt because the thin spouts of water that emerge from them look odd. If it is to be successful, a rock fountain should glisten with moisture in the sunlight, and, if it is tall and slender, it should release the water as if it were the source of a strong spring. Flatter, chunkier rocks are more suitable if they are the source of an emerging jet of water, which gives extra height and dominance to the focal point.

Some suppliers have stocks of pre-drilled rocks to make life easier for the water gardener, but it is worth looking at a selection of rocks from other sources, and only if you are unable to have it drilled should you resort to the more limited range of pre-drilled rocks.

The method of installation will depend entirely on the size and weight of the rock you have chosen. A small rock fountain can sit on an existing cobble fountain with the delivery pipe extended through the hole drilled in the rock. The main essential is to ensure that the wire mesh or grid, which is intended to bear the weight of cobbles in a cobble fountain, is strong enough to bear the weight of a small rock. A very large, heavy rock will have to be supported on piers, in which case the method of installation would be identical to that of a millstone fountain with a heavy stone. The former method is described opposite.

BELOW: **A drilled rock fountain is a modified cobble fountain. This drilled rock fountain is an ideal feature to bring interest to a small corner.**

YOU WILL NEED

- Spade
- Plastic dustbin (trash can)
- Soft sand
- Spirit level
- Timber for tamping the backfill
- Rake
- 2 bricks or a piece of broken paving
- Submersible pump
- Rigid delivery pipe with flow adjuster
- Sheet of polythene (polyethylene)
- Scissors
- Galvanized metal mesh in two grades, both larger than the diameter of the dustbin
- Wire cutters
- Drill
- Large rock
- Cobbles

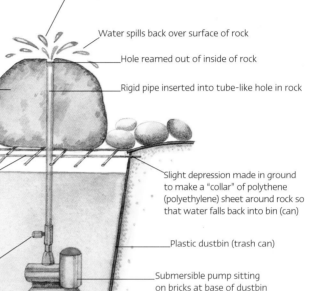

Water spout

Water spills back over surface of rock

Hole reamed out of inside of rock

Rigid pipe inserted into tube-like hole in rock

Rock

Cobbles, rocks, or shingle or gravel to cover up polythene (polyethylene) "collar"

Slight depression made in ground to make a "collar" of polythene (polyethylene) sheet around rock so that water falls back into bin (can)

Top of dustbin (trash can) covered with galvanized grid strong enough to support rock

Plastic dustbin (trash can)

Submersible pump sitting on bricks at base of dustbin (trash can)

Flow adjuster on pump outlet

1 Mark out the diameter of the plastic dustbin (trash can) on the ground and dig out a hole slightly wider and deeper than its dimensions.

2 Place a shallow layer of sand at the bottom of the hole. Put the dustbin (trash can) in the hole to ensure that the rim is just level with the surrounding soil. Check that the sides are level by placing a spirit level across the top of the dustbin. If any corrections are necessary, lift out the bin and make adjustments to the bottom of the hole.

3 Backfill the gap between the bin and the sides of the hole with soil and ram firm with a cut-down broom handle. Mound the surrounding soil slightly to make an even saucer shape and rake to remove any stones.

4 Place two bricks on the bottom of the dustbin (trash can) to act as a plinth for the pump. This will save the pump intake becoming clogged with any debris that accumulates at the bottom of the bin.

5 Check that the length of rigid plastic pipe used for the fountain spout from the pump will be high enough to extend above the dustbin (trash can) and up through the hole drilled into the piece of rock.

6 Place the polythene (polyethylene) sheet over the dustbin (trash can) as well as the surrounding area.

Cut a hole in the centre that is slightly wider than the fountain pipe. Fill the dustbin with water.

7 Lay the polythene (polyethylene) sheet over the bin, with the fountain pipe protruding from the hole.

8 Place a piece of galvanized mesh large enough to rest on the rim of the bin over the hole and the delivery pipe from the pump.

9 Place a smaller mesh on top of the larger one to catch any small cobbles used for the surface of the fountain. The small mesh would not be strong enough on its own to support the weight of large, wet cobbles.

10 Drill the hole through the centre of the piece of rock you have chosen. Position this over the fountain pipe, ensuring that the top of the pipe does not show above the surface of the rock.

11 Turn on the pump to check the flow of water over the surface of the piece of rock.

12 Completely hide the surface of the polythene (polyethylene) and mesh with a layer of cobbles around the edge of the piece of rock.

13 Add additional cobbles and plants to the surrounding area, if you wish. Connect the pump cable to a convenient waterproof switch so that the pump can be controlled easily.

MAKING A STONE TROUGH

Small containers, such as stone troughs and barrels, can be used to create miniature water gardens. When planted appropriately, with miniature waterlilies and small marginals, they provide a feature with clear water that does not get too hot in summer.

Genuine stone troughs are increasingly hard to obtain and are, in any case, very heavy. Simulated stone troughs can, however, be made fairly easily by coating old glazed sinks, which are sometimes available in recycling yards, with hypertufa.

YOU WILL NEED

- Glazed sink
- Bricks or blocks to lift sink off the ground
- Wooden bung
- Hammer
- Screw and screwdriver
- Silicon sealant
- Sphagnum peat or peat substitute
- Coarse sand or fine grit
- Cement

- Container in which to mix the hypertufa
- Scoring tool, such as a glass- or tile-cutter
- Industrial glue
- Paintbrush
- Rubber gloves
- Liquid fertilizer or antiquing fluid to paint on the outer surface of the trough
- Black bitumen paint

1 Stand the sink on a plinth that is smaller in width and length than the sink so that the coating does not stick to the support.

2 Hammer a cylindrical piece of wood into the outlet pipe at the bottom of the sink in order to retain the water.

3 Secure the bung by inserting a screw through the outlet pipe with a screwdriver. Seal around the bung with a silicon sealant.

4 Pour equal parts of sphagnum peat or peat substitute, sand or grit and cement into a plastic bucket in order to make the hypertufa.

5 Mix the hypertufa into a stiff mixture by slowly adding water and stirring.

6 Score the glazed exterior surface, including the rim, with a tile- or glass-cutter. Coat the sides and the rim of the sink with an industrial glue and allow it to become tacky.

7 Wearing rubber gloves and working from the bottom up, apply the stiff mixture of hypertufa to the sides and rim. The covering should be just thick enough to give a rough texture; if it is too thick it will not adhere. Protect the trough from rain and strong sunshine until the hypertufa is thoroughly dry; this could take as long as a week.

8 Coat the outside walls and rim with proprietary liquid fertilizer to encourage algae and moss to develop on the surface. Alternatively, you can paint the trough with antiquing fluid to create an aged effect. Paint the inside of the trough with black bitumen paint and allow to dry. Carefully move the trough to its permanent position and partly fill with water before planting with aquatics in small containers. A small amount of duckweed or other floater can be planted on the surface to reduce light and consequent water greening; this should be removed later, when the other plants become established.

INSTALLING A TSUKUBAI
or Japanese spill basin

One of the most symbolic features involving moving water in the Japanese garden is the *tsukubai*, a stone basin that is constantly replenished with water in which visitors wash their hands before entering the tea house. The basin is usually made from a hollowed-out rock, but any basin that is dignified enough, including a stone trough, could be used.

A vital element of this feature is a constant supply of clean water, and, because the reservoir for a pumped recirculating system will be protected from debris and from light by a covering of cobbles, the necessary water can be provided by a small feature in the garden. Another important characteristic of the *tsukubai* is that the basin should be no higher than 20–30cm (8–12in), so that the visitor has to stoop in humility to use it. The apparent source of water is through a hollow bamboo pipe, though which the water pours into the basin so

BELOW: **This is a perfect combination of materials for a Japanese feature: natural stone, bamboo and a cut-leaved Japanese maple (*Acer japonicum*).**

that the water is never still. The stones around the reservoir, whose positioning has symbolic meaning in the true *tsukubai*, act in a similar way to the cobbles in a cobble fountain, with the water draining over and through them to the reservoir below. The effect is made even more interesting if the reservoir is deep enough so that the sound of the water falling through the cobbles onto the hidden surface beneath is audible.

This feature and a *shishi-odoshi*, or deer scarer, must be carefully integrated into the landscape if they are to be reasonably true to the authentic Japanese style. Flowering plants do not play a major part in such a scheme, but ferns, bamboos and Japanese maples (*Acer japonicum*) will help to create the elements of balance and harmony that lie at the heart of the Japanese landscape. To complete the picture, a bamboo ladle should be placed beside the *tsukubai*.

YOU WILL NEED

- Plastic dustbin (trash can)
- Spade
- Soft sand
- Spirit level
- Timber for tamping the backfill
- Rake
- Cloth
- 2 bricks or a piece of broken paving
- Submersible pump
- Flexible delivery pipe, about 1cm (½in) in diameter
- 2 lengths of bamboo tube, one 60–90cm (2–3ft) and at least 2.5cm (1in) in diameter; the other about 30cm (1ft) long and 2.5cm (1in) in diameter (the *tsukubai* is available in kit form from most good garden centres)
- Sheet of polythene (polyethylene)
- Scissors
- Galvanized metal grid or mesh larger than the diameter of the dustbin
- Wire cutters
- Spill basin, such as a small basin-shaped rock or a trough no higher than 20–30cm (8–12in)
- Selection of cobbles in various sizes

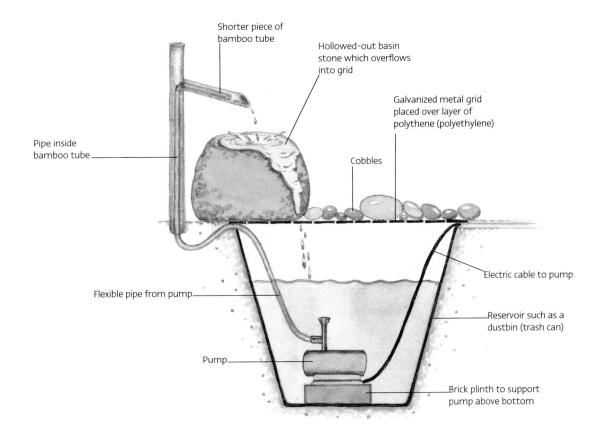

Shorter piece of
bamboo tube

Hollowed-out basin
stone which overflows
into grid

Galvanized metal grid
placed over layer of
polythene (polyethylene)

Pipe inside
bamboo tube

Cobbles

Electric cable to pump

Flexible pipe from pump

Reservoir such as a
dustbin (trash can)

Pump

Brick plinth to support
pump above bottom

1 Choose a small, level site in an area of paving or in front of a border so that the feature will provide a focal point. The cobbles can extend as far as you wish, but the area need be no more than a circle with the diameter of the plastic dustbin (trash can).

2 Mark out the diameter of the plastic dustbin (trash can) and dig out a hole slightly wider and deeper than its dimensions. At the same time, dig out a shallow, saucer-shaped depression to surround the hole. When this depression is lined it will allow any water blown from the basin to drain back into the reservoir.

3 Place a shallow layer of sand at the bottom of the hole. Put the dustbin (trash can) in the hole and check that the rim is just lower than the depression. Check that the sides are level with a spirit level. If necessary, lift out the bin and make adjustments to the base of the hole.

4 Backfill the gap between the bin and the hole sides with soil and ram firm with a piece of timber, such as a cut-down broom handle.

5 Rake the surrounding soil and remove any stones. Remove any soil that may have fallen into the bin (can) during backfilling and raking, and wipe out the inside with a cloth.

6 Before lowering the submersible pump onto two bricks or a piece of broken paving, which will act as a plinth at the bottom of the bin (can), attach a flexible delivery pipe to the pump outlet. Take the pipe over the side of the reservoir and push it through a rigid tube of bamboo, 60–90cm (2–3ft) tall, which is stood in an upright position next to the reservoir. Then, push the pipe through to a further bamboo tube positioned to spill into the basin. These *tsukubai* spouts are available ready-made from most good garden centres.

7 Lay the polythene (polyethylene) sheet over the depression and over the dustbin (can) and cut out a hole, 5cm (2in) smaller than the diameter of the bin.

8 Lay the galvanized metal grid or mesh, which should be larger than the diameter of the dustbin (trash can), over the polythene (polyethylene). Fill the dustbin with water.

9 Position a spill basin or trough at the side of the grid, but make sure that it slightly overhangs the reservoir so that it will overflow onto the cobbles.

10 Test the flow of water, adjusting the flow regulator on the pump or moving the position of the spout so that the water falls into the saucer part of the spill basin. Arrange the cobbles over the metal grid.

INSTALLING A SHISHI-ODOSHI
or a Japanese deer scarer

This is an appealing refinement to the *tsukubai*, and it was originally used as a means of scaring away deer and wild boar because it emits an intermittent click as a pivoted length of bamboo cane strikes a stone. Water is fed through a thick bamboo pipe onto an angled length of thinner bamboo, which is set on an axle and whose first node or joint has been scraped or cut away on the inside. Water from a thin spout collects in the front of the pivoted portion, which is forced to the ground by the weight of the water. As the water runs out, the back portion of stem, which is now heavier than the tip, drops quickly to the ground, where it strikes against a rock producing a sharp clicking sound. The striking rock and surrounding smaller rocks are placed on the mesh or grid suspended over a sunken reservoir as described for a cobble fountain.

Installation is basically the same as constructing a cobble fountain, but the delivery pipe is led into a bamboo cane as described for a *tsukubai*.

RIGHT: **The careful placing of rock and limited planting is a feature of certain Japanese garden styles. Movement and noise are created by the clacking of the "deer scarer".**

LEFT: **Notice the role of the "deer scarer" in this garden, forming a focal point with its contrasts of texture and colour as well as providing movement and interest.**

YOU WILL NEED

- Plastic dustbin (trash can)
- Spade
- Soft sand
- Spirit level
- Timber for tamping the backfill
- Rake
- Submersible pump
- 2 bricks or a piece of broken paving
- Flexible delivery pipe

- *Tsukubai* kit, available from most garden centres
- *Shishi-odoshi* kit, available from most garden centres
- Polythene (polyethylene) sheet
- Scissors

- Galvanized metal grid or mesh larger than the diameter of the dustbin
- Wire cutters
- Large stone
- Cobbles

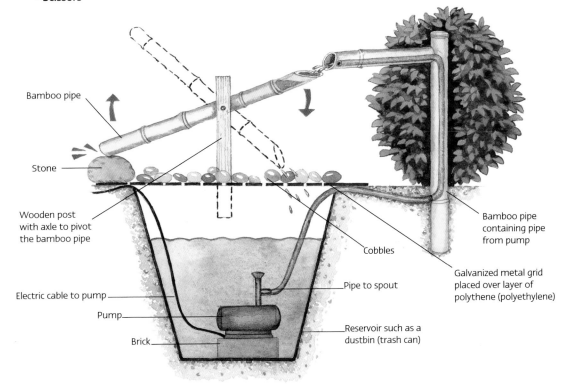

Bamboo pipe

Stone

Wooden post with axle to pivot the bamboo pipe

Electric cable to pump

Pump

Brick

Cobbles

Pipe to spout

Bamboo pipe containing pipe from pump

Galvanized metal grid placed over layer of polythene (polyethylene)

Reservoir such as a dustbin (trash can)

1 Mark out the diameter of the plastic dustbin (trash can). Dig out a hole slightly wider and deeper than its dimensions. Dig out a shallow, saucer-shaped depression around the hole. When this is lined it will allow any water to drain back into the reservoir.

2 Place a shallow layer of sand at the bottom of the hole. Put the dustbin (trash can) in the hole to check that the rim is just lower than the shallow depression. Check that the sides are level with the spirit level. If necessary, lift out the bin and make adjustments to the base of the hole.

3 Backfill the gap between the bin and the sides of the hole and ram firm with a cut-down broom handle.

4 Rake the surrounding soil to make an even saucer shape and remove any stones.

5 Before lowering the submersible pump onto two bricks or a piece of broken paving, which will act as a plinth, attach the delivery pipe to the pump outlet. Take the pipe over the side of the bin and push it through a hollow, vertical bamboo pipe and then through a

horizontal pipe, as for a *tsukubai* mechanism (see p.147). The bamboo pipes can be hidden among bushes or wedged between some rocks to one side of the reservoir. The tipping mechanism into which the water falls is easy to construct from a piece of bamboo pipe and a wooden post with a metal rod to create a pivot, but it is simpler to buy the mechanism ready-made from a good garden centre. Insert the post into the ground on one side of the reservoir, and set up the pipes so that the water will spill into the tipping piece of bamboo tube.

6 Lay the polythene (polyethylene) sheet over the depression and cut out a hole, 5cm (2in) smaller than the diameter of the bin. Lay the metal grid, which should be larger than the diameter of the dustbin (trash can), over the polythene. Fill the dustbin with water.

7 Position the stone to one side of the grid so that it will be struck by the tipping piece of pipe. Test the flow of water, adjusting the flow regulator on the pump or the position of the bamboo spout so that the water falls into the tipping pipe. Arrange cobbles over the grid.

The choice of plants for the water and surrounding area is more than just an aesthetic consideration. The

PLANTING WATER AND ROCK GARDENS

health of a water feature depends on good planting, and oxygenating and shade plants should be a priority. Once these mainstays of the scheme are in place, there is scope for greater creativity, such as using plants to produce reflections in the water.

OPPOSITE: **The careful selection of aquatic plants makes this informal composition look natural rather than planned.**

PLANNING PLANTING SCHEMES

The most commonly available aquatics are rampant native species, but they can be grown in small pools if they are containerized in aquatic planting baskets and divided regularly. Containers enable you to exploit the plants' lush growth, but at the same time prevent them from swamping the pool. Containers also allow a greater number of plants to be used in a small space.

Knowing the shape and colour of the leaves will be helpful in making your choice, because intensity of flower colour is not common in temperate aquatics. Visits to nurseries, flower shows and gardens will

BELOW: **The choice and arrangement of the plants is of vital importance when you are designing a planting scheme for the waterside.**

prove invaluable as you draw up a list of plants. However, a mixed planting scheme should not only blend your favourite species, but also keep together plants from the same type of habitat.

Maintaining interest all year round is a challenge in the water garden because most aquatics die down in late autumn and the old leaves turn straw-coloured. However, winter interest can be enhanced if the surrounding area is considered along with the surface of the water and its margins. In winter, the coloured stems and tree outlines come to the fore, making this one of the best times to enjoy reflections.

CHOOSING COLOURS

Although an informal pool allows greater freedom in the choice of plants than a formal one, it can soon become a tangled mix of uncoordinated plants and rank growth. The careful selection of shapes and more subdued colours are the chief attractions of an informal scheme, while stronger, more intense colours are more likely to be the focus in a formal pool. Subdued colours work well in temperate climates, where the pale tones and subtle textures harmonize with each other and are enhanced by the quality of the light.

Finding colours that harmonize can be difficult. It can be useful to refer to a colour wheel in order to help develop an appreciation of colour harmonies. Adjacent colours harmonize with each other because they share a pigment; opposite colours contrast with or intensify each other. You should also consider texture and tonal variations, which allow a much broader palette of colours to be used than appears in a simplified colour wheel. White waterlilies come in useful here, breaking up any potential clashes in colour harmony by reflecting light.

SPECIMEN PLANTING

An informal scheme lends itself to group plantings rather than to a collection of single specimens, but there is still a place for the occasional specimen plant, particularly in small schemes. Some excellent specimen plants include the arum lily (*Zantedeschia*), arrowhead (*Sagittaria*), horsetail (*Equisetum*), zebra rush (*Schoenoplectus lacustris* subsp. *tabernaemontani* 'Zebrinus'), and lizard's tail (*Saururus cernuus*). In tropical pools there are few plants to match the impact

FAR LEFT: **Where space permits, planting in groups is often more dramatic than specimen planting, especially with plants like this goatsbeard (*Aruncus*).**

LEFT: **Two classic and contrasting moisture-lovers jostle for space in this planting, the regal fern (*Osmunda*) forming a perfect background for the exotic Japanese iris (*Iris ensata*).**

of lotus (*Nelumbo*) as either a specimen or a group, with their combination of leaves like upturned umbrellas and brightly coloured flowers. Each of these plants combines an attractive shape with good flower colour.

PLANT DIVERSITY

The diversity of plants for water gardens is enormous. Leaf sizes range from the minuscule leaves of duckweed (*Lemna*) and watermeal (*Wolffia*) to the gigantic leaves of Amazonian waterlily (*Victoria amazonica*). The water garden includes some of the most beautiful flowers in the plant kingdom. Waterlilies (*Nymphaea*), for instance, display the most delicate, fragrant and exotic blooms, while lotus (*Nelumbo*) is surely one of the most exquisite combinations of leaf, flower and seed-heads.

The extent and speed with which floating plants can spread is equally dramatic. In warm, nutrient-rich tropical rivers plants such as water lettuce (*Pistia*) and water hyacinth (*Eichhornia*) can cover and choke vast areas of water in a single summer. Even in cooler temperate waters duckweed (*Lemna*) and fairy moss (*Azolla*) can cover the surface of a small pool in a matter of weeks. The nature of their habitat, where there is

constant water and food both in and around the margins of a pool, makes the careful choice of species particularly important. Many pools are spoiled when they become choked with vigorous species, which can be almost impossible to thin out if they are left unattended for two or three seasons.

GETTING THE BALANCE RIGHT

The construction of a new pool to encourage an increased range of wildlife to the garden or to create an architectural feature will require a diverse range of water plants if it is to be successful. Any expanse of fairly shallow water will quickly go green unless it is adequately stocked with plantlife or contains a sophisticated filtration system. The healthy, balanced pool depends on each layer of water depth being planted so that the water surface, the deep water and the shallow margins are inhabited with the particular type of plant that thrives in those conditions. The mixed planting will help in the establishment of a biological balance that contributes to clear water and provides a home for the myriad beneficial submerged organisms on which a natural food chain or eco-system depends.

PLANT TYPES AND ENVIRONMENTS

Water plants are categorized into the following groups: submerged, deep-water plants, floating plants and marginals. A successful planting scheme will include plants from each group, so that the pool and its immediate surroundings together form a complete environment. Achieving the correct balance among the plants is an important part of keeping the pool water clear and in preventing a build-up of algae.

SUBMERGED PLANTS

These plants are referred to as oxygenators. They are the workhorses or "weeds" of the pool, suppressing algae in their search for nutrients and providing a home for fish fry amid their strands of fine foliage.

The primary role of this group of aquatic plants is not aesthetic. It is to provide a living filtration system in the water through the leaves and roots. The leaves give off oxygen in the presence of sunlight, an important contribution to a pool that is heavily stocked with fish. In addition, the roots absorb nutrients from fish waste, thereby helping to prevent a build-up of toxic material and contributing to a balanced cycle of life within the pool. During the night, oxygenators deplete the water of oxygen and give off carbon dioxide, and this can result in some very low levels of oxygen during sultry nights in summer. This condition can be alleviated if there is a fountain in the pool and it is kept running through the night to help to replace lost oxygen.

As well as supplying oxygen, these plants play a vital role in the water gardener's perennial battle with green water. Oxygenators seek nutrients from the water in the form of dissolved mineral salts, which are also the main diet of the tiny, single-celled algae that cause water to go green so quickly. If there are no oxygenators, the algae have no competition for their food. In a well-established pool the oxygenators leave few dissolved salts, and the algae are starved. It is for this reason that the water in a freshly constructed pool goes cloudy soon after the pool is filled. Even if oxygenators are introduced at once, mineral salts are present in high concentrations in tapwater and the young plants will have made inadequate growth to use them up. This can be the most frustrating time for new pool owners, and many people are tempted to change the water in an effort to return to clear water. This desire must be resisted at all costs, because the problem will certainly recur shortly after replacing the water if tapwater is used. The answer is to be patient, and quite unexpectedly, the pool will become clear as quickly as it clouded weeks before. The algae will have been starved out and are unlikely to reappear unless large volumes of tapwater are introduced.

Sometimes the oxygenators can grow beyond the surface of the water and creep out into the margins. A plant called diamond milfoil (*Myriophyllum aquaticum*) is particularly prone to this aerial growth, and when the leaves are as attractive as those of milfoil, there is no harm in letting it sprawl. It is, however, essential to cut it back in autumn because the decaying, frost-damaged leaves will blacken and rot in the water, which has the effect of deoxygenating the water. This autumn cutting back of vigorous growth applies to all the other oxygenators.

Good aquatic centres will usually have about six species of oxygenator from which you can choose, and they are mainly native plants. Buy several species so that if any one type fails, it is likely that another will flourish. They are normally sold as bunches of unrooted cuttings with a weight, used as the clasp to keep the cuttings together and prevent them from floating if they become dislodged from the bottom. More oxygenators are now being sold in small cubes of rockwool so that they can be just thrown into the pool and will develop in the small amount of soil that inevitably accumulates on the bottom.

RIGHT: *Eichhornia crassipes*, the water hyacinth, is a tender free-floating plant which will not survive winter outdoors in temperate climates. In very warm summers, it produces pale blue, hyacinth-like flowers, which grow to a height of 15–23cm (6–9in).

If you are planting in containers, keep the same species together so that vigorous types do not smother more delicate ones. If you are using a planting crate, bear in mind that a medium-sized crate will hold five bunches, one in the centre and one in each corner. For a new pool, aim for five bunches to every square metre (10 square feet) of pool surface.

Many oxygenators have exquisite foliage, which, when it is submerged, does not require fibrous tissue to maintain its shape. When suspended in water, the leaves are often thin and translucent. Some genera, such as *Cabomba*, are used in aquaria because of the delightful arrangement of their whorled leaves. In outdoor pools the fine leaves of oxygenators make superb retreats for fish fry to escape the cannibalism of larger fish. The leaves also make hidden depositories for fish eggs.

FLOATING PLANTS

Although there are several aquatic plants with floating leaves, this group contains free-floating plants that are not anchored to the bottom. Wherever you see this type of plant, the water will invariably be crystal clear. The floating leaves will have so reduced the amount of daylight entering the water that insufficient of the sun's energy is available for the algae to survive. The suspended, fine, hair-like roots of floating plants also use up considerable quantities of dissolved nutrients at the surface of the water where algae would otherwise flourish. This makes them useful in establishing a newly constructed pool. Some floating plants have extensive fine roots which make homes for fish fry and tiny, almost microscopic, life. Newly introduced fish also like the protective surface cover, especially in a new pool where the submerged plants have not yet developed.

The main problem is the ability of floaters to colonize large surfaces of water. In some tropical and subtropical countries it is illegal to introduce these plants to waterways, which become completely impassable. In a large natural pool, therefore, floaters should be introduced with great care. In smaller pools, where the plants can be easily netted off, the advantages outweigh any problems. In temperate climates most species sink to the bottom in winter, reappearing in the warmer spring days by floating to the surface.

In addition to contributing to clear water, many floating plants are extremely attractive in their own right, especially when they are viewed at close quarters on the surface of a raised pool.

One of the most common examples of a floating plant in temperate climates is duckweed (*Lemna*). There are different types of duckweed. It exhibits an extraordinary ability for rapid reproduction by offsets, which is the most common method for this group of plants, and can be something of a pest in a large ornamental pool. However, the smaller, ivy-leaved species, *L. trisulca*, is less invasive. For warmer pools the tender water hyacinth (*Eichhornia*) has the bonus of a flower that can be produced if the weather is very hot and sunny for a prolonged period. Because there is such a small choice of hardy floaters, you may have to use the more tender species that have only a limited time outdoors in temperate pools. As most of these become available only when the water is really warm in early summer, they are on sale for a limited time.

There are two other tender floaters: fairy moss (*Azolla*) and water lettuce (*Pistia*). The tender species will probably die out in winter and are unlikely to cover too much of the pool's surface. Fairy moss will sink to the bottom as spores, reappearing in spring if conditions are right. Keep water hyacinth and water lettuce indoors in a light, airy, frost-free place. The plants survive best when left on a muddy seed tray rather than in cold water.

Planting floaters is simple. Empty out the bag of plants on to the surface of the water. The water hyacinth and water lettuce may exhibit an initial lack of buoyancy if they have been in a bag for some time, but they will soon right themselves. In an exposed pool they tend to be blown all over the surface, but can be kept together in a floating wooden frame, anchored to the bottom.

ABOVE: **The young leaves of autumn starwort (***Callitriche hermaphroditica***), an oxygenating plant, are a delicacy for goldfish.**

ABOVE: **The waterlily epitomizes the special nature of aquatic planting, and when seen at close quarters there are few flowers to match its beauty.**

DEEP-WATER PLANTS

The plants in this group grow in deep water, which is usually defined as water 30–60cm (12–24in) deep in ornamental pools. Although waterlilies (*Nymphaea*) are the best known example of this group, they are often given a section of their own in catalogues, leaving a small selection of other plants that have surface leaves but roots that are anchored in the deeper water.

Deep-water plants are grown not only for their flowers but also for the valuable shade that is cast by their leaves in summer, which makes a contribution to clear water at a time it is most needed. The leaves in this group are floating and flat, providing resting platforms for a variety of creatures and, on the undersides, a depository for eggs. The leaves prefer still water and, unlike the totally submerged plants, are less tolerant of currents. They can survive the worst temperate winters because the thick rhizomes are below the ice layer.

Deep-water plants are particularly beneficial because they both decorate the pool and provide shade. Fish and other aquatic creatures enjoy this shade, and it can provide useful cover when herons are regular visitors. When you are creating a planting plan for the pool's surface, aim to cover between one-third to one-half of the water with leaves. Intersperse clumps of plants with equal areas of clear water to provide the best effect, because a pool completely dominated by surface leaves loses much of its impact. A good plant for deeper water is Cape pondweed or water hawthorn (*Aponogeton distachyos*). In addition to its dark green, strap-like leaves, this intriguing plant produces scented white flowers earlier than the waterlilies,

with a second flush in autumn as the water cools down. For this reason, *Aponogeton* is recommended for pools where there is inadequate sunshine for waterlilies to flower successfully.

New deep-water plants should be purchased in late spring, just as growth has started. Avoid disturbing plants in winter in case a cut or damaged root begins to rot in the cold water rather than healing quickly as it is more likely to do when in active growth. Deep-water plants are often sold as bare-rooted specimens, having been freshly divided from the parent plant. Buying containerized plants saves root disturbance, but established plants in containers are heavy and the extra expense is seldom justified as bare-rooted plants soon catch up in growth if they are planted at the right time. Deep-water plants require good root systems so that the nutrient reserves support the leaves as they try to reach the surface, and the largest size of planting crate should be used. Try to provide at least 30 litres (about 8 gallons) of compost (soil mix) in a crate about 40cm (16in) in diameter and 20cm (8in) deep. A larger container is even better.

WATERLILIES

Although classified as deep-water plants, waterlilies are generally given a section of their own. The beauty of the waterlily has exercised the skills of the writer and painter alike, with its perfect blooms, subtle perfume and range of colours, which change slightly each day in the flower's brief life on the surface. It is not only the exquisite blooms that make the waterlily the most popular aquatic plant, but also the spread of the leaves, which provide vital shade in high summer.

Waterlilies are divided into hardies and tropicals, with the tropicals further divided into day- and night-blooming plants. Hardy forms can remain outdoors in temperate winters quite satisfactorily, even if the surface of the water is frozen for significant periods. The tropicals, which tend to hold their flowers above the surface of the water, are often treated as annuals, particularly in climatic zones that are only marginally tropical.

Waterlily breeding is going through something of a revival, particularly in North America, where tropicals can be grown in the southern states. All waterlilies enjoy full sun and still, warm water, which should be free from the turbulence of a fountain or strong winds. A little time spent dead-heading and removing old and yellowing leaves will be amply rewarded by more flowers, and the sight of overgrown leaves thrusting above the surface and very few flowers is a sign of neglect.

Like the marginal plants, waterlilies can be planted in three ways, but by far the most common method is to use containers. Different waterlilies vary considerably in vigour and the depth of water in which they will thrive.

MARGINALS

The fringe of the water garden is home to a group of plants that play a vital part in the aesthetic impact of the pool. The shallow water and the nearby water-logged soil are inhabited by marginals, which thrive in various conditions, from having hardly any water at one extreme to having a depth of water 15–23cm (6–9in) above their root systems. The plants in this latter group tolerate different amounts of water over their root systems, and it is important not to drown the very shallow water plants. Short or seasonal variations in water level can be tolerated, and deciduous shallow-water marginals will tolerate more water in winter over their crowns than in summer. Slightly deeper water in winter also helps to protect plants such as arum lilies (*Zantedeschia*) from severe frost and winds. Vigorous species of marginal will be prevented from invading the centre of the pool if the water is too deep for them to survive, hence the importance of having marginal shelves only 23cm (9in) deep in a new pool. Natural

LEFT: **The Amazon waterlily (*Victoria amazonica*) makes a striking addition to a tropical pool. It should be grown at a minimum temperature of 25°C (77°F).**

pools with shallow, saucer-shaped sides will gradually become swamped by vigorous marginals, such as reedmace (*Typha*) and reeds (*Phragmites*), which form floating rafts of thick root systems that will eventually encroach on the centre of the pool.

The range of marginal plants has for many years been limited to a core list of indigenous species, but as interest in water gardening has expanded, so the range of available marginals has become more extensive. There is now a greater international exchange of

FAR LEFT: **Irises must rank as one of the waterside favourites, for both wet and moist soil.**

LEFT: **The familiar florists' arum lily (*Zantedeschia*) is hardier when it is just submerged to protect the crown. Graceful *Z. aethiopica* 'Crowborough' is ideal for situations such as this.**

ABOVE: **As the soil becomes less saturated away from the margins of the pool, there are several moisture-loving iris, such as the Siberian iris (*Iris sibirica*), which are suitable for such conditions and best planted in drifts.**

RIGHT: **The flowers of candelabra primulas look stunning against a dark background.**

looked after more easily as competition for space becomes more intense. The fast rate of growth of the indigenous marginals is not always considered when space is allocated for different plants. Tempting though it is to have an established pool quickly, if too many rampant growers are close together, the lush growth will obscure the light and compete for space with the smaller plants, and the ultimate height that some of these plants achieve may be out of scale when there is only a small surface area visible. If the taller plants are planted into small, inadequate containers, their lank, sappy growth will make them susceptible to being blown over, and you will probably have to re-pot them in a matter of weeks. Many of the species that grow to 1–1.2m (3–4ft) are more appropriate to larger wildlife pools, where they can be planted directly into the soil. Make sure that around smaller ornamental pools there are sufficient carpeting species, such as speedwell or brooklime (*Veronica*), to help soften edges and keep the growth in scale with the area of the pool.

MOISTURE-LOVING PLANTS

The plants in this group are not strictly aquatic plants, but they play a crucial role in the successful transition from the water to the drier regions of the garden. Moisture-lovers are mainly used in informal water gardens in the rich soil that has ample reserves of water without being waterlogged. Although many of them will survive in drier soils, their performance in both size and flowering never reaches the same potential if they do not have adequate and constant moisture.

Several woody plants are included in this group, such as dogwood (*Cornus*), alder (*Alnus*) and willow (*Salix*). These species should be planted in the same way as ordinary terrestrial plants: dig out a planting hole, add moisture-retentive organic matter and firm in the roots. Unlike aquatics, which are planted in the growing season, moisture-loving plants are best planted in autumn or spring.

OTHER POOLSIDE PLANTS

The emphasis in any water-garden planting is naturally given to the main groups of plants that can thrive in aquatic conditions. The planting in the immediate surrounds where the soil can be quite dry is equally important if the full potential of the design is to be realized. Trees and shrubs form the framework to water gardens, providing height, which in turn creates a sense of scale. There is such a wide diversity in the

species, and breeding programmes of specialist growers have introduced new cultivars, notably of *Iris*, monkey flower (*Mimulus*) and *Lobelia*. Towards the end of summer, displays of marginals not only look depleted, they often look starved, and it is best to avoid making new purchases at this time of year. Buy in spring or early summer when the plants have fresh new growth thrusting from the compost (soil mix), and they will quickly become established in the pool as the days get longer and the water warms up.

For your initial planting, choose the well-tried native species because they will grow well and require little pampering. Save some of the prime positions for special favourites or for less vigorous plants that can be

characteristics of trees and shrubs, that there can be few water gardens that would not benefit from their inclusion in one form or another.

One of the main advantages of woody plants in an aquatic surround is the winter interest. As aquatics and moisture-loving herbaceous plants die down in winter, the woody stems persist on shrubs, and, when these are coloured or form a tracery of branches, they come into their own among dead, brown vegetation. In addition to winter interest, the use of woody plants can exploit reflection. The light bark colours of certain birch species are very useful in this respect and large shrubs or small trees with catkins are also most effective.

Although deciduous trees are associated with leaves blowing into the water in autumn, their dappled shade can be a valuable compensation for the margins of some pools. There are several moisture-loving plants that scorch badly in full sun, and the dappled light below trees is ideal for these plants. Avoid planting the very thirsty species of trees and shrubs, like many willows and poplars, close to a pool. If a liner weeps moisture from the slightest imperfection in the manufacture, the roots of adjacent trees will find this water and inevitably make the seepage worse in time.

Conifers are valuable in providing single specimens for reflection or making hedges to enhance a formal scheme and providing shelter from wind. Avoid siting a pool too near overhanging branches as, despite retaining their leaves in the winter, they constantly shed bud scales and needles, making the water surface very dusty. There are several slow-growing, dwarf conifers that can be grown amongst rocks at the side of a watercourse. As many of them are quite tolerant of dry conditions, they make a good choice for raised mounds of soil for rock gardens where there is limited moisture and it is much harder for roots to reach the water table.

GRASSES AND FERNS

There is a particular affinity between the waterside and ornamental grasses and ferns. The very fine flowers of grasses can be lost in a mixed border where the variety of colours and leaf shapes make the detail of the flowers difficult to see. Provide a backdrop of a water surface and their effect is enhanced. Some of the grasses that actually like quite dry conditions can also be used in an informal setting to suggest a boggy area without the soil being at all moist. Where there is ample moisture, there are numerous species of ornamental rushes and sedges that will occur naturally by water.

LEFT: **Bowles' golden sedge (*Carex elata* 'Aurea') is a striking marginal, which is grown for its bright golden yellow leaves.**

ALPINES

There are few informal schemes where rock and water are combined that would not look very stark and bare without alpines. The soil edges immediately outside lined pools are the classic situation for scrambling types of alpine. These plants are adapted to use the available moisture present in the soil in late winter and spring to flower and seed quickly in native habitats which dry out as the summer progresses. The scrambling types will be of greatest use to the water gardener as they soften and hide stream and pond edges and bring a riot of colour to a rock formation in spring.

BELOW: **The daisy-like fleabane (*Erigeron karvinskianus*) is a superb plant, which will seed itself among the crevices and dry crannies in rocks.**

PLANTING AQUATICS

Unlike terrestrial plants, water plants have no need to develop an extensive root system to seek out moisture. As the planting medium is permanently waterlogged, the need for drainage or moisture-retaining materials in the compost (soil mix) is superfluous. This means that quite large plants can be grown in relatively small containers specially adapted for aquatic growth. As this growth is rapid for a short season, the vigorous species will need dividing and replanting every year with fresh compost.

AQUATIC PLANTING CRATES

OPPOSITE: **A planting basket placed on the marginal shelf allows the plant to be immersed at just the right depth.**

Planting baskets for aquatics are available in a variety of shapes and sizes, and they differ from ordinary plant containers in having lattice sides, which make it possible for the gases and chemicals that are produced in the compost (soil mix) to pass easily into the pool water and so prevent the soil inside the container from stagnating. In addition to the round crates, there are also square and curved ones, which are ideal for standing on a curved marginal shelf. The wider the base of the planting basket, the more stable it will be, and this is important if a tall plant is likely to be buffeted by wind. These planting baskets are made of plastic, and although they are mostly black, you can sometimes buy green ones.

To prevent the compost (soil mix) in the basket from leaching out into the water, the baskets are lined with a permeable lining, such as hessian (burlap) or polypropylene mesh. Liners are sold at aquatic centres, ready cut into squares of different sizes. More expensive containers are available that have smaller louvred mesh sides, and these do not need a lining.

The containers range from 40cm (16in) in diameter, which are suitable for medium to large waterlilies, to 4cm (1½in) in diameter, which are used for cuttings or aquarium plants. The vigorous plants soon become potbound and suffer through having insufficient nutrients, and the regular division and repotting of these plants into fresh compost (soil mix) is essential.

PLANTING MEDIUM

Soil suitable for aquatic plant containers can be taken from the garden, provided the soil is not too rich in nutrients and is free from pesticide and herbicide residues. The soil should preferably be on the heavy

TYPES OF AQUATIC PLANTING BASKET

There are aquatic planting baskets for every type of aquatic, from vigorous waterlilies to small oxygenators. Some baskets are contoured to fit on the shelves of curving preformed units.

This is the largest type of basket which is suitable for vigorous waterlilies. Note the handles for lifting and the wide mesh which will require an inner lining of hessian (burlap)

These standard square and round fine-mesh containers require no lining. They are commonly available in a variety of diameters

This fine-mesh contoured container is useful for a marginal shelf in pools with a curved outline

side and neither extremely acid nor extremely alkaline. Avoid peaty soils, which decompose very rapidly, or sandy soils which have little or no nutrient value. If your soil is a heavy loam, it will probably be suitable. If you are using garden soil, sieve it through a coarse sieve to remove stones and any loose organic matter. An ideal home-made aquatic compost (soil mix) can be made from old turves that have been stacked for a few months and are rotting down into a condition described as a fibrous loam.

Proprietary multi-purpose or soil-based composts (soil mixes) should be avoided, because these contain too many nutrients and materials that are not necessary for submerged conditions.

If you are uncertain whether your garden soil is suitable, you can buy bags of aquatic compost (soil mix). The content of these proprietary aquatic composts can vary enormously, and they are expensive if you have a large pool to plant.

PLANTING TIME

Aquatics should be planted while in growth and not touched during their dormant period. The warmer the water, the more quickly the new plant will become established, and the ideal time is late spring when there is plenty of sunshine, long hours of sunlight and

OTHER PLANTING EQUIPMENT

Other pieces of equipment, such as long-sleeved gloves and planting mats and liners for aquatic planting baskets, will prove very useful when planting up a water garden.

Long-sleeved plastic or PVC gloves that reach to the elbows provide valuable protection when working in pond water

Border planting mats made from natural jute or coconut material can be draped over the muddy margins of a pool to provide extra grip for pond plants and to help prevent erosion. They will degrade in the water over two years

Hessian (burlap) liners can be cut into squares for baskets of different diameters. They prevent the compost (soil mix) from escaping through the sides of the container. Very steep pond borders can also be covered in this finer-weave material to make planting pockets which will rot in time when the plant roots have stabilized the banks

warmer water. If the planting is left until autumn, the water will still be warm, but will be gradually cooling down and the plant may not have time to become established before winter. If the temperature falls sharply and the plants are slightly tender, as are some waterlilies, they will not have had sufficient time to build up reserves in their root systems. If containerized plants are bought, the planting time is less important.

DIRECT PLANTING

In a natural or wildlife pool with a minimum covering of 15cm (6in) of soil over the liner, aquatics can be planted directly into this soil. In such conditions plants will spread rapidly, and direct planting is ideal only in very large pools where there is a deep area of water into which the plants cannot spread and which prevents the entire pool from becoming overgrown. A

RIGHT: **A good mixture of marginals and alpines is essential for a rocky water-course in which extremes of dry and moist soils are found.**

small pool can be planted by this method, but the range of suitable plants is limited and regular cutting back will be essential.

PERMANENT PLANTING BEDS

These beds are better suited to large pools, where the number of aquatic containers might be excessive. The beds can be free-standing in the deep water near the centre for plants like waterlilies, or built with a retaining wall to enclose the soil between the side of the pool and the wall. The retaining walls can be built with a variety of natural and man-made materials such as rocks, walling stones, bricks and concrete blocks. If the walls are mortared for extra strength to resist the pressure of roots, it is important that small holes are left in the sides for gases and salts in solution to escape into the water. The walls can be built onto flexible liners, and if this is done the liner should be protected by a layer of polythene (polyethylene) or by a spare piece of liner. The top of the walls should finish a few centimetres under the water level so that they are not seen.

DEPTH OF PLANTING

Most marginal plants will tolerate a certain depth of water above their crown or growing point when they are placed on a marginal shelf in a container. However, the question of depth is more important when you are planting waterlilies, which vary considerably in their tolerance. If you buy from a reliable aquatic supplier, the information will be printed on the plant label, and if you are in any doubt, ask the supplier. The suggested depth will refer to the depth of water above the growing point or crown; it does not refer to the base of the container. Err on the side of shallow planting rather than immersing the plant too deeply, especially with a young, bare-rooted waterlily that has just been containerized.

The danger of planting too deeply in the early stages can be avoided by propping up the container on some bricks or blocks on the floor of the pool so that the growing point is covered by no more than 10–15cm (4–6in) of water. As the plant begins to grow, the bricks can be removed one by one from the supporting pier beneath until, by the time the plant is growing strongly, the container is resting on the bottom of the pool.

If young plants are planted into permanent beds, the water level should be reduced initially, then topped up gradually as the plants get stronger.

PERMANENT PLANTING BED

Marginal planting beds, which are permanent, can be made with bricks or walling stones. This type of planting bed is suitable for formal ponds.

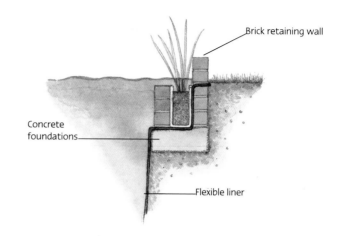

Brick retaining wall

Concrete foundations

Flexible liner

TEMPORARY PLANTING

A planting basket placed on a marginal shelf can be used to help amphibians gain access to and from the pool if a roofing tile or small slab is placed on the compost (soil mix).

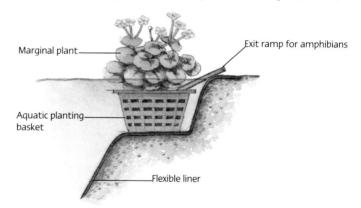

Marginal plant

Exit ramp for amphibians

Aquatic planting basket

Flexible liner

PLANTING DEPTHS

Young waterlilies in planting baskets should be supported on a brick pier at first before being placed on the bottom of the pool when they are growing vigorously.

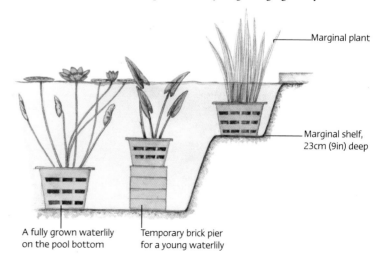

Marginal plant

Marginal shelf, 23cm (9in) deep

A fully grown waterlily on the pool bottom

Temporary brick pier for a young waterlily

PLANTING TECHNIQUES

Aquatic plants can be planted in a number of ways: in aquatic crates, in permanent beds or directly in the soil. The method depends on whether you are planting a submerged or deep-water aquatic, a marginal or a moisture-lover. If you are planting in a basket, the golden rule is always to firm in the compost (soil mix) well. If this is not done, there will be a great reduction in volume when the compost is submerged and large amounts of air are expelled.

OXYGENATORS

If oxygenators are purchased as bunches of unrooted cuttings and are to be planted in a newly installed pool, they will stand a better chance of survival and will begin to develop more readily if they are planted in a container. A medium-sized container, about 20cm (8in) square, will be adequate. It should be lined with a square of permeable material, such as hessian (burlap) or polypropylene, and filled to the brim with soil or aquatic compost (soil mix). Firm down the compost, make some holes with a dibber (dibble), then push the bunches into position. They are usually best arranged with one in the centre and one in each corner, and the bottom of the stems should be just buried. Firm in the stems and top-dress the compost with a layer of washed pea gravel about 2.5cm (1in) thick.

The gravel not only prevents soil particles from floating about when the container is immersed but also stops inquisitive fish from disturbing the surface of the soil. Place the containers on the bottom of the pool as quickly as possible after planting, because the plants curl up very quickly when they are out of water.

If the pool is well established, weigh down the bunches with a small weight which holds the ends of the stems together, and throw them into the centre of the pool, where they will settle into the thin layer of mud on the bottom. Individual plants bought in plugs of rockwool can be simply thrown into the pool.

PLANTING AN OXYGENATOR

The unrooted cuttings of oxygenating plants will flourish best in a new pond if they are first planted in an aquatic container before being placed at the bottom of the pond.

1 Fill a small planting crate with aquatic planting compost (soil mix) to the brim of the container.

2 Using a wooden dibber (dibble), make a hole in the centre of the compost (soil mix) deep enough for the bunch of oxygenating plants to be inserted so that the clasp holding the bunch together is buried in the compost.

3 Firm the compost (soil mix) around the bunch thoroughly so that there is no danger of it floating out when the container is submerged.

4 Place a layer of small chippings or washed pea shingle or gravel over the top of the compost (soil mix). This prevents the particles of soil escaping into the water and gives some protection from inquisitive fish. Immerse in the pond as soon as possible because the soft leaves of submerged plants will desiccate very rapidly when out of water.

MARGINALS

These plants can be planted in three main ways: in a special planting basket, in a permanent bed or directly in the soil at the bottom of the pond. Most are planted into planting crates of various sizes, which makes it possible to move them around on the marginal shelves. The size of the container will relate to the vigour of the plant, because this will determine its ultimate spread and height.

When you are choosing the container, take into account how much restraint is required and the depth of water in which the container is to be positioned. Many marginals require only shallow water over their crowns, and this factor will affect the depth of the container when it is standing on a typical marginal shelf, 23cm (9in) deep. Ensure that the plant is securely held in the soil, which must be covered with a good layer of gravel if it is to be submerged. Do not bury the roots too deeply and ensure that they are spread out adequately in the container.

Marginals can also be planted into permanent beds, which are constructed when the pool is built. Permanent planting beds can be built behind the rocks when constructing a pond, or more substantial planting beds can be made by building retaining walls with brick or walling stones. These are made when the pool is originally constructed and should be built so that the tops of the retaining walls are just below the waterline. Planting into this type of permanent bed allows some intermingling of species and looks more natural. Greater care is required in the plant choice and positioning so that the vigorous species do not overrun their neighbours.

Some marginals can be planted in the soil that covers the whole submerged area of a wildlife pool. There are no restrictions on the root systems of such plants, which will spread very rapidly. This may be acceptable in a wildlife pool but is not recommended in a small ornamental pool.

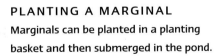

PLANTING A MARGINAL

Marginals can be planted in a planting basket and then submerged in the pond.

1 Half-fill a medium-size planting crate with aquatic planting compost (soil mix).

2 Check that there is ample depth in the container to bury the plant to the same depth as its previous planting, taking care not to bury too deeply.

3 Place the plant near the centre of the container and add the compost (soil mix) so that the loose compost reaches the rim.

4 Firm the compost (soil mix) thoroughly around the roots and base of the leaves.

5 Spread a layer of washed pea shingle or gravel over the compost (soil mix) to prevent the soil particles from floating.

6 Place the freshly potted plant on to the marginal shelf of the pond.

WATERLILIES AND OTHER DEEP-WATER AQUATICS

Some waterlilies have thick, flattish, creeping roots; others have pineapple-shaped roots. When planting, the fleshy rhizomes of the creeping root type should be laid horizontally under about 2.5cm (1in) of soil, while the more upright, pineapple-shaped root is planted vertically or at a slight angle, with the crown or growing point almost exposed at the surface. Whatever the type of root, ensure the crown is planted shallowly.

Before planting, trim off the fibrous roots and examine the root carefully for any signs of damaged or diseased tissue. Cut out any suspicious material and dust the exposed tissue with fungicide. The leaves are often damaged in transport, and it is far better to remove these leaves before planting than to allow them to rot off. Even if all the foliage is dead or damaged, the plant can still survive at planting time. During planting, keep the foliage cool and damp, and never leave plants exposed to sun or drying wind.

When you are planting a waterlily in a container, choose a large size of crate, and firm the soil thoroughly around the rootstock because, once all the air is expelled by firming and the soil is saturated, the volume will shrink considerably. If the soil has been inadequately firmed, containers will only be half full a short time after immersing. It is, therefore, a good idea to water thoroughly before planting and to add any extra soil that may be needed. Finally, when the soil has been firmed, add a layer of pea gravel about 2.5cm (1in) deep. Plant shallowly, using bricks under the container, which can be gradually removed when growth starts. Containerized planting for deep-water plants largely follows the method described above for waterlilies.

The technique for planting tropical waterlilies is similar to that for hardy plants, although it varies in a few important ways. The tropicals are generally more vigorous and faster growing than the hardy plants, and they should be given large containers. In most temperate climates their cultivation

is restricted to pools in conservatories where water temperatures of 24–29°C (75–85°F) can be guaranteed. In temperatures below 21°C (70°F) the young tropicals frequently go dormant. In temperate climates they should be planted later than the hardy waterlilies so that the warmer water will encourage rapid development.

The hardy plants are sold as rootstocks of the parent plant, but tropicals are sold as complete young plants. These are planted into containers as described for

PLANTING A WATERLILY

Increasingly, waterlilies are being sold in aquatic baskets ready for planting; these will be adequate until the plant needs dividing.

1 Do not plant the young containerized plant too deeply until it is established. Build a temporary brick pier so that the top of the container will be approximately 15cm (6in) below the surface of the water.

2 Remove any old or damaged leaves which will soon rot in the water. Gently place the container on top of the support.

3 As the plant grows and the leaf stems elongate, remove one layer of bricks at a time until the plant is strong enough to be placed on the pool bottom.

the hardies, but a sachet of slow-release fertilizer should be added to the planting medium. They are planted shallowly and, unlike the hardies, do not need to be gradually introduced to deeper water. They flourish in surface water that warms up quickly in the sun. For both hardy and tropical waterlilies, anticipate the problem of reaching the deeper area of the pool with a container full of compost (soil mix) which is often heavy. For larger pools, you will need to wear waders to reach the deeper area.

MOISTURE-LOVERS

These plants are usually planted in soil that is not saturated at the edges of the pool. For this reason, they are treated in the same way as other herbaceous plants. Moisture-loving plants are frequently planted in soil conditions which will be compacted if you are working in one area for any length of time and it is useful to work from temporary planks or permanent stepping stones, such as partially buried railway sleepers (ties), for access to the planting bed.

NON-AQUATIC PLANTS

Disguising the edges of rigid stream units and informal preformed pools is often difficult as the soil can be quite dry in these areas. The technique for planting these areas involves procedures which are almost completely opposite to those required for aquatics. Whereas aquatic plants will have no need to develop an extensive root system in search of water, the terrestrial plants will need help in their initial stages to survive and grow in a dry environment, particularly when planted on any form of raised soil bed like a rock garden. At the same time as needing water to grow, these plants also need good drainage in order for oxygen to be available for the roots, an element which aquatics are specially adapted to take in through leaves or roots when present in the pool water.

The steps for planting shown here will assume that the plants are already growing in containers such as rigid or flexible plastic pots. Although the sizes vary considerably from an alpine to a shrub, the technique is basically the same. With most types of soil, especially heavy clay, you should add plenty of coarse grit to the bottom of the hole when planting plants such as alpines that prefer dry conditions, as good drainage is essential and they are likely to rot if the soil becomes waterlogged in winter. In light, sandy soils, they should be happy, but you will need to make sure they are watered regularly until established.

PLANTING A MOISTURE-LOVER

When planting moisture-loving plants, remember to leave enough room for larger plants such as *Gunnera* and *Rheum*.

Dig out a hole that is large enough to accommodate the roots. Plant the young plant in the hole to the same depth as it had been planted before. Spread out the roots in the planting hole and take care not to plant too deeply. Cover the roots with the damp soil surrounding the plant in the bed and firm gently. Water in the plant with a fine rose on a watering can.

PLANTING AN ALPINE

Scrambling alpines can be used to soften and disguise the edge of a pool.

1 Dig a hole slightly larger than the spread of the roots alongside the edge.

2 If the soil is heavy, add a smaller layer of coarse grit to the bottom of the hole.

3 Remove the young alpine from its pot, teasing out a few roots so that they spread more widely into the hole. Spread a

well-drained compost (soil mix) around the roots, taking care not to bury the growing point or stems of the plant. Firm in well as the plant is more likely to establish quickly in dry areas if the soil is in firm contact with the roots. Water well and keep moist until the plant can support itself. Do not water for too long a period as this discourages the young plant from becoming self-sufficient.

4 Top-dress the plant with a collar of coarse grit for a more finished effect.

PROPAGATION TECHNIQUES

Most aquatic plants grow so easily that propagation is more often used to replace the existing stock than to increase the quantity of plants. Rejuvenating through propagation is important for containerized plants such as waterlilies and marginals, which quickly use up the nutrients in their compost and become overcrowded, when they are susceptible to pests and diseases.

BY RUNNERS AND OFFSETS

Removing runners from parent plants is an easy method of propagating floating plants. Simply snap off a plantlet when the parent is in full growth in summer. Place the parent and offset back in the pool, where the young plant will need no special care as it has its own root system.

BY WINTER BUDS

Most floating and some submerged plants develop special overwintering buds, known as turions, at the tips of the shoots. These can be simply removed and rooted, providing another method of propagation. The

buds usually form in mid-autumn, when they should be cut off and dibbled into a small container full of aquatic compost (soil mix). When growth begins the following spring, each one can be potted up individually and placed on the pool bottom.

FROM SEED

Propagating by seed is seldom practised because most of the plants are more easily divided. The main exceptions are plants that are treated as annuals, such as bachelor's buttons (*Cotula coronopifolia*), and a few deep-rooted plants with thick rootstocks that are difficult to split, such as skunk cabbage (*Lysichiton*).

Because the seed of aquatic plants tends to lose its viability quickly if it is allowed to dry out, it should be sown as soon as it is ripe in summer or early autumn. Seed of submerged plants and deep-water plants, such as waterlilies, should be sown onto a layer of compost (soil mix) about 8cm (3in) deep in a washing-up bowl or seed pan, then lightly covered with 3mm (⅛in) of

finely sieved aquatic compost (soil mix). Water the compost with a fine rose until the water level covers the compost by 2.5cm (1in). For marginal seeds, the compost can be slightly deeper and 2.5cm (1in) of water should be placed in the bowl so that the seed tray is only just submerged.

Place the container in a frost-free greenhouse and replenish the water regularly to maintain the same level as at sowing. When the seedlings are large enough to handle, prick them out into 8cm (3in) pots of aquatic compost and return to the washing-up bowl. Keep the water covering the pots at the same level as before and grow on until they are large enough to be transferred to a small aquatic planting crate.

LEFT: **Species of *Iris* can be propagated by division, either of the rhizome or offsets, in late summer or by seed in autumn. Named cultivars should be propagated by division only.**

ABOVE: **The delicate pink flowers of pink or thrift (*Armeria maritima*), an evergreen, clump-forming perennial, appear in summer. It can be propagated by seed in the autumn.**

PROPAGATING FROM SEED

For most aquatic plants, it is generally best to sow seed as soon as it has been gathered so that it is fresh. Propagation from seed is a perfect way of obtaining large quantities of any one plant if you are planning to plant large areas. The best time to collect seed from the plant is just as it begins to disperse the seed naturally. The following sequence is especially suitable for marginal plants.

1 Fill a seed pan to the brim with aquatic compost (soil mix).

2 Firm the compost (soil mix) thoroughly using a square, flat piece of wood which will ensure that the corners are adequately compressed.

3 Sow the seeds evenly across the surface of the compost (soil mix), leaving a small gap between each seed.

4 Using a fine sieve, cover the seed with a shallow covering of sieved compost (soil mix), using just enough compost to cover the seed.

5 Using a fine rose on a watering can, water the compost (soil mix) thoroughly and evenly.

6 After watering, place the seed pan in a watertight container. For the seed of marginal plants, pour approximately 2.5cm (1in) of water into the surrounding container so that the seed tray containing the seeds is only just submerged. Maintain this water level in the container and no further watering should be necessary on the surface of the compost (soil mix). If the seed is from a submerged plant or a deep-water aquatic, such as a waterlily, then submerge the seed pan in 2.5cm (1in) of water. Use fine sharp sand on the compost surface to prevent particles of soil floating in the water.

SOFTWOOD CUTTINGS

Oxygenating plants are propagated by taking cuttings. They produce masses of young, soft growth in summer, and this can be cut off into pieces 15–23cm (6–9in) long. Bunch the shoots together and bind them with florist's wire near the base before inserting them into small aquatic baskets full of aquatic compost (soil mix). Top-dress with pea gravel, and then submerge the baskets.

TAKING SOFTWOOD CUTTINGS

This is a very simple method of propagating aquatics, from submerged oxygenating plants to several of the marginals that make soft sappy growth in the summer.

1 Remove a young shoot approximately 15–23cm (6–9in) long from the parent plant and make a cut with a sharp knife just underneath a leaf joint on the stem to leave one cutting of about 15cm (6in) long.

2 Using a sharp knife, trim off the young leaves at the base as close as possible to the stem.

3 Having filled a small container with fine-mesh sides with aquatic compost (soil mix), make a hole in the centre of the compost deep enough for the base of the cutting to be inserted securely.

4 Firm the compost (soil mix) around the cutting to make the stem more secure.

5 Top-dress the compost (soil mix) with washed pea shingle or gravel to prevent particles of soil from floating to the surface. Water the plant thoroughly with a fine rose on a watering can. If it is a submerged plant, the cutting can be placed under water immediately. If it is a marginal plant, then partially submerge the container in water 5cm (2in) deep and spray the cutting regularly with a fine mist spray until it has rooted. Keep the cuttings indoors out of direct sunlight, preferably inside a large, clear plastic bag. Remove this daily and spray the plants with a fine mist until they have rooted. If possible, store in a cool greenhouse while the cutting is taking root.

DIVIDING WATERLILIES AND DEEP-WATER PLANTS

Division is by far the most common method of propagation, and it simply consists of splitting the root system into two or more parts with a sharp knife, a spade or two forks placed back to back so that the roots are prized apart.

Waterlilies will soon become overgrown in containers, and will often develop roots outside the container. Overgrown plants tend to make leaves at the expense of producing flowers. If the leaves start to stick out of the water, then the waterlily is in need of dividing.

For plants such as waterlilies, which have thick roots, division involves cutting the root into sections so that each piece has a growing bud. You will need to lift the waterlily rootstock out of the pond and clean it thoroughly first by hosing it down. Remove the old leaves and cut the plump sections of the waterlily root-stock into sections, approximately 5–8cm (2–3in) in length. Make sure that each section of the rootstock has new growth at its tip. Trim back the thin roots on the underside of the rootstock.

Fill a small basket with aquatic compost (soil mix) and firm in thoroughly. Press the piece of young root onto the compost so that the growing tip is above the surface and at the same angle as it was in the water. Top-dress with 2.5cm (1in) of pea shingle or gravel and water in thoroughly. After the division has been planted, the basket is submerged in the water so that the growing point is covered by no more than 5–8cm (2–3in) of water.

Some types of waterlily form tuberous roots, and it is possible to cut off individual side shoots flush to the tuber. The species *Nymphaea tuberosa* develops small nodes on the tuber, and these can be snapped off and planted individually. Any exposed or cut surfaces should be dusted with charcoal before pressing them firmly onto the aquatic compost (soil mix) and treating them as the rhizomatous waterlilies.

DIVIDING A WATERLILY

When the leaves of waterlilies start to stick out of the water, this is an indication that the plant needs dividing.

1 Cut off the end of the rootstock which contains the growing point. Cut off the smaller, thin feeding roots from the thick rhizome as close to the rhizome as possible.

2 Further reduce the rhizome to no more than 5–8cm (2–3in) long, making a clean cut with a sharp knife.

3 Cut off the leaves and flowers at the base of their stems, leaving no more than 2–3 young developing leaves.

4 Fill a large, fine-mesh container nearly to the rim with aquatic compost (soil mix) and firm in well.

5 Firm the young stem into the surface of the compost (soil mix) and position it so that the growing point is directed away from the corner of the container.

6 Top-dress with pea shingle before submerging the container in the pool.

DIVIDING MARGINALS

Many marginal plants are propagated easily by division, and vigorous plants in small containers will benefit from this procedure on an annual basis. You will need to remove the plant from the pond first of all in order to assess how potbound the specimen is and whether there is a suitable point to make the division.

To divide a marginal, discard the older inner pieces and select the more vigorous and younger outer portions. Pot these up into a container of aquatic compost (soil mix), planting at the same depth as before, and immerse in water so that the water just covers the crown. Cut back aerial shoots to within 5cm (2in) of the water level.

There are slightly different methods for dividing marginal plants, depending on whether they are clump-forming, fibrous-rooted or have thick rhizomatous roots.

DIVIDING A CLUMP-ROOTED MARGINAL

Several marginals are clump-forming in habit. Clump-forming plants tend to form clumps with several crowns or growing points, which are clustered together. This differs from other common types of marginal which form thick rhizomatous roots, with the buds and growing points distributed along the length of the root.

If the plant is not too old, the clump can be teased apart by gently pulling the roots between thumb and finger. In older or more vigorous plants, it is often necessary to break up the crown with a hand fork, or, if this is still not strong enough, the pieces may need cutting apart with a knife.

1 Vigorous marginals that are grown in small containers should be divided annually. Remove the plant from the pond and assess how potbound it is. This is also the time to check whether there is a suitable point to make the division.

2 After removing from the container, tease the leaves apart and cut through the roots on the outside of the clump with a large knife.

3 Having removed a young portion of the plant with healthy leaves and a growing point, half-fill the original container with fresh aquatic compost (soil mix).

4 Place the young piece of the divided plant into the container and add more compost (soil mix) to bury the roots. Firm as much compost as possible into the container.

5 Top-dress the compost (soil mix) with pea shingle or gravel before putting the plant back into the pool. This top-dressing ensures that the particles of soil do not escape into the water.

DIVIDING A FIBROUS-ROOTED MARGINAL

Fibrous-rooted aquatics are less common than fibrous-rooted terrestrial plants. This is because the fibrous root system is more suited to dry soils. However, there are some aquatics with fibrous root systems, and these can be propagated through division.

1 Tease out the stems and roots that have become intertwined. Spread the roots out on a flat surface and cut through a portion of the young growth at the edge which has growing points and healthy leaves.

2 Fill a medium-size, fine-mesh container with aquatic compost (soil mix) to about half full.

3 Place the young portion of the divided plant into the container and cover the roots with compost (soil mix).

4 Firm in the newly divided plant well so that the compost is fairly compact.

5 Top-dress with pea shingle or gravel to ensure that the compost (soil mix) does not escape when the basket is submerged.

DIVIDING A MARGINAL WITH THICK RHIZOMATOUS ROOTS

Many marginal aquatics have thick, hard rhizomatous roots which grow in a straight line on the surface of the mud. This type of root system is quite common among marginal plants, notably the many species of *Iris* that prefer their roots on the surface of the mud.

1 Remove the younger pieces of rhizomatous root which contain 2–3 leaves.

2 Cut up the root so that each piece contains a leaf.

3 Trim off the fibrous roots on the underside of the rhizome to within 2.5cm (1in).

ABOVE: *Iris pseudacorus* var. *bastardii* is a rhizomatous iris with lovely, soft yellow flowers. It can be propagated by division.

RIGHT: *Iris versicolor* is a rhizomatous iris which can be easily propagated by division.

4 Fill a small container that has fine-mesh sides with aquatic compost (soil mix) to the rim of the container.

5 After firming the compost (soil mix) in the container, make a small depression in the compost (soil mix) with a dibber (dibble) to enable the rhizome to be half buried in the depression.

6 Firm the root thoroughly into the depression on the compost so that the cutting is stable. It is also important to firm the compost (soil mix) in very well in order to minimize the reduction in volume which can occur when the basket is placed in the pool, and large amounts of air are expelled from the compost.

7 Top-dress the compost (soil mix) with washed pea shingle or gravel to increase the stability of the young division and prevent compost floating to the surface. Place in shallow water to the depth of the container in a shaded position until it develops enough roots to survive in strong sun, and then place on the marginal shelf.

PLANT PESTS AND DISEASES

The plants in and around the pool are not subject to many serious pests and diseases. Fish can keep several pests down, but where they cannot cope, use biological methods of control rather than chemicals, which are lethal to fish and other beneficial organisms.

PESTS

It is difficult to control pests with chemicals, especially if you have fish. In most cases, where pest damage is serious, it is easier to handpick infected areas.

Aphids In serious cases, jet insects off soft aquatic growth with a garden hose. Aphids overwinter on nearby plums or cherries, and you may need to spray the trees with a winter wash to kill overwintering eggs.

Brown China mark moth The larvae of this moth form floating shelters from cut pieces of foliage and eat large holes in the edges of waterlily leaves, often completely skeletonizing the leaf. The moths, about 2.5cm (1in) long, have irregular white patches on brownish-orange wings and are usually seen on late-summer evenings. The eggs hatch out beneath the leaf surface into creamy coloured caterpillars that crawl about in their shelters. Remove damaged leaves and in autumn net off the shelters to which the overwintering pupae are attached.

Caddis-fly The damage is caused by the larvae of this insect, which grow into small, dull-coloured moths. The eggs are laid in early evening in long, jelly-like tubes, the larvae emerging after about ten days and spinning protective cases around themselves. These are made of small sticks embedded in pieces of shell and

sand and covered in leaf fragments. The larvae swim or float around in these structures, feeding on vegetation and devouring young waterlily leaves as they grow to the surface. They pupate inside leaves at the water's edge. Control is almost impossible, but a good population of carp, orfe or goldfish will help.

Leafhoppers These weaken plants in the same way as aphids by sucking sap through leaves and tender young growth. Waterlilies that have become overgrown and whose leaves are growing above the surface are very prone to attack. Use a strong jet of water to wash off the insects and, more importantly, divide waterlilies regularly so that vulnerable growth is not allowed to develop.

Leaf-mining midge The larvae eat serpentine channels just under the surface of waterlily leaves. Eggs are laid on the leaf surfaces and the mites tunnel away at the tissue. The leaf starts to rot between the channels, leaving no more than skeletonized remains. Cut off affected leaves immediately. If this is not enough, remove the entire plant and submerge it in a large bucket containing an insecticide suitable for killing greenfly. Wash the plant thoroughly in clean water before returning it to the pool.

Snails In an ornamental pool with limited vegetation, water snails are a pest, although in a large wildlife pool, they are a valuable part of the food chain. The most common species is the freshwater whelk or common water snail, which has a tall, pointed and spiralling shell, about 2.5cm (1in) high when mature. They are very fond of soft plant tissue, particularly young waterlily leaves. Under

RIGHT: **The offspring of this adult caddis-fly will wreak havoc to underwater foliage.**

FAR RIGHT: **The damage caused by leafhoppers is similar to that by aphids. This leafhopper is jumping from leaf to leaf.**

any mature waterlily leaf, you will see the eggs in a jelly-like tissue. Trap them overnight on floating lettuce leaves, and net them off in the morning.

Waterlily beetle These dark brown beetles are about 5mm (¼in) long and lay clusters of eggs on the surface of waterlily leaves. Shiny, black larvae with yellow bellies hatch out after about seven days and feed voraciously on the leaves which gradually rot away. After summer, the larvae pupate on any foliage above the water level and the hatched beetles overwinter on dead foliage at the waterside. Remove this brown foliage in autumn. In summer, remove damaged leaves and jet the leaves regularly to control the spread. Raise the water level for a day to submerge the waterlily leaves and drown the larvae.

DISEASES

Water gardening is free from several of the common garden diseases which plague plants when they are not fully nourished and watered. Occasional disease is best treated by removing the plants from the water and treating them in a bucket of dilute fungicide, returning them to the pond after a thorough rinsing.

Iris leaf spot Older leaves of many ornamental plants are prone to leaf spots, but the strong sword-shaped leaves of iris look particularly disfigured when they are infected. This is largely because the spots become elongated along the direction of the veins on the leaf. The brown oval spots appear at random, and the centre of the spot is often lighter in colour, sometimes showing the spores of the fungus. In severe cases the spots coalesce and the leaf dies. A wide spectrum fungicide, such as dithiocarbonate, should be used to control it, but make sure that there is no spray drift onto the pool surface.

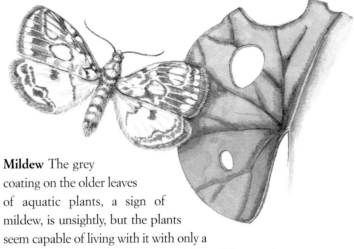

Mildew The grey coating on the older leaves of aquatic plants, a sign of mildew, is unsightly, but the plants seem capable of living with it with only a little loss of vigour. Marsh marigolds (*Caltha*) are the most susceptible, often developing mildew in mid- to late summer. If the old, infected leaves are completely removed, the plant will recover very quickly and fresh green leaves will soon appear. The rapid re-growth shown by most aquatics means that this method of control is more advisable than spraying with a fungicide.

Waterlily crown rot The first symptoms are yellowing leaves, which sometimes become mottled. The leaf stems then become soft and blackened, and later break away from the crown. The crown will be soft and gelatinous with black tissue inside and have a vile smell. Remove the plant at once; if this is done early enough, it should not spread to other waterlilies, especially if these are different species or cultivars. If other plants remain unaffected for a few weeks, it is safe to replace the lost plant.

Waterlily leaf spot More common, but less serious than crown rot, leaf spot appears as dark patches or as dry, brown edges which eventually rot. In time, the whole leaf rots away. Remove infected leaves at once, and, if there are no fish, apply a weak fungicidal spray.

ABOVE: **The China mark moth and its caterpillars can do untold damage, as this waterlily leaf clearly shows.**

FAR LEFT: **The tunnel marks made by the larvae of leaf mining moths are often found on bramble leaves.**

LEFT: **The damage to these cherry leaves is caused by one of the many leaf-mining moths.**

A garden using both water and rock involves almost opposite ends of the cultivation spectrum. Alpines are suited

PLANT DIRECTORY

to the dry soil along some pool edges, but most of this section covers aquatic plants. The growth of most temperate aquatics can be restrained by a basket, but care is required for exotic plants as they can get out of control.

OPPOSITE: **A massed planting of candelabra primulas looks spectacular in the moist soil by the side of a pond.**

FREE-FLOATING PLANTS

It is particularly important to introduce floating plants when you are establishing a new pond. These plants not only reduce algae by cutting down light and absorbing mineral salts through their suspended roots, but also provide valuable homes for fish fry. The reduction of surface light is an important part of the planting strategy, although totally covering the water's surface would do more harm than good by blocking out too much energy-giving light. Between one-half and two-thirds of the surface area should be covered by the leaves of either surface floaters or waterlilies. This cover is difficult to achieve on a new pond and you may have to resort to using more floaters than will ultimately be necessary and later netting off when the pond becomes more established. A selection of the more common and widely available floaters is given here.

Azolla (Azollaceae)

Mosquito fern, water fern, fairy moss
The genus contains eight species of dainty, green, floating plants. They quickly reproduce by division, and their rapid rate of reproduction means they should be netted off a small pond as soon as they swamp the surface.
Propagation: By division.
Hardiness: Half hardy to frost tender.

Azolla filiculoides (syn. *A. caroliniana*)

This small, perennial, half hardy fern forms clusters of soft, pale green fronds, 1–5cm (½–2in) long, which turn purplish-red in autumn. Each leaf is attached to a single fine root. It can be invasive, so thin regularly. It survives cold winters by producing overwintering bodies, which sink to the bottom of the pool, but resurface when the water warms up in late spring.
Cultivation: Grow in full sun.
Height: To 5cm (2in); *spread:* indefinite.

Eichhornia (Pontederiaceae)

Water hyacinth, water orchid
There are seven species in this genus of tropical, mainly floating plants

Azolla filiculoides

Eichhornia crassipes

from South America, where they root into any shallow mud and form huge colonies, which can swamp rivers and lakes, becoming a major problem.
Propagation: By breaking off young offsets, which is very easily done.
Hardiness: Borderline hardy.

Eichhornia crassipes (syn. *E. speciosa*)

Water hyacinth
This tender plant will not survive winter outdoors in temperate climates. It is available in summer and for a few months in hot weather provides a striking sight on the pool surface. It bears rosettes of shiny, pale green leaves, the swollen, spongy bases of which act as floats. In very warm summers it produces pale blue, hyacinth-like flowers to 15–23cm (6–9in) high. Long, feathery roots, purplish-black in colour, provide a perfect medium for spawning goldfish. It spreads by means of fast-growing stolons, and in some countries with warm climates is prohibited because it chokes waterways. This is not a problem in temperate climates, and it will only be successful in areas with sunny, warm weather. Overwinter in a frost-free greenhouse on trays of moist soil.

Hydrocharis morsus-ranae

Cultivation: Grow in full sun and warm water, preferably 18°C (64°F).
Height: 15–23cm (6–9in); *spread:* 15–30cm (6–12in).

Hydrocharis (Hydrocharitaceae)

Frogbit
The two species of submerged or free-floating plants in this genus are native to temperate and subtropical parts of Europe, Africa, Asia and Australia. These plants have short, stolon-like stems, which form mats just under the surface of the water.
Propagation: By removing offsets, which is easily done.
Hardiness: Hardy.

Hydrocharis morsus-ranae

Frogbit
Rather like a tiny waterlily, this graceful little floater has kidney-shaped, shiny green leaves, 3cm (1¼in) long, in a rosette and small white flowers which have a yellow centre.
Cultivation: Grow in full sun in water to 30cm (12in) deep.
Spread: Indefinite.

Lemna (Lemnaceae)

Duckweed, frog's buttons
The genus contains 13 species of small, temperate and tropical floating plants, found in almost all parts of the world. They form green floating mats in still or slow-moving water. The flowers are small and have no decorative merit.
Propagation: By removing young plants.
Hardiness: Hardy to half hardy.

Lemna minor

Lesser duckweed
This is the most widespread of all the duckweeds. It has light green, ovate leaves, about 5mm (¼in) across, with a single rootlet hanging down from each one. It is a valuable food for goldfish.
Cultivation: Grow in full sun or shade.
Spread: Indefinite.

Lemna trisulca

Star duckweed, ivy-leaved duckweed
This species is the easiest to control because it reproduces more slowly than the other duckweeds. The light green, almost transparent leaves are elliptical in shape, about 1cm (½in) across, with the young plants growing at right angles to the old ones.
Cultivation: Grow in sun or shade.
Spread: Indefinite.

Pistia stratiotes

Stratiotes aloides

Trapa natans

Pistia (Araceae)

Water lettuce, shell flower
There is only one species in this genus. It is a floating plant, which is found growing throughout the world in tropical and subtropical areas. It produces rosettes of leaves, which resemble those of lettuces. Radiating stolons terminate in new plantlets, each in turn producing further plantlets, which result in this plant being a nuisance in warm tropical waters.
Propagation: By removing the young plantlets.
Hardiness: Frost tender.

Pistia stratiotes

A deciduous, perennial, floating aquatic, this species is evergreen in tropical waters which are warmer than 19–21°C (66–70°F). The slightly overlapping, wedge-shaped, velvety, sessile leaves grow to approximately 25cm (10in) in length and are 10cm (4in) wide. They have crenated tips and are a soft shade of

pale green on the upper side and whitish green on the underside. The tiny greenish flowers are produced at various times in leaflike spathes in the leaf axils.
Cultivation: Grow in warm water, with a minimum temperature of 10–15°C (50–59°F), in full sun.
Height: 10cm (4in); *spread:* indefinite.

Salvinia (Salviniaceae)

This is a cosmopolitan genus of ten species of free-floating aquatic ferns, which are found in tropical and subtropical areas. Some species can be grown in temperate regions, where they have become naturalized. Second only to the water hyacinth in its rate of growth, the plants have become a pest in southeastern Africa and southern India. The floating leaves are soft to the touch and have a covering of silky hairs.
Propagation: By separating the stems in spring or summer.
Hardiness: Half hardy.

Salvinia natans

This attractive species bears roundish, green leaflets, up to 2.5cm (1in) long, which have shiny brown hairs on the underside. The plant also has a submerged, root-like frond.
Cultivation: Grow in full sun in water with a minimum temperature of 10°C (50°F).
Height: 2.5cm (1in); *spread:* indefinite.

Stratiotes (Hydrocharitaceae)

Water soldier, water aloe
The single species in this genus is a semi-submerged or floating aquatic plant that is native to Europe and northwestern Asia. The sword-like leaves resemble pineapple tops.
Propagation: By separating runners from the parent plant.
Hardiness: Hardy.

Stratiotes aloides

This semi-evergreen, perennial floater can form quite extensive

stands of prickly rosettes on the surface of the water. These are formed by long, olive-green leaves, approximately 50cm (20in) long and 2cm (¾in) wide, with serrated edges. The tips of the leaves frequently emerge above the water's surface. In summer the whole plant tries to surface in order to produce cup-shaped, white, sometimes pink-tinged flowers about 4cm (1½in) across.
Cultivation: Grow in water to 1m (3ft) deep and in sun so that it will produce flowers.
Height: 40cm (16in); *spread:* indefinite.

Trapa (Trapaceae)

Water chestnut
There are 15 species of temperate and subtropical floaters in this genus. All species within this genus colonize shallow, still water. This plant is rich in fat and starch, and for this reason the plants are eaten in continental Asia, Malaysia and India.
Propagation: By seed sown in spring.
Hardiness: Frost hardy to frost tender.

Trapa natans

Jesuit's nut, water caltrop
An annual floating plant, this frost hardy species forms rosettes of pale green, glossy, diamond-shaped leaves, 2.5cm (1in) across, with conspicuous veins and serrated edges. The leaves are carried on long, reddish, inflated petioles. The inconspicuous white flowers produce fruits like thorny black chestnuts, 5cm (2in) in diameter, with four spikes.
Cultivation: Grow in full sun in water with a minimum temperature of 10°C (50°F).
Spread: Indefinite.

Lemna minor

Salvinia natans

OXYGENATING PLANTS

Oxygenators are the first group to be planted in a new pool. They are sold in bunches of unrooted stems, about 23cm (9in) long, nipped together at the base by a piece of lead. The weight prevents them from floating to the surface if they are loosened after planting. They are available throughout summer, and in a new pool it is best to give them a start by planting them into crates on the bottom. In an established pool, however, where some mud will have accumulated on the bottom, they can simply be weighted down and dropped into the pool over as wide an area as possible. They should not be planted deeper than 1–1.2m (3–4ft) deep, and they do best at depths between 45–60cm (18–24in). A medium-size planting crate will hold five or six bunches of oxygenators, and in general this planted crate will be adequate for 1 square metre of surface area; this is equivalent to one bunch to each square foot of surface area.

Callitriche
(Callitrichaceae)
Water starwort
The 25 species in this genus are distributed throughout the world, except South Africa. They are small, slender plants, and they generally grow in a tight mass in a wide range of habitats, but mainly in temperate locations. Most species are recognizable by their terminal rosettes of leaves, which, when floating on the water, give rise to the common name.
Propagation: By softwood cuttings.
Hardiness: Hardy.

Callitriche hermaphroditica (syn. *C. autumnalis*)
Autumn starwort
This hardy species has light green, linear leaves, 1–2cm (½–¾in) long, held opposite each other on thin, branching stems, to 50cm (20in) long. The mass of stems provides homes for minute life, while the young leaves are a delicacy for goldfish. This species is the exception to the rule in not forming rosettes of floating leaves.
Cultivation: Grow in sun or partial shade in water to 50cm (20in) deep.
Spread: Indefinite.

Ceratophyllum demersum

Ceratophyllum
(Ceratophyllaceae)
The genus contains about 30 hardy species of submerged rootless aquatics, found around the world. They grow only in submerged conditions and are unable to tolerate even the shortest time out of water. They flourish in cold water and shade, conditions that could inhibit other species.
Propagation: By detaching small pieces of stem and floating them in the water.
Hardiness: Hardy to frost tender.

Ceratophyllum demersum
Hornwort
The leaves usually form clusters 30–60cm (1–2ft) long. The whorls of slender, rather brittle, forked, dark green leaves, 1–4cm (½–1½in) long, crowd towards the apex. Hornwort is hardy, and useful in more shaded ponds. It is often found free-floating or loosely anchored in the bottom mud in both still and moving water. It has inconspicuous flowers, which are borne in the leaf axils. To overwinter, the tips of the shoots shorten and thicken and then break off before sinking to the bottom. *C. submersum* is slightly more vigorous, with stems reaching nearly 1m (3ft) and leaves growing to 2.5–5cm (1–2in) in length.
Cultivation: Grow in sun or shade in water to 1m (3ft) deep.
Spread: Indefinite.

Egeria
(Hydrocharitaceae)
The two species of evergreen or semi-evergreen submerged plants in this genus were originally native to the warm and temperate zones of South America, but they have become established elsewhere, sometimes becoming so invasive that they are regarded as pests.
Propagation: By softwood cuttings.
Hardiness: Hardy to frost tender.

Egeria densa (syn. *Elodea densa*)
Argentinian water weed
This frost-tender species has long, branching stems, to 1m (3ft) long, with whorls of narrow, dark green leaves, each 2.5cm (1in) long and with a pointed tip that usually curls backwards. Plants may produce insignificant white flowers on the surface of the water in summer.
Cultivation: Grow in full sun.
Spread: Indefinite.

Hottonia
(Primulaceae)
The genus contains two species of submerged plants which have primula-like flowers, held above the water. The two species are mainly found in bright, clear pools or slow-moving ditches in temperate areas of the northern hemisphere.
Propagation: By seed or by division.
Hardiness: Hardy to half hardy.

Callitriche hermaphroditica

Hottonia palustris

Ceratophyllum submersum

Hottonia palustris
Water violet
In summer, the fully hardy water violet bears beautiful spikes of violet flowers, which have yellow throats. The flower spikes are held well above the surface of the water on stalks that grow to 30–40cm (12–16in) tall. The submerged, bright green leaves are finely divided and reach a length of 2–13cm (¾–5in). They are arranged in an attractive, comb-like fashion.
Cultivation: Grow in full sun and clear water.
Height: 1m (3ft); *spread:* indefinite.

Lagarosiphon
(Hydrocharitaceae)
Curly water thyme
There are nine species of tender, submerged plants in this genus. They are native to central Africa and Madagascar, but they have also established themselves in Europe and New Zealand. Similar to *Egeria*, curly water thyme is an excellent oxygenator for fish bowls, pools and aquaria.
Propagation: By softwood cuttings, which is easily done.
Hardiness: Hardy to half hardy.

Lagarosiphon major (syn. Elodea crispa)
This hardy, semi-evergreen perennial has narrow, strongly recurved, fresh green leaves, 5–25mm (¼–1in) long, borne in spirals along the stem. The dense masses of submerged stems should be cut back every autumn.
Cultivation: Grow in full sun.
Height and spread: 1m (3ft).

Myriophyllum aquaticum

Myriophyllum
(Haloragaceae)
Milfoil
The 40 species of submerged aquatics in this genus are mainly from the southern hemisphere. The submerged stems are often long, bearing finely divided, almost feathery leaves, which are extremely attractive. The milfoils show a great diversity of habit, and many love to creep out of the water and scramble onto the surrounds of the pool.
Propagation: By softwood cuttings, which is easily done.
Hardiness: Hardy to frost hardy.

Myriophyllum aquaticum (syn. M. brasiliense, M. proserpinacoides)
Diamond milfoil, parrot's feather
This species is slightly tender and must be well submerged in temperate climates if it is to survive the winter. It is, nevertheless, extensively used in outdoor pools, where the graceful foliage and stems take root in the wet soil above the water line. The stems can grow to 50cm–1.5m (20–60in) long, with leaves 2.5–5cm (1–2in) long and borne in whorls of four to six, divided into four to eight bright green segments.
Cultivation: Grow in sun or partial shade and thin clumps regularly.
Spread: Indefinite.

Potamogeton
(Potamogetonaceae)
There are 80–100 species of submerged aquatic plants in this genus, and they are found in temperate regions throughout the world. They are vigorous rhizomatous perennials, and only a few are suitable as oxygenators in decorative ponds as they can quickly choke other growth.
Propagation: By stem cuttings in early summer.
Hardiness: Hardy to frost tender.

Potamogeton crispus
Curled pondweed
The stems of this hardy species can grow to 4m (13ft) or more, and bear narrow, stalkless leaves, each about 8cm (3in) long and 5–10mm (¼–½in) wide. They are almost translucent, with wavy edges, and vary from green to reddish-brown.
Cultivation: Grow in full sun if possible, but it tolerates cloudy water better than any other oxygenator.
Spread: Indefinite.

Ranunculus
(Ranunculaceae)
This large genus contains about 400 species of temperate and tropical moisture-loving and aquatic species, which have a big impact in the garden.
Propagation: By softwood cuttings for the submerged species.
Hardiness: Hardy.

Ranunculus aquatilis
Water crowfoot
This hardy, submerged, clump-forming perennial bears flat, kidney-shaped, floating leaves, 3–8cm (1¼–3in) long, and threadlike, submerged leaves. The buttercup-shaped, white flowers, held above the water, are 2cm (¾in) across with a yellow base to the petals.
Cultivation: Grow in full sun in water to 1m (3ft) deep at a depth of 15–60cm (6–24in), where it can root in the mud.
Spread: Indefinite.

Ranunculus aquatilis

DEEP-WATER PLANTS

There are a few species of water plants that prefer deeper water than the marginals and that will grow in the same conditions as waterlilies. They are usually grouped in a section called deep-water plants in aquatic catalogues; although it is not a large category, these plants make a valuable contribution to the appearance of the pool in providing a welcome change in shape from the pads of waterlilies when you are selecting the surface leaves. As well as being decorative, their leaves also provide valuable shade.

Aponogeton
(Aponogetonaceae)

The genus contains some 44 species of rhizomatous perennials, which are found in mainly tropical and subtropical areas, but there is one hardy species, which is used extensively in cold-water ponds.
Propagation: The hardy species is propagated by seed or by dividing the rhizomes into sections with a bud.
Hardiness: Hardy to frost tender.

Aponogeton distachyos

Water hawthorn, Cape pondweed
This frost-hardy perennial aquatic has oblong, bright green leaves, to 20cm (8in) long by 8cm (3in) wide, which can become almost evergreen in mild winters. The strongly scented flowers are often produced in two flushes, the main flush in spring and a second as a most welcome surprise in the autumn. The beautiful white flowers, which have purple-brown anthers, are 10cm (4in) long and are held above the water. A very tolerant plant, particularly of shade, it extends the flowering season, and its long leaves add interest to the water surface.
Cultivation: Grow in sun or shade in water to 60cm (2ft).
Spread: 1.2m (4ft).

Euryale (Nymphaeaceae)

Fox nuts, Gorgon plant
The genus contains a single species of large aquatic plants, which are native to India, Bangladesh and China. The floating leaves are spiny, and this has given rise to the common name Gorgon plant, a reference to the mythological snake-haired Gorgon.
Propagation: By seed.
Hardiness: Frost tender.

Euryale ferox

This is a spectacular plant. The large, puckered leaves, 60cm–1m (2–3ft) in diameter, have prominent veins and spines. The flowers are relatively small – 5cm (2in) across – for such a large-leaved plant. They are violet-magenta in colour and mature to a berry containing seeds the size of a pea.
Cultivation: Grow in full sun in water about 1m (3ft) deep and with a minimum temperature of 5°C (41°F).
Spread: 1.5m (5ft).

Nuphar (Nymphaeaceae)

Cow lily, spatterdock
There are 25 species of aquatics in the genus, and they are found in temperate areas of the northern hemisphere. They bear some resemblance to waterlilies but have tougher floating leaves and will grow in conditions that are either too deep or too shaded for waterlilies.
Propagation: By division of the rhizome during summer.
Hardiness: Hardy to frost hardy.

Nuphar japonica

Japanese pond lily
This hardy species is much smaller than the other nuphars. It has wavy, heart-shaped, submerged leaves, which are a delicate purplish colour, and dark green, oblong, surface leaves, with arrow-shaped bases, 40cm (16in) long. The red-tinted yellow flowers are 5cm (2in) across.
Cultivation: Grow in full sun in water 30–60cm (1–2ft) deep.
Spread: 1m (3ft).

Aponogeton distachyos

Nuphar lutea

Nuphar lutea
Yellow pond lily
A common hardy species, this nuphar survives in deep and slow-moving water. The leathery floating leaves are 40cm (16in) long, and the bowl-shaped yellow flowers are 5cm (2in) across.
Cultivation: Grow in sun or partial shade in water 30–60cm (1–2ft) deep.
Spread: 2m (6½ft).

Nymphoides
(Menyanthaceae)
Floating heart
There are 20 species of submerged aquatics in this genus. They originate from temperate and subtropical areas around the world, and they resemble miniature waterlilies. They are often found in shallow, still waters, spreading very quickly to form a carpet of leaves.
Propagation: By dividing the long, thin roots in early spring.
Hardiness: Hardy to frost tender.

Nymphoides peltata
Yellow floating heart,
water fringe
This hardy species spreads rapidly by means of the extensive runners that carry the small, heart-shaped leaves, which are about 5cm (2in) across. The leaves are often mottled and splashed with brown. The yellow flowers, 2cm (¾in) in diameter, are fringed and held just above the water; they appear in summer.
Cultivation: Grow in full sun in water no deeper than 45cm (18in).
Spread: Indefinite.

Victoria amazonica

Victoria (Nymphaeaceae)
Giant waterlily, water platter
The genus contains two species of tropical aquatics with very large floating leaves. The species are native to tropical America.
Propagation: By seed.
Hardiness: Frost tender.

Victoria amazonica
Amazon waterlily, royal water lily
The rounded, floating leaves can reach up to 1.8m (6ft) across and are reddish-purple underneath. The leaves are covered with large prickles and the rims are vertical. The white, waterlily-like flowers appear in summer.
Cultivation: Grow in full sun in water 1m (3ft) deep and with a minimum temperature of 25°C (77°F).
Spread: 6m (20ft).

Victoria 'Longwood'
This cultivar was raised at Longwood Gardens in Philadelphia in the United States. It is an amazing plant, with a very fast rate of growth, quickly developing enormous, circular, floating, glossy green leaves. These can grow to 1.2–1.8m (4–6ft) in diameter, with upturned rims. The large nocturnal flowers, 25–40cm (10–16in) in diameter, last only two nights, and they turn from white to pink then purplish-red.
Cultivation: Grow in full sun in water 1m (3ft) deep and with a minimum temperature of 22°C (72°F).
Spread (in a single season): 7m (23ft).

Euryale ferox

Nymphoides peltata

WATERLILIES

In addition to the grouping of waterlilies (*Nymphaea*) by colour, the following are further subdivided into hardy and tropical plants. All the hardy types will succeed without protection in temperate regions outdoors; the tropical plants, on the other hand, will need to be grown in a sunny glasshouse in all but the most favoured locations.

The flowers vary in size, but they are generally always in proportion to the leaf, ranging from 2.5cm (1in) across in the pygmy varieties, to 30cm (1ft) across in some of the tropicals. There are waterlilies suitable for every size of pond, from barrels and tubs to extensive pools. All should be given a sunny, sheltered position without any water turbulence on their leaves. The planting depth given here refers to the depth of water above the crown or growing point and not to the depth of pond. The spread refers to the average area that the leaves will eventually cover, although in small planting containers they may not achieve these sizes. This selection includes species and cultivars that should be commercially available, although the tropical types are less easy to source in temperate areas.

PINK
Hardy waterlilies

Nymphaea 'Amabilis'
The star-shaped flowers, which grow to approximately 15–19cm (6–7½in) across, have pink petals with lighter tips surrounding deep yellow stamens. The nearly round leaves are green, 24cm (9½in) in diameter and reddish-purple when young.
Approximate spread: 1.5–2.3m (5–7½ft).
Suggested planting depth: 30–45cm (12–18in).

Nymphaea 'American Star'
The star-like flowers, which grow to about 15–18cm (6–7in) in diameter, have pink petals with light tips surrounding deep yellow stamens. The young leaves are reddish-purple, turning green as they mature. They are round in shape and 25–28cm (10–11in) across.
Approximate spread: 1.2–1.5m (4–5ft).
Suggested planting depth: 30–45cm (12–18in).

Nymphaea 'Comanche'

Nymphaea 'Caroliniana Perfecta'

Nymphaea 'Attraction'
Cup-like, later star-shaped, pink flowers are 15–20cm (6–8in) across with slightly lighter outer petals and glowing orange stamens. The oval leaves are 25–30cm (10–12in) long, light bronze when young, turning mid green with age. One of the best pinks for cut flowers although the central petals can "burn" on hot days.
Approximate spread: 1.2–1.5m (4–5ft).
Suggested planting depth: 30–45cm (12–18in).

Nymphaea 'Caroliniana Perfecta'
The cup-like, salmon-pink flowers of this waterlily are approximately 13–15cm (5–6in) across and have a sweet scent. The leaves are nearly round, 23–25cm (9–10in) across, bronzy at first, turning dark green with reddish brown undersides.
Approximate spread: 1.2–1.5m (4–5ft).
Suggested planting depth: 30–45cm (12–18in).

Nymphaea 'Comanche'
The cup-like, later stellate, flowers are 13–15cm (5–6in) across. They change from yellow apricot to gold orange, flushed with pink, then finally to deep orange, flushed with red. The stamens are yellow. The leaves are nearly round, 30cm (12in) across, bronzy when young with a few purple flecks. This is the largest and one of the showiest of the changeable cultivars.
Approximate spread: 1.2–1.5m (4–5ft).
Suggested planting depth: 30–45cm (12–18in).

Nymphaea 'Darwin' (syn. *N.* 'Hollandia')
The double, peony-style flowers, 15–19cm (6–7½in) across, have light pink inner petals and lighter pink, almost white outer petals surrounding pinkish-yellow stamens. The new leaves are brownish, turning green as they mature. They are round in shape and 25–28cm (10–11in) across.
Approximate spread: 1.2–1.5m (4–5ft).
Suggested planting depth: 30–60cm (1–2ft).

Nymphaea 'Attraction'

Nymphaea 'Laydekeri Lilacea'

Nymphaea 'Fabiola' (syn. N. 'Mrs Richmond')

The peony-shaped flowers, 15–18cm (6–7in) across, have pinkish-red, highly flecked petals surrounding orange stamens. The longish leaves, 30cm (12in) long, turn from bronzy purple to green.
Approximate spread: 1.5m (5ft).
Suggested planting depth: 30cm (12in).

Nymphaea 'Firecrest'

The star-shaped flowers, 14–15cm (5½–6in) across, have lavender pink petals surrounding orange and pink stamens. The round leaves, 23cm (9in) in diameter, change from deep purple when young to green.
Approximate spread: 1.2m (4ft).
Suggested planting depth: 23–30cm (9–12in).

Nymphaea 'Laydekeri Lilacea'

The cup-like, lilac-pink flowers are 6–9cm (2½–3½in) across with deep yellow stamens. The leaves are nearly round, 18–20cm (7–8in) across, purplish when young, turning olive-green with a few purple mottles.
Approximate spread: 1–1.2m (3–4ft).
Suggested planting depth: 15cm (6in).

Nymphaea 'Marliacea Carnea' (syn. N. 'Apple Blossom Pink')

The cup-shaped, light pink flowers, 12–13cm (4.5–5in) across, have yellow stamens. Purplish when young, the mature leaves are oval, deep green, and 19–20cm (7½–8in) long.
Approximate spread: 1.2–1.5m (4–5ft).
Suggested planting depth: 30–45cm (12–18in).

Nymphaea 'Pink Sensation'

Nymphaea 'Mrs. George C. Hitchcock'

A night-blooming cultivar which holds its large, soft-rose flowers, 25–28cm (10–11in) across, well above the water where the dark orange stamens are seen to good effect. The wavy, copper-green leaves, which are 38cm by 34cm (15in by 13½in), are flecked with darker green on the upper side and purplish brown beneath. This is a very reliable waterlily which flowers well into autumn.
Approximate spread: 2.2–2.4m (7–8ft).
Suggested planting depth: 45cm (18in).

Nymphaea 'Odorata Turicensis'

The fragrant, star-shaped flowers, 13–15cm (5–6in) across, have lovely soft pink petals surrounding deep yellow stamens. The round, green leaves are 13–15cm (5–6in) across and have bronzy red undersides.
Approximate spread: 2.4m (8ft).
Suggested planting depth: 23–30cm (9–12in).

Nymphaea 'Perry's Pink'

The star-shaped flowers, 15–18cm (6–7in) across, have rich pink petals and yellow to orange stamens. There is an unusual red dot in the centre of each flower. The new leaves are reddish-purple, turning green as they mature, and are round in shape, to 28cm (11in) across. Plant in a large container for the best flowering.
Approximate spread: 1.2–1.5m (4–5ft).
Suggested planting depth: 30–60cm (1–2ft).

Nymphaea 'Pink Sensation'

The cup-shaped flowers, which become star-shaped, are 12–15cm (5–6in) across and have pink petals surrounding yellow and pink stamens. Purplish when young, the round leaves mature to green and are up to 25cm (10in) in diameter. This is one of the best pinks, and the flowers stay open late into the afternoon.
Approximate spread: 1.2m (4ft).
Suggested planting depth: 30–45cm (12–18in).

Nymphaea 'Pygmaea Rubra'

The small, cup-like flowers, 6cm (2½in) across, have outer petals that are a white-blushed pink in colour as they open and become rich maroon red later. The stamens are yellow. Bronzy when young, the leaves are round and green when mature, and 15–18cm (6–7in) across.
Approximate spread: 75cm (30in).
Suggested planting depth: 15–23cm (6–9in).

Nymphaea 'Rose Arey'

Nymphaea 'Marliacea Carnea'

Nymphaea 'General Pershing'

Nymphaea 'Ray Davies'

The peony-shaped, almost double flowers, which are 15–18cm (6–7in) across, have yellow and pink petals surrounding yellow stamens. The young leaves are slightly bronzed, later turning to glossy green, and 25–28cm (10–11in) in diameter.
Approximate spread: 1.5m (5ft).
Suggested planting depth: 30cm (12in).

Nymphaea 'Rose Arey'

The star-shaped, sweetly scented flowers are 18–20cm (7–8in) in diameter and have golden stamens. The flowers change towards the margins from pink to orange-pink. The purple young leaves mature to round plain green leaves, 23cm (9in) in diameter.
Approximate spread: 1.2–1.5m (4–5ft).
Suggested planting depth: 38–60cm (15–24in).

Tropical waterlilies

Nymphaea capensis var. zanzibariensis

This is a day-blooming and free-flowering form that has larger flowers than *N. capensis*, reaching 18–25cm (7–10in) across. The hybrid 'Wild Rose' was introduced in 1941 by George Pring who was the famous American breeder of tropical waterlilies. The flowers have an almost bi-colour effect, which is caused by the large pink petals being flushed with yellow at their base and combined with a mass of golden stamens that are tipped with pink. The blooms are held at a height of 20–25cm (8–10in) above the water. The leaves are a dark green, flecked with reddish brown above, and light green, flushed with red, underneath.
Approximate spread: 1.5–2.4m (5–8ft).
Suggested planting depth: 45cm (18in).

Nymphaea 'Froebelii'

Nymphaea 'James Brydon'

Nymphaea 'Emily Grant Hutchings'

The large, cup-like flowers, 15–20cm (6–8in) across, are dark pink with red stamens. The leaves are round, 25–30cm (10–12in) across, bronzy green on top with olive-green undersides.
Approximate spread: 2–2.2m (6–7ft).
Suggested planting depth: 45cm (18in).

Nymphaea 'General Pershing'

The cup-like, scented flowers, which later become flat, are 20–28cm (8–11in) in diameter and have lavender-pink petals surrounding yellow stamens. The round leaves, 23–25cm (9–10in) across, are olive green with purple blotches.
Approximate spread: 1.5–2m (5–6½ft).
Suggested planting depth: 30–45cm (12–18in).

RED
Hardy waterlilies

Nymphaea 'Andreana'

At first cup-like, the peony-style flowers, 13–18cm (5–7in) across, have reddish-orange inner petals and peach-yellow outer petals surrounding deep yellow stamens. The nearly round leaves, 18–20cm (7–8in) in diameter, are green with reddish-brown blotches.
Approximate spread: 1–1.2m (3–4ft).
Suggested planting depth: 30–35cm (12–14in).

Nymphaea 'Arethusa'

The globe-shaped flowers, 13–14cm (5–5½in) across, have dark red petals in the centre with lighter outer petals surrounding orange-red stamens. The round green leaves, 20cm (8in) across, have purple blotches.
Approximate spread: 1–1.2m (3–4ft).
Suggested planting depth: 30–38cm (12–15in).

Nymphaea 'Charles de Meurville'

One of the first waterlilies to flower, the star-shaped flowers, 15–18cm (6–7in) across, have dark, pinkish-red inner petals and pink outer petals around orange stamens. The almost plum-coloured blooms are occasionally streaked with white. The leaves, 25cm (10in) long and 20cm (8in) wide, are dark green with light green veins.
Approximate spread: 1.2–1.5m (4–5ft).
Suggested planting depth: 45–60cm (18–24in).

Nymphaea 'Conqueror'

The star-like flowers, 18–20cm (7–8in) in diameter, have white-flecked, almost crimson petals surrounding long yellow stamens. The round leaves, 25–28cm (10–11in) in diameter, are bronze when young, maturing to deep green.
Approximate spread: 1.5m (5ft).
Suggested planting depth: 30–35cm (12–14in).

Nymphaea 'Escarboucle'

At first cup-shaped, the flowers become star-shaped, about 15–18cm (6–7in) across, with bright vermilion-red petals, the outer ones tipped with white, and deep orange stamens. The brown-tinged young leaves mature to round, green leaves, 25–28cm (10–11in) in diameter. This is one of the best reds for medium and large pools, and it stays open later in the afternoon than most other red varieties.
Approximate spread: 1.2–1.5m (4–5ft).
Suggested planting depth: 30–60cm (1–2ft).

Nymphaea 'Froebelii'

The cup-shaped flowers, which become star-shaped, are 10–13cm (4–5in) across, with burgundy-red petals and orange-red stamens. The young leaves are bronze-red, becoming green, round and 15cm (6in) across. It is ideal for cooler situations and for barrels or small pools.
Approximate spread: 90cm (3ft).
Suggested planting depth: 15–30cm (6–12in).

Nymphaea 'James Brydon'

The cup-shaped flowers, 10–13cm (4–5in) across, have bright rose-red petals and orange-red stamens. Purplish-brown young leaves, blotched with dark purple, mature to round, green leaves 18cm (7in) in diameter. It is ideal for barrels or medium-size pools, both for its flower shape and its free-flowering habit.
Approximate spread: 1–1.2m (3–4ft).
Suggested planting depth: 30–45cm (12–18in).

Nymphaea 'Laydekeri Fulgens'

The cup-shaped flowers of this waterlily, which grow to 13–15cm (5–6in) in diameter, have striking burgundy-red petals surrounding orange-red stamens. The purplish young leaves, which are blotched with dark purple, mature to round, green leaves, reaching 18–20cm (7–8in) in diameter. This is one of the first waterlilies to bloom in spring.
Approximate spread: 1.2–1.5m (4–5ft).
Suggested planting depth: 30–45cm (12–18in).

Nymphaea 'Lucida'

The star-shaped flowers, which are 13–15cm (5–6in) in diameter, have red inner petals and pink-veined, whitish-pink outer petals surrounding yellow stamens. The mature oval leaves grow to 25cm (10in) long and 23cm (9in) wide, with large purple blotches. Suitable for any sized pool, this is a free-flowering form, which has particularly attractive leaves.
Approximate spread: 1.2–1.5m (4–5ft).
Suggested planting depth: 30–45cm (12–18in).

Nymphaea 'Newton'

The star-shaped, red flowers, 15–20cm (6–8in) across, are unusual for a hardy, being carried well above the water when young and floating on the surface on the third day. The narrow petals increase the tropical look and are complemented by deep yellow stamens. The nearly-round leaves are 23cm (9in) across and mid green in colour with purple blotches and brownish red undersides.
Approximate spread: 1.1–1.5m (3½–5ft).
Suggested planting depth: 30cm (12in).

Nymphaea 'Charles de Meurville'

Nymphaea 'Escarboucle'

Nymphaea 'Lucida'

Nymphaea 'Radiant Red'
The star-shaped flowers, 13–15cm (5–6in) in diameter, have long sepals, slightly flecked, deep red petals and orange stamens. The new leaves, which are bronze before turning green, are almost round in shape and reach up to 25cm (10in) in diameter.
Approximate spread: 1–1.2m (3–4ft).
Suggested planting depth: 30–45cm (12–18in).

Nymphaea 'René Gérard'
The star-shaped, rosy-red flowers, 15–23cm (6–9in) across, have flecked, paler red outer petals and yellow stamens. The round, plain green leaves are bronzed when young and grow to 25–28cm (10–11in) across.
Approximate spread: 1.5m (5ft).
Suggested planting depth: 30–45cm (12–18in).

Nymphaea 'Vésuve'
The star-shaped, scented flowers, 17cm (6½in) across, have inward-pointing, red petals, which deepen with age, and orange stamens. The almost circular, green leaves are 23–25cm (9–10in) across. It opens early in the morning and closes late in the afternoon.
Approximate spread: 1.2m (4ft).
Suggested planting depth: 30–45cm (12–18in).

Nymphaea 'William Falconer'
The cup-like flowers, 10–13cm (4–5in) in diameter, have very deep red petals

Nymphaea 'William Falconer'

and burgundy-red stamens. The new leaves are purple, maturing to green, and are almost round, 25cm (10in) in diameter. It is ideal for cool areas because it dislikes too much heat and will stop flowering in very hot spells.
Approximate spread: 1m (3ft).
Suggested planting depth: 30–45cm (12–18in).

Tropical waterlilies

Nymphaea 'Evelyn Randig'
The cup-like flowers, which later become star-like, are 18–23cm

Nymphaea 'Jennifer Rebecca'

(7–9in) in diameter and have deep raspberry-pink petals surrounding deep yellow stamens. The beautiful dark green, round leaves, which reach 35–38cm (14–15in) across, have purple blotches covering half of the leaf.
Approximate spread: 1.5–2.2m (5–7ft).
Suggested planting depth: 38–45cm (15–18in).

Nymphaea 'H.C. Haarstick'
A night-blooming waterlily with a pungent scent, the large, flat flowers, 25–3cm (10–12in) across, have red petals surrounding orange-red stamens. The large, round leaves grow to 40cm (16in) and have a reddish-brown tinge and wavy, toothed margins.
Approximate spread: 1.8–3.6m (6–12ft).
Suggested planting depth: 45cm (18in).

Nymphaea 'Jennifer Rebecca'
This is a night-blooming waterlily with dark red flowers shaped like a sunflower, 20–25cm (8–10in) across, and with deep pink stamens. The nearly round leaves, 38cm (15in) across, are reddish brown and sharply dentate, with the edges of the older leaves becoming distinctly wavy.
Approximate spread: 2.2–2.7m (7–9ft).
Suggested planting depth: 45cm (18in).

Nymphaea 'Maroon Beauty'
A night-blooming waterlily, this has huge, flat flowers, measuring 20–25cm (8–10in) across, with deep red petals surrounding reddish-brown and red stamens. The reddish-brown, round leaves are 38cm (15in) in diameter, with toothed leaf margins which become wavy edged as the leaves get older.
Approximate spread: 2.2–2.7m (7–9ft).
Suggested planting depth: 30–45cm (12–18in).

Nymphaea 'Mrs C. W. Ward'
The reddish-pink flowers of this tropical waterlily are star-shaped and 15–20cm (6–8in) in diameter. The flowers have yellow stamens and a most pleasant fragrance. The leaves are egg-shaped and grow to 30–38cm (12–15in) in length. They are green on the top and red underneath with slightly wavy edges. This waterlily requires plenty of space to flourish.
Approximate spread: 2.4m (8ft).
Suggested planting depth: 45cm (18in).

Nymphaea 'Red Flare'
The large, flat, night-blooming flowers, 18–25cm (7–10in) across, have deep red petals and light pink or yellowish stamens. The older leaves, 25–30cm (10–12in) across, become round with a reddish-bronze hue and a few purple blotches, and they have heavily serrated and wavy edges.
Approximate spread: 1.5–1.8m (5–6ft).
Suggested planting depth: 30–45cm (12–18in).

WHITE
Hardy waterlilies

Nymphaea alba
White waterlily
The cup-shaped flowers, 10–13cm (4–5in) in diameter, have rather concave, white petals surrounding yellow stamens. The fresh green leaves, 30cm (12in) across, are red when young and tend to hug the water's surface. This waterlily is not really suitable for small ornamental ponds.
Approximate spread: 1.7m (5½ft).
Suggested planting depth: 60cm (2ft).

Nymphaea 'René Gérard'

Nymphaea 'Gladstoneana'

Nymphaea 'Hermine'

Tropical waterlilies

Nymphaea dentata 'Superba'

This is a night-blooming waterlily which is native to Egypt and also to other parts of Africa. It is sometimes referred to as the "White Nile Lotus". It has large, fragrant white flowers, which grow to 20–25cm (8–10in) in diameter. The flowers are held on hairy flower stalks above the surface of the water. The petals open flat, displaying the attractive yellow stamens. The large leaves are 33cm by 30cm (13 by 12in), dark green above with toothed edges and prominent leaf veins on the underside. This waterlily needs a minimum temperature of 27°C (80°F) to flower well.
Approximate spread: 1.5–1.8m (5–6ft).
Suggested planting depth: 45cm (18in).

Nymphaea 'Marliacea Chromatella'

Nymphaea 'Albatros'

The star-shaped flowers, 15–20cm (6–8in) across, have white petals surrounding yellow stamens. The round, olive-green leaves, 20–25cm (8–10in) across, have a few purple blotches.
Approximate spread: 1–1.5m (3–5ft).
Suggested planting depth: 30cm (12in).

Nymphaea 'Gladstoneana'

The star-shaped flowers, 13–18cm (5–7in) in diameter, have white petals surrounding yellow stamens. Bronzed young leaves mature to almost round, wavy-edged green leaves, 28–30cm (11–12in) across, with crimped margins along the lobes. It is very free flowering and best suited to larger pools.
Approximate spread: 1.5–2.4m (5–8ft).
Suggested planting depth: 45–60cm (18–24in).

Nymphaea 'Hermine'

The elegant, star-shaped flowers, 10–15cm (4–6in) across, have long, white petals which are surrounded by golden yellow stamens. The mature leaves are round and green. This magnificent waterlily is moderately vigorous and should be grown in a medium-size pool.
Approximate spread: to 1.8m (6ft).
Suggested planting depth: 15–45cm (6–18in).

Nymphaea 'Marliacea Albida'

The cup-shaped flowers, 13–15cm (5–6in) in diameter, have white petals surrounding yellow stamens. The slightly bronzed young leaves mature to round, green leaves, 23cm (9in) in diameter. This is a good choice for small pools where there is limited space.
Approximate spread: 1–1.2m (3–4ft).
Suggested planting depth: 30–45cm (12–18in).

Nymphaea odorata var. *minor*

The small, star-shaped flowers, which are 8cm (3in) in diameter, have white petals surrounding prominent golden-yellow stamens. The green leaves are almost round, 8–10cm (3–4in) in diameter, and have dark red undersides. It is a most successful waterlily in tubs or shallow pools, but must have full sun.
Approximate spread: 60cm (2ft).
Suggested planting depth: 23–30cm (9–12in).

Nymphaea tuberosa 'Richardsonii'

The peony-like flowers, 10–23cm (4–9in) in diameter, have white petals surrounding yellow stamens. The round, mid-green leaves are 38cm (15in) across.
Approximate spread: 1.8–2.2m (6–7ft).
Suggested planting depth: 30cm (12in).

Nymphaea 'Virginia'

The fragrant, star-shaped, almost double flowers, 15–18cm (6–7in) in diameter, have creamy, pale yellow petals in the centre and pure white petals on the outside surrounding yellow stamens. The young leaves are green with heavy purple blotching, which becomes restricted to the perimeter of the mature, egg-shaped leaves, which are 25cm (10in) long and 21cm (8½in) wide. This is a classic, free-flowering waterlily.
Approximate spread: 1.5–1.8m (5–6ft).
Suggested planting depth: 30–60cm (1–2ft).

Nymphaea 'Sir Galahad'

This tropical waterlily is vigorous and suitable for a large pool. The star-shaped, white flowers open at night and are held well above the large, waxy leaves, which have crinkled edges. In cold climates, grow under glass in a heated pool.
Approximate spread: to 3m (10ft).
Suggested planting depth: 20–90cm (8–36in).

Nymphaea 'Wood's White Knight'

A full peony-shaped white flower 25–30cm (10–12in) across with yellow stamens and a strong, pungent smell. The nearly-round leaves, 30–38cm (12–15in) across, have wavy and scalloped edges. A superb white for the larger pool.
Approximate spread: 2.4–3m (8–10ft).
Suggested planting depth: 45cm (18in).

YELLOW
Hardy waterlilies

Nymphaea 'Charlene Strawn'

The star-shaped, sweetly-scented flowers, 15–20cm (6–8in) across, have yellow petals surrounding yellow stamens. The nearly round green leaves are 20–23cm (8–9in) in diameter, displaying purple specks when young. This is one of the most fragrant waterlilies.
Approximate spread: 1–1.5m (3–5ft).
Suggested planting depth: 30cm (12in).

Nymphaea 'Marliacea Chromatella'

The cup- to star-shaped flowers, 15cm (6in) in diameter, have broad, incurved, canary-yellow petals and golden stamens. The coppery young leaves with purple streaks mature to attractive purple-mottled, round, green leaves, 15–20cm (6–8in) in diameter.
Approximate spread: 1.2–1.5m (4–5ft).
Suggested planting depth: 30–45cm (12–18in).

Nymphaea 'Sir Galahad'

Nymphaea 'Wood's White Knight'

Nymphaea 'Sioux'

Nymphaea 'Leopardess'

Nymphaea 'Odorata Sulphurea Grandiflora' (syn. *N.* 'Sunrise')

The cup-shaped, later star-shaped, sweet-smelling flowers, which are 15–18cm (6–7in) in diameter, have yellow petals and yellow stamens. The speckled, purple-blotched young leaves mature to broadly ovate green leaves, 25cm (10in) long. The flowers tend to open for only a short time from late morning to early afternoon.
Approximate spread: 1–1.2m (3–4ft).
Suggested planting depth: 30–45cm (12–18in).

Nymphaea 'Pygmaea Helvola' (syn. *N.* × *helvola*)

The cup-shaped, later star-shaped, flowers, which are no more than 5–8cm (2–3in) in diameter, have yellow petals and yellow stamens. The leaves are oval, 13cm (5in) long and 9cm (3½in) wide, heavily mottled and purple-blotched with purple undersides. This delightful small waterlily is a perfect plant for a barrel or sink.
Approximate spread: 60cm (2ft).
Suggested planting depth: 15–23cm (6–9in).

Tropical waterlilies

Nymphaea 'Afterglow'

The flat, sunflower-shaped flowers, 15–25cm (6–10in) in diameter, have yellow petals and golden orange stamens. The leaves are green and nearly round, 28cm (11in) in diameter, with wavy margins and purple undersides. This is a very colourful tropical waterlily.
Approximate spread: 1.8–2.4m (6–8ft).
Suggested planting depth: 30cm (12in).

Nymphaea 'Saint Louis'

The fragrant, star-shaped flowers, 20–28cm (8–11in) across, have lemon-yellow petals and golden-yellow stamens. The purple-blotched young leaves mature to broadly ovate, green leaves, which are occasionally wavy edged and to 50cm (20in) long.
Approximate spread: 2.4–3m (8–10ft).
Suggested planting depth: 38–60cm (15–24in).

CHANGEABLES
Hardy waterlilies

Nymphaea 'Aurora'

The cup-like, later flatter, flowers, 10–12cm (4–4½in) across, have petals that change from yellow-apricot to orange-red then deep burgundy-red on the third day. The leaves, 15–16cm (6–6½in) across, are green with the new leaves blotched purple.
Approximate spread: 1m (3ft).
Suggested planting depth: 25–30cm (10–12in).

Nymphaea 'Indiana'

The cup-like flowers, which when fully open can reach up to 9–10cm (3½–4in) across, have apricot petals, which change to apricot orange, then deep orange-red surrounding glowing orange stamens. The almost round leaves are quite small, eventually reaching 15cm (6in) in diameter. They are initially bronzy green with heavy mottling then become green with purple blotches.
Approximate spread: 75cm (30in).
Suggested planting depth: 23cm (9in).

Nymphaea 'Sioux'

The star-like flowers, 13–15cm (5–6in) across, have long petals, which deepen each day from yellowish-apricot to orange-red then apricot-orange surrounding golden yellow and orange stamens. The round leaves have a dappled purple perimeter when young, maturing to plain green, 20–23cm (8–9in) in diameter.
Approximate spread: 1.2m (4ft).
Suggested planting depth: 23–30cm (9–12in).

BLUE
Tropical waterlilies

Nymphaea 'Blue Beauty'

The fragrant, day-blooming, star-shaped flowers, 20–28cm (8–11in) across, have mauve petals surrounding yellow stamens. The oval, dark green, wavy-margined leaves grow to 35cm (14in) across and have brown speckling on the upper surface. It requires a minimum water temperature of 10°C (50°F).
Approximate spread: 1.2–2.2m (4–7ft).
Suggested planting depth: 38cm (15in).

Nymphaea caerulea

The day-blooming, star-shaped flowers, 15cm (6in) across, have pale blue petals surrounding yellow stamens. The oval, mid-green leaves are 30–40cm (12–16in) long and have purple spotting on the undersides.
Approximate spread: 2.4–3m (8–10ft).
Suggested planting depth: 30–40cm (12–16in).

Nymphaea 'Leopardess'

A day-blooming cultivar with cup-like flowers, 10–13cm (4–5in) across, which are clear blue with purple-tipped petals and yellow stamens. The nearly round, green-blotched purple leaves are green underneath with heavy speckles of purple and 25–30cm (10–12in) across.
Approximate spread: 1.2–1.5m (4–5ft).
Suggested planting depth: 30–45cm (12–18in).

Nymphaea 'Rhonda Kay'

This day-blooming cultivar has star-shaped, violet-blue flowers, 15cm (6in) across, held high above the water, with deep yellow stamens. The leaves are mid-green, slightly longer than they are wide at 28–30cm (11–12in) across.
Approximate spread: 1.8–2.7m (6–9ft).
Suggested planting depth: 45cm (18in).

Nymphaea micrantha

This day-blooming species from the west coast of Africa is free flowering, and can be confused with *N.* × *daubenyana*. The cup-like, later star-shaped, flowers are 2.5–10cm (1–4in) across and pale blue to white with creamy white stamens. The nearly round leaves, 8cm (3in) across, are pale green with reddish under-sides. It is the parent species to many wonderful cultivars.
Approximate spread: 60–75cm (2–2½ft).
Suggested planting depth: 30–45cm (12–18in).

Nymphaea 'Blue Beauty'

Nymphaea 'Rhonda Kay'

LOTUS

The genus (*Nelumbo*) contains two species of rhizomatous marginals from Asia, north Australia and eastern North America, where they are found in the shallow margins or muddy banks of pools. They have circular leaves, held horizontally well above the water. Their showy, solitary flowers are borne on long stalks, and develop distinctive "pepper pot" seed-heads. The flowers of the American species, *N. lutea*, approximately 20cm (8in) in diameter, are sulphur-coloured with dark yellow stamens. The Asiatic species, *N. nucifera*, has larger flowers, nearly 30cm (12in) across, with pink or white petals, deep rose on opening, but becoming paler with age. By the end of the third day, the petals are almost creamy white with a rosy-pink blush at the edges.

Lotus need ample sunshine or a high light intensity to ripen the thick roots in the mud. They need a minimum winter temperature of 5°C (41°F), but they will only do their best with a summer temperature of around 20°C (68°F). They can be grown in a large container of rich loam, with at least 30cm (12in) of soil under a covering of 8–15cm (3–6in) of water. Scoop out a depression in the compost for the rootstock, taking care not to damage the crown or growing point. Cover the rhizome with compost, leaving the growing point just sticking out above the surface. Add water and, when there is no danger of frost, stand outside in a hot sunny position. Propagate by dividing the fragile roots, which resent disturbance. In spring, plant the divisions just under the soil surface and just submerge until growth starts.

WHITE

Nelumbo nucifera 'Alba Grandiflora'
The large, white flowers are cup-shaped, 30cm (12in) in diameter, with golden stamens. The leaves grow to 40–58cm (16–23in) across.
Height: 1.2–1.8m (4–6ft); *spread:* indefinite.

Nelumbo nucifera 'Alba Striata'
The fragrant, globe-shaped, white flowers are 25–30cm (10–12cm) across, with the outer petals flushed with pale green and prominent, uneven red margins. The leaves can be as much as 70cm (28in) across.
Height: 1.2–1.5m (4–5ft); *spread:* indefinite.

Nelumbo 'Shiroman' (syn. *N.* var. *alba plena*)
The large, fully double, creamy white flowers are 25cm (10in) in diameter, but have little fragrance. The leaves grow to 62cm (25in) across.
Height: 1–1.5m (3–5ft); *spread:* indefinite.

Nelumbo leaves and seedhead

PINK AND RED

Nelumbo 'Charles Thomas'
The pink flowers are 15–20cm (6–8in) across, deeper at first, then change to a paler lavender-pink. The leaves grow to 35–56cm (14–22in) across.
Height: 60cm–1m (2–3ft); *spread:* indefinite.

Nelumbo 'Maggie Belle Slocum'
The large lavender-pink flowers are 25–30cm (10–12in) in diameter, and the inner petals beautifully rolled. The leaves are 50–62cm (20–25in) across. This lotus is good for tub culture.
Height: 1.2–1.5m (4–5ft); *spread:* indefinite.

Nelumbo nucifera 'Momo Botan'
The peony-like, double, deep rose-pink flowers with yellow bases are 13–15cm (5–6in) in diameter. The leaves have a diameter of 30–38cm (12–15in). The flowers last longer than most other lotuses, also staying open later into the day. This is particularly good for barrels.
Height: to 60cm–1.2m (2–4ft); *spread:* indefinite.

Nelumbo nucifera 'Mrs Perry D. Slocum'
The huge, double flowers are 30cm (12in) across. They open rose pink and change to creamy yellow. The leaves have a diameter of 45–58cm (18–23in). Because it is a changeable bicolor lotus, there are often different coloured flowers on the plant at the same time.
Height: 1.2–1.5m (4–5ft); *spread:* indefinite.

Nelumbo nucifera 'Pekinensis Rubra'
The slightly fragrant deep rose flowers are 20–30cm (8–12in) in diameter and turn pink as the flower matures. The leaves are 50–60cm (20–24in) across.
Height: 1.2–1.8m (4.6ft); *spread:* indefinite.

Nelumbo nucifera 'Rosea'
The fragrant flowers, which are 20–25cm (8–10in) in diameter, resemble those of a rose and have rose-pink petals and a yellow centre. The leaves are 45–50cm (18–20in) in diameter.
Height: 1.2–1.5m (4–5ft); *spread:* indefinite.

Nelumbo nucifera 'Rosea Plena'
This free-flowering lotus is a double form of *N. nucifera* 'Rosea'. The flowers, 25–33cm (10–13in) across, are a very deep rose pink, and the petals yellow towards the base. The leaves are 45–50cm (18–20in) in diameter.
Height: 1.2–1.5m (4–5ft); *spread:* indefinite.

YELLOW

Nelumbo lutea 'Flavescens'
The yellow flowers are 15–20cm (6–8in) across, with a red spot at the base of each petal. The leaves, like the flowers, have a red spot, and grow to a diameter of 33–43cm (13–17in).
Height: 1–1.5m (3–5ft); *spread:* indefinite.

Nelumbo lutea

MARGINALS

The word "marginal" is used to describe water garden plants that thrive with their roots and the basal part of their stem totally submerged in water or waterlogged soil. Different marginals tolerate different depths of water, and it is important to check that plants which prefer shallow water are not drowned by being too deep, even though in most cases short or seasonal changes in level will be tolerated; deciduous marginals will tolerate more water over their crowns in winter than in summer. Slightly deeper levels of water in the winter will also help to protect certain plants from frost and chilling winds. A good example is *Zantedeschia* (arum lily), which would never survive a severe winter in an ordinary soil outdoors but will be protected under a minimum of 15cm (6in) of water.

Vigorous species of marginals are prevented from invading the centre of the pond when the water becomes too deep for them to survive, which is why it is important to have marginal shelves that are no more than about 23cm (9in) deep when you are making a new pond.

Late spring is a good time to select and purchase marginals, when the new growth is thrusting from the fresh compost. Because so many marginals are vigorous growers it is best to plant them in aquatic containers. The depth of water given for the following marginals is the depth above the crowns and not the actual depth of water. Some containers are as much as 23cm (9in) deep, and the depth of the container should be added to the depth recommended here.

Acorus (Araceae)

The genus contains two perennial species originating in eastern Asia and widespread in the northern hemisphere, where they grow in shallow margins of lakes and ponds. The sword-shaped leaves bear a strong resemblance to those of *Iris*, and they have a distinctive, strong smell when bruised.
Propagation: By dividing the rhizomes into pieces, each containing two or three buds.
Hardiness: Hardy to half hardy.

Acorus calamus

Sweet flag, myrtle flag
This hardy, widespread plant is a vigorous species, ideal for a wildlife pool. Like many vigorous, temperate marginals, it is a good cover plant for waterfowl but does not have the piercing root tips and almost uncontrollable spreading habit of *Typha* (reedmace). The long, glossy sword-shaped leaves have a distinct midrib, and part of the leaf edge is noticeably crinkled. The flower is inconspicuous and unusual, resembling a small brown horn, which emerges at an angle just below the tip of a leaf.
Cultivation: Grow in full sun in water to 23cm (9in) deep.
Height: 60cm–1m (2–3ft); *spread:* indefinite.

Acorus calamus 'Argenteostriatus'

This is a much superior form for pools, where the cream-striped leaves make a striking impact in the margins. The variegation is maintained throughout summer, unlike the similar *Iris pseudacorus* 'Variegata' (variegated flag iris), which goes green by midsummer. It is slightly slower growing than *A. calamus*.
Cultivation: Grow in full sun in water to 23cm (9in) deep.
Height: 60cm–1m (2–3ft); *spread:* 60cm (2ft).

Acorus gramineus

Japanese rush
This is a much smaller plant than *A. calamus*, with a rather fan-like habit and glossy, sedge-like leaves that are semi-evergreen. It is slightly vulnerable in severe winters if the roots are not covered with water about 5–8cm (2–3in) deep. It will tolerate a very wide range of soil conditions, from being submerged in shallow water to being grown as a pot plant. There are some excellent cultivars, including 'Variegatus' (variegated Japanese rush), with striped creamy leaves, and 'Hakuro-nishiki', with pale green variegated leaves.
Cultivation: Grow in full sun in pond margins.
Height: 8–35cm (3–14in); *spread:* 10–15cm (4–6in).

Alisma (Alismataceae)

The nine species of aquatics in the genus are found across the world, but mainly in the northern hemisphere, where they grow in the muddy edges of marshes and lakes. The seeds,

Acorus calamus

Alisma plantago-aquatica

which are valuable food for wildlife, are the main method of propagation. They are produced in abundance and are capable of floating some distance. Unlike most aquatic seeds, they remain viable for up to a year.
Propagation: By seed or by division.
Hardiness: Hardy.

Alisma plantago-aquatica

Water plantain
This deciduous perennial has rosettes of oval, grey to grey-green, semi-upright, ribbed leaves, which have long leaf stalks that emerge well above the water. The tiny pinky-white flowers have three petals and are arranged in whorls on a pyramidal spike in midsummer.
Cultivation: Grow in a sunny position in water to 15cm (6in) deep.
Height: 75cm (30in); *spread:* 45cm (18in).

Butomus (Butomaceae)

A genus containing a single species of marginal perennial, which is found widely distributed in Europe, western Asia and north Africa and which has naturalized along the St Lawrence river near Montreal in North America.
Propagation: By removing the bulbils, which grow along the roots, and potting these individually in small pots of aquatic compost, or by dividing the rootstock in mid-spring.
Hardiness: Hardy.

Butomus umbellatus

Flowering rush, flowering gladiolus
Often found growing singly in the wild among a clump of reedmaces, it has long, dark green, pointed, narrow twisted leaves, with sheathed, triangular bases. The elegant flowers are borne above the leaves in a rounded pink flower-head.
Cultivation: Grow in rich mud or shallow water no deeper than 8–15cm (3–6in).
Height: 1m (3ft); *spread:* 45cm (18in).

Butomus umbellatus

Calla (Araceae)

A genus containing one species of perennial marginal from central and northern Europe, northern Asia and North America, where it is found in swamps, bogs and wet woods. In mild winters it is semi-evergreen.
Propagation: By dividing the surface root in spring, making sure that each piece contains a bud.
Hardiness: Hardy.

Calla palustris

Bog arum
The bog arum has conspicuous, long, creeping surface roots and round to heart-shaped, glossy, mid-green leaves, which are firm and leathery. The flowers, which appear in spring, resemble small, flattened arum lilies, and they are followed by clusters of red or orange berries.
Cultivation: Grow in full sun in water no deeper than 5cm (2in).
Height: 25cm (10in); *spread:* indefinite in the right conditions, but usually about 30cm (12in).

Caltha (Ranunculaceae)

This is a widespread and common genus containing ten species of temperate marginals, which are extremely popular in both decorative and wildlife ponds.
Propagation: By seed (apart from the double forms) or by division immediately after flowering.
Hardiness: Hardy to frost hardy.

Caltha palustris

Marsh marigold, kingcup
Indispensable for the pond margins, the native hardy marsh marigold needs little introduction. It has long-stalked lower leaves and stalkless upper leaves. The leaves are nearly round, heart-shaped at the base, and have toothed margins. The beautiful, waxy, yellow, buttercup-like flowers can appear as early as late winter in a mild season but are generally at their peak in mid-spring, when they brighten the spring garden, particularly when they are planted near the blue flowers of *Muscari* (grape hyacinth). They look best in groups in a sunny or partly shaded position at the very edge of the water, and they tolerate waterlogged or even slightly submerged conditions in winter and a degree of drying out in the summer. The white marsh marigold, *C. palustris* var. *alba*, differs from the common marsh marigold in having white flowers with yellow centres and a slightly more compact habit. The

double form, *C. palustris* 'Flore Pleno', covers its foliage with a mass of double yellow flowers, often producing a second flush in the summer.
Cultivation: Grow in sun or partial shade in water no deeper than 10–15cm (4–6in).
Height: 15–30cm (6–12in); *spread:* 45cm (18in).

Caltha palustris var. *palustris* (syn. *C. laeta*, *C. polypetala*)

Giant marsh marigold
This massive plant is suitable only for growing by the side of large ponds, where it can send its large yellow flowers on long stems as high as 1m (3ft). The dark green leaves are as much as 25–30cm (10–12in) across, forming strong hummocks of foliage.
Cultivation: Grow in sun in water to 10–13cm (4–5in) deep.
Height: 1m (3ft); *spread:* 75cm (30in).

Canna (Cannaceae)

Indian shot plant
The genus contains nine species that are native to tropical and subtropical America and that are used mainly as decorative terrestrial plants, but there is one species suitable for immersing in pools for the summer where it makes a showy specimen plant.
Propagation: By seed or by division of the rhizomes in spring so that each section has a prominent "eye".
Hardiness: Half hardy to frost tender.

Canna glauca

This tender species has long, slender stems with long, greyish, pointed leaves with whitish margins to 45cm (18in) long. Yellow flower spikes are produced intermittently throughout the summer. Several excellent

Caltha palustris

Carex riparia

Carex pendula

cultivars have been produced at Longwood Gardens in Pennsylvania, including *C.* 'Endeavour' (bright red), *C.* 'Erebus' (bright pink) and *C.* 'Taney' (bright orange).
Cultivation: Grow in a sunny position in containers of rich soil and submerged in water no deeper than 30cm (12in).
Height: 1.2–1.8m (4–6ft); *spread:* 50cm (20in).

Carex (Cyperaceae)

Sedge
This is a large genus, containing about 1,000 species of mainly temperate marsh plants, found throughout the world. They prefer slightly acid conditions, but some species are able to thrive in shallow water. All have grasslike, narrow leaves and triangular flower stalks bearing flowers in brownish spikes. See also the section on ornamental grasses.
Propagation: By division of the strong rhizomes.
Hardiness: Hardy to frost tender (unless otherwise stated).

Carex elata 'Aurea' (syn. *C. stricta* 'Aurea', *C. stricta* 'Bowles' Golden')

Bowles' golden sedge
This plant is particularly valuable in bringing a touch of yellow to the water's edge. It grows in dense tufts of bright grassy leaves. The flowers appear in early spring before the leaves turn bright yellow.
Cultivation: Grow in full sun or partial shade submerged in shallow water to 15cm (6in) deep or in an ordinary soil, kept constantly moist.
Height: 38cm (15in); *spread:* 45cm (18in).

Carex pendula

Pendulous sedge, drooping sedge
Ample space by the waterside and partial shade is required for the long spikes of pendulous flowers, which are held on stems 1m (3ft) long above the thick tufts of grassy leaves.
Cultivation: Grow in water no deeper than 2.5–5cm (1–2in).
Height: 60cm–1m (2–3ft); *spread:* 1.5m (5ft).

Carex pseudocyperus

Hardy to frost hardy, this is one of the more graceful of the sedges. It has bright green, grassy leaves, and the flowers form drooping dark green spikelets in the summer.
Cultivation: Grow in partial shade.
Height and spread: 60cm–1m (2–3ft).

Carex riparia

Great pond sedge
A coarse, tough plant, this is suitable only for the margins of a large wildlife pool. It has acutely triangular stems and leaf blades with a deep midrib. It often forms dense masses of leaves supporting a further cluster of foliage and flowers above.
Cultivation: Grow in sun or shade in water to 10–15cm (4–6in) deep.
Height: 1.5m (5ft); *spread:* 1–1.2m (3–4ft).

Colocasia (Araceae)

Taro
The genus of seven tropical species from Asia contains some species that thrive in shallow water and make bold architectural plants. In temperate areas they should be grown in reliably frost-free conservatories.
Propagation: By division of the rootstock in spring.
Hardiness: Frost tender.

Colocasia esculenta (syn. *C. antiquorum*)
Green taro
This striking plant forms an erect, tuberous rootstock, which bears long-stalked, arrow- to heart-shaped leaves that resemble elephants' ears. The leaf stalks are 8–25cm (3–10in) in length and the leaf blade grows up to 1m (3ft) long. The leaves vary in colour, often having prominent veins, which add to the ornamental value. The flowers, which are rather insignificant spathes, are borne during the summer. *C. esculenta* 'Fontanesii' has heart-shaped leaves with dark green veining and margins and violet leaf stalks.
Cultivation: Grow in partial shade to protect the leaves from sun scorch.
Height: 1.5m (5ft); *spread:* 60cm (2ft).

Colocasia esculenta

Cyperus involucratus

Equisetum hyemale

Cotula (Asteraceae)
Brass buttons
A cosmopolitan genus of about 75 mainly terrestrial species, which are found mostly in the southern hemisphere. One species can be considered as a true aquatic.
Propagation: By seed.
Hardiness: Frost hardy to half hardy.

Cotula coronopifolia
Bachelor's buttons, golden buttons
The various common names give a clue to the flower shape of this bright little marginal. It is an annual or short-lived, half-hardy perennial with several creeping succulent stems and strongly

Cotula coronopifolia

scented, toothed leaves. The plant is covered with masses of disc-shaped yellow flowers about 1cm (½in) in diameter. It tends to die down in the winter but regenerates easily in the spring from the masses of self-sown seed produced throughout the year.
Cultivation: Grow in full sun in shallow water 8–10cm (3–4in) deep.
Height: 15–30cm (6–12in); *spread:* to 30cm (12in).

Cyperus (Cyperaceae)
This large genus contains about 600 predominantly tropical species with a very wide distribution but only a few

temperate species. They are often referred to as umbrella sedges, and some are impressive in stature and can be grown as specimen clumps in conservatories or outdoor ponds.
Propagation: By seed or by division in the spring.
Hardiness: Hardy to frost tender.

Cyperus involucratus (syn. *C. alternifolius*)
Umbrella plant
This distinctive, tender perennial, which originates from Africa, can be grown as a houseplant as long as it is kept in a saucer of water, and is often, in fact, sold as a houseplant. In warm sheltered pools in subtropical gardens it makes an elegant marginal, the erect stems topped with several dark green radiating leaves. In the summer, tiny yellow flowers form clusters, 13cm (5in) across, at the top of the stems in the leaf axils, and turn brown after pollination.
Cultivation: Full sun or partial shade. Requires a minimum temperature of 5–10°C (41–50°F).
Height and spread: 60–75cm (24–30in).

Cyperus longus
Sweet galingale
The sweet galingale is one of the few hardy members of the genus and is a particularly attractive colonizer of muddy banks. It can spread very quickly so should be kept restricted to containers in small ponds. The almost triangular stems bear interesting, bright green, stiffly ribbed leaves that radiate from the top of the stem like the ribs of an umbrella. The brown flowers are rather inconspicuous spikelets interspersed among the leaves. It is an excellent plant for the wildlife

pool, particularly in late summer and autumn when the arching brown flowers come into their own.
Cultivation: Grow in full sun or partial shade.
Height: 60cm–1.2m (2–4ft); *spread:* 1m (3ft) or more.

Cyperus papyrus
Egyptian paper reed, giant papyrus
When grown in a sheltered, tropical situation or in a conservatory in temperate areas, this will make a tall, elegant specimen. It produces a thick rootstock with long, triangular, pithy stems, bearing mop-head tufts of fine long pendulous leaves and spikelets of brown flowers.
Cultivation: Grow in full sun and protect from wind.
Height: 3.6–4.5m (12–15ft); *spread:* 60cm–1.2m (2–4ft).

Equisetum (Equisetaceae)
Horsetail
The genus contains about 25 species from wet places in most regions of the world except Australia and New Zealand. Do not introduce any of the species into marginal beds where there is no restriction to their spreading.
Propagation: By division from spring to autumn.
Hardiness: Hardy.

Equisetum hyemale
Scouring rush, rough horsetail
This is an evergreen species. The hollow, leafless stems are ridged. A brownish pollen cone is produced at the tip of the spikes.
Cultivation: Grow in moist soil or covered with up to 20cm (8in) of water.
Height: 1.2m (4ft); *spread:* indefinite.

Eriophorum angustifolium

Glyceria maxima var. *variegata*

Equisetum scirpoides

A smaller species with fine, multi-branched, soft stems, which can be impressive in a half barrel or stone trough of water. The semi-prostrate, light green stems will spread indefinitely unless grown in a container.
Cultivation: Grow in full sun or partial shade in shallow water no deeper than 5cm (2in).
Height: 15cm (6in); *spread:* indefinite.

Eriophorum (Cyperaceae)

Cotton grass
A genus of 20 species found in bogs, marshes and shallow water margins of lakes and pools in most northern temperate regions. It spreads rapidly, particularly in acid conditions.
Propagation: By breaking off pieces from the clumps of spreading rootstocks.
Hardiness: Hardy.

Eriophorum angustifolium

Common cotton grass
Cotton grass is a widespread plant found in bogs, grown for the conspicuous white tassels of cotton-like flowers. Out of flower it is a rather dull plant, with short, leafy and angled stems, which will spread to form large clumps.

Houttuynia cordata 'Chameleon'

Cultivation: Grow in full sun and where it will not be covered by more than 5cm (2in) of water for any length of time.
Height: 30cm (12in); *spread:* indefinite.

Glyceria (Poaceae)

Manna grass, sweet grass
A widespread genus of 16 temperate species of aquatic grasses that quickly colonize the edges of streams and ponds. All species are extremely rapid spreaders and need to be kept in check.
Propagation: By dividing the creeping rootstocks.
Hardiness: Hardy to frost tender.

Glyceria maxima var. variegata (syn. G. spectabilis 'Variegata')

This highly ornamental, hardy aquatic grass deserves a place in the ornamental pond provided it is planted in an aquatic container. It has very striking leaves, which are striped cream, white and green, and in spring the young leaves are flushed with pink. The flowers form greenish spikelets in summer. It is very easy to grow.
Cultivation: Grow in full sun (for the best leaf colours) in water to 15cm (6in) deep.
Height: 60cm (2ft); *spread:* indefinite.

Houttuynia (Saururiaceae)

The genus contains a single species of temperate aquatic plant from eastern Asia. It flourishes in wet soil or the shallow margins of ponds and streams, producing extensive mats of shallow rhizomes.
Propagation: By dividing rhizomes in spring.
Hardiness: Borderline hardy.

Houttuynia cordata

This useful clump-forming, hardy perennial has spreading roots and erect, leafy red stems. The bluish-green, leathery, pointed leaves give off a pungent smell when crushed. In spring spikes of rather insignificant flowers surrounded by white bracts are produced. It is on the borderline of hardiness and requires the protection of a thick, leafy mulch in autumn. *H. cordata* can be invasive and should be grown in a container in a small pool.
Cultivation: Grow in a partially shaded position in water no deeper than 2.5–5cm (1–2in).
Height: 45–50cm (18–20in); *spread:* indefinite.

Houttuynia cordata 'Chameleon' (syn. H. c. 'Tricolor')

The leaves of this colourful cultivar are splashed with crimson, green and cream.
Cultivation: Grow in full sun (for the complete colour range) in water no deeper than 2.5–5cm (1–2in).
Height: 45–50cm (18–20in); *spread:* indefinite.

Iris (Iridaceae)

This is a large, widely distributed genus containing about 300 mainly temperate, moisture-loving species, and it is one of the most important groups in the water garden. All species have a wide tolerance of degrees of moisture, but the three described here are the most suitable for growing with their roots submerged in water. Some other species are described in the section on moisture-loving plants.
Propagation: By division of the rootstock in spring.
Hardiness: Hardy to frost tender. (Those described here are hardy.)

Iris laevigata

This species produces clumps of sword-shaped, soft green leaves. The sparsely branched stems bear between two and four broad-petalled, beardless, blue flowers in early summer. When it is not in flower, *I. laevigata* can be confused with *I. ensata* (syn. *I. kaempferi*), the Japanese iris, which has large, showy flowers but is not a true marginal, dying if the roots remain underwater in winter. The leaves of *I. laevigata* lack a midrib, while those of *I. ensata* have a distinct midrib. Of the many excellent cultivars of *I. laevigata*, one of the most impressive is 'Variegata', which has pale, lavender-blue flowers and lovely cream-and-white-striped leaves. 'Atropurpurea' has single, purple flowers; 'Richard Greany' has sky-blue single flowers; 'Snowdrift' has beautiful white single flowers; and 'Weymouth Blue' has blue single flowers.
Cultivation: Grow in water no deeper than 8–10cm (3–4in).
Height: 60cm–1m (2–3ft); *spread:* indefinite.

Iris pseudacorus

Flag iris
This vigorous perennial is often seen in sunny or shaded positions in ditches and along the margins of natural ponds and lakes. The strong, stiff, bluish-green, sword-shaped

Iris laevigata 'Snowdrift'

Juncus ensifolius

leaves, to 1m (3ft) long, emerge from a thick rhizome, which will spread for some distance, binding the soil surface. The tall, branched flower stems bear as many as ten beardless flowers on each stem. Each flower is yellow, with brownish veins and a deeper orange spot in the throat. It is ideal for the margins of a wildlife pool.
Cultivation: Grow in 15–30cm (6–12in) of water.
Height: 1–1.8m (3–6ft); *spread:* indefinite.

Iris pseudacorus var. *bastardii*
This form is not quite as vigorous as *I. pseudacorus* but has lovely, creamy yellow flowers, much lighter in colour.
Cultivation: Grow in 15–30cm (6–12in) of water.
Height: 1–1.8m (3–6ft); *spread:* indefinite.

Iris pseudacorus 'Variegata'
This is an excellent variegated form, which is suitable for small pools if it is grown in a container. The leaves have a striking, creamy-striped variegation, which appears in spring and gradually fades as the summer advances.
Cultivation: Grow in 15–30cm (6–12in) of water.
Height: 1–1.8m (3–6ft); *spread:* indefinite.

Iris versicolor
Blue flag
This free-flowering species is similar in vigour to *I. laevigata* and can spread extensively. The flowers are violet blue with yellow patches at the petal bases. The sword-shaped leaves are to 60cm (2ft) long.
Cultivation: Grow in permanently wet soil or with no more than 10cm (4in) of water above the roots.
Height: 60cm (2ft); *spread:* indefinite.

Juncus (Juncaceae)
Bog rush
This is a large cosmopolitan genus, containing more than 220 species, which are more prevalent in the northern hemisphere, where they occur mainly in marshes and bogs. Commonly referred to as rushes, their appearance is more similar to that of grasses, and they often have flattened leaves sheathed at the base.
Propagation: By dividing the grassy clumps in spring.
Hardiness: Hardy.

Juncus effusus
Common rush, soft rush
Forming ornamental tufts or clumps of green spikes, this species is used in large wildlife pools. It produces brown flower spikes.
Cultivation: Grow in full sun or partial shade with 8–13cm (3–5in) of water over the roots.
Height: 1m (3ft); *spread:* indefinite.

Juncus effusus f. *spiralis*
Corkscrew rush
This is a hardy form with dark green, needlelike leaves that are contorted or corkscrew-like. They create a point of interest in the shallows of a small pond.
Cultivation: Grow in full sun with no more than 8–13cm (3–5in) of water over the crown.
Height: 45cm (18in); *spread:* 30–40cm (12–16in).

Juncus ensifolius
This small member of the rush family is a charming hardy marginal for the side of a small pool and is particularly good for the side of a stream. It prefers very damp, mostly wet banks, where it

Iris versicolor

looks best in groups. It produces neat tufts of grassy foliage and attractive round brown flower spikes.
Cultivation: Grow in full sun in water no deeper than 5cm (2in).
Height: 30cm (12in); *spread:* indefinite.

Lysichiton (Araceae)
Skunk cabbage
The genus contains two temperate species of perennial bog plants from North America, Siberia and Japan. The unfortunate common name refers to the scent of the flowers.
Propagation: The thick roots grow deeply into a moist soil and become difficult to divide; propagation is best by seed.
Hardiness: Hardy.

Lysichiton americanus
Yellow skunk cabbage
This impressive plant provides an early spring display of yellow, aroid-like flowers, which are followed by huge, almost stalkless, paddle-like leaves capable of growing to almost 1.2m (4ft) high and spreading to 90cm (3ft).
Cultivation: Grow in full sun in no more than 2.5cm (1in) of water.
Height: 1.2m (4ft); *spread:* 1m (3ft).

Lysichiton camschatcensis
White skunk cabbage
This species, which has white flowers, is less vigorous than the more common *L. americanus* and is therefore more suitable for the margins of a small pond. The leaves are mottled and paddle-shaped, growing semi-upright from ground level with little or no leaf stalk.
Cultivation: Grow in full sun. It is on the borderline of tolerance to having shallow water over the roots, but provided there is a deep saturated soil it will not mind short periods of being submerged by shallow water.
Height and spread: 60–75cm (24–30in).

Iris laevigata 'Atropurpurea'

Mentha (Lamiaceae)

This is a genus of 25 species of temperate, aromatic plants, which prefer moist conditions and spread rapidly by underground rhizomes. The genus includes one species that will thrive in aquatic conditions and is now widely available as a marginal.
Propagation: By dividing the long, thin roots in spring and summer.
Hardiness: Hardy.

Mentha aquatica
Water mint
Common in ditches and alongside running water, water mint has lilac-coloured flowers, produced in terminal whorls above hairy, egg-shaped leaves with serrated margins.
Cultivation: Grow in full sun or partial shade. It can survive in a wide range of water depths but does best in water no deeper than 15cm (6in).
Height: 1m (3ft); *spread:* 1m (3ft) or more.

Menyanthes (Menyanthaceae)

Bog bean, marsh trefoil, buck bean
The single species in the genus is a temperate aquatic, distributed throughout North America, northern Asia, Europe and northwestern India. It is common in shallow pools and acid bogs, where its thick, spongy, creeping rootstocks quickly colonize the edges.
Propagation: By dividing the extensive roots in spring.
Hardiness: Hardy.

Menyanthes trifoliata
This excellent hardy perennial will quickly colonize the shallow waters at the margins of a large, sunny pool, as its thick, spongy rootstock spreads just underneath the surface of the water. The attractive foliage is clover-like, shiny, olive-green leaves, made up of three leaflets, with a long leaf stalk that clasps the spreading roots with a broad sheath. The flowers are particularly appealing. Dense spikes of dainty, frilled, white to purplish flowers emerge from pink buds and are held above the surface of the water. In a large, wildlife pool it provides excellent cover for submerged creatures in the shallow margins and can spread to form clumps of 1m (3ft) across or more in one year.
Cultivation: Grow in sun in water about 5cm (2in) deep. Containerize in a small pool and cut back hard any escaping roots each spring.
Height: 25–40cm (10–16in); *spread:* indefinite.

Mentha aquatica

Menyanthes trifoliata

Mimulus (Scrophulariaceae)

Musk, monkey flower
The genus contains about 150 temperate and subtropical species, native to North America, South Africa and Asia but not occurring naturally in Europe. Most of the species appreciate moisture-rich conditions, and a few make striking marginal plants.
Propagation: By seed.
Hardiness: Hardy to frost tender.

Mimulus guttatus (syn. *M. langsdorffii*)
Monkey musk, common monkey flower
This is a hardy species which originates from western North America. It grows submerged in water during the winter and produces aerial shoots in summer. It grows from robust stems, which have oval, toothed leaves and masses of yellow flowers. The flowers are marked with a pair of reddish-brown, hairy ridges.
Cultivation: Grow in full sun.
Height: 35–100cm (14–40in); *spread:* 50–120cm (20–48in).

Mimulus luteus
Yellow monkey flower
This is a vigorous, hardy species, which has prostrate, smooth, hollow stems. These stems root at the nodes and carry several bright yellow flowers with deep-red or purple spots.
Cultivation: Grow in full sun or light dappled shade.
Height: 10–30cm (4–12in); *spread:* 60cm (2ft).

Mimulus ringens
Allegheny monkey flower, lavender musk
This hardy species has branching square stems with dark green, narrowly oblong leaves. The blue to bluish-violet, snapdragon-like flowers are about 2.5cm (1in) long with a very narrow throat.
Cultivation: Grow in full sun in moist soil or in shallow water no deeper than 8–13cm (3–5in).
Height: 45cm (18in); *spread:* 30cm (12in).

Myosotis (Boraginaceae)

Forget-me-not
This genus of 50 temperate species, which are most commonly found in Europe and Australia and naturalized in North America, includes a few attractive aquatic forms that are indispensable to the water gardener.
Propagation: By stem cuttings from the young growth in spring or by division in spring or early summer.
Hardiness: Hardy.

Myosotis scorpioides
Water forget-me-not
This attractive hardy marginal has a slightly looser and more delicate habit of growth than most of the more rampant marginals. It bears the most delightful light blue flowers with yellow centres in midsummer. The angular stems are almost upright, becoming fully erect at the tips. The loose habit of growth combined with the delicacy of the small leaves and flower colourings makes this one of the

Mimulus guttatus

Orontium aquaticum

Ranunculus lingua

most sought-after marginals for ponds of all sizes. 'Mermaid' is an improved cultivar that is more free-flowering than the species.
Cultivation: Grow in full sun or light dappled shade in no more than 8cm (3in) of water.
Height: 23–30cm (9–12in); *spread:* 30cm (12in).

Orontium (Araceae)
Golden club
The genus contains a single species from temperate areas of eastern North America, where it grows in bogs or shallow water.
Propagation: By sowing seed as soon as it is ripe in midsummer.
Hardiness: Hardy.

Orontium aquaticum
This hardy species produces large, bluish-green, velvety, lance-shaped leaves with a silvery sheen on the undersides. The shades of the leaves are best appreciated when the plant is grown as a specimen. The white-stalked, pencil-shaped flowers that emerge from the water, tipped with yellow, resemble small golden pokers.
Cultivation: Grow in full sun in water between 38–45cm (15–18in) deep. In water deeper than 30cm (12in) the leaves float on the surface.
Height: 45cm (18in); *spread:* 75cm (30in).

Peltandra (Araceae)
Arrow arum
The genus contains two species from temperate North America, closely related to the arums. They are suitable

for muddy margins or shallow water, scrambling over the surface, with the long rhizomes rooting at the nodes.
Propagation: By dividing sections of the rhizomes in spring so that each section contains a bud.
Hardiness: Hardy.

Peltandra sagittifolia (syn. *P. alba*)
White arrow arum
The hardy species has strong, bright green, arrow-shaped and veined leaves growing from a short rhizome. The arum-like flowers are white, about 8–10cm (3–4in) long, and are followed by fleshy red berries in late summer.
Cultivation: Grow in full sun in water no deeper than 10–15cm (4–6in).
Height: 45cm (18in); *spread:* 60cm (2ft).

Peltandra undulata (syn. *P. virginica*)
Green arrow arum
This species is distinguished from *P. sagittifolia* by its narrower and greener flower spathe, which produces red rather than green berries. The firm leaves are narrowly arrow shaped.
Cultivation: Grow in full sun in water no deeper than 10–15cm (4–6in).
Height: 75cm (30in); *spread:* 60cm (2ft).

Persicaria (Polygonaceae)
The large genus contains about 80 species, some of which were previously classified as *Bistorta*, *Polygonum* and *Tovara*. The species are found in tropical and temperate areas throughout the world, and many are excellent moisture-loving plants, with one species suitable for marginal planting.
Propagation: By stem cuttings in midsummer.
Hardiness: Hardy to frost hardy.

Persicaria amphibia
Amphibious bistort, willow grass
A hardy, stem-rooting perennial, this is useful for pools with a

Peltandra undulata

fluctuating water level. The lance-shaped leaves clasp the stem with long petioles that emerge from a papery sheath. The flowers form neat pink spikes.
Cultivation: Grow in full sun in water 30cm–1m (1–3ft) deep.
Height: 30–60cm (1–2ft); *spread:* indefinite.

Pontederia (Pontederiaceae)
This genus of shallow-water plants from temperate and subtropical areas in North and South America contains just five species. They are useful plants for both formal and informal water gardens, having a strong shape and blue flower in late summer.
Propagation: By division in late spring.
Hardiness: Hardy to frost hardy.

Pontederia cordata
Pickerel weed
This hardy, perennial marginal is undoubtedly one of the most decorative blue-flowered plants available from aquatic suppliers. It is a robust, tidy plant. The thick, creeping rootstock supports shiny, erect, heart-shaped leaves, which are olive green with exquisite swirled markings. A delightful soft blue flower spike appears from a leaf bract at the top of the stem.
Cultivation: Grow with up to 13cm (5in) of water above its crown. Plant in full sun so that it shows off its full flowering potential.
Height: 45–60cm (18–24in); *spread:* 75cm (30in).

Ranunculus (Ranunculaceae)
There are about 400 species of temperate and tropical moisture-loving and aquatic plants in this large, cosmopolitan genus. Of these, almost 40 grow in water.
Propagation: By division in spring and summer.
Hardiness: Hardy.

Ranunculus flammula
Lesser spearwort
This hardy perennial member of the buttercup family is suitable for a small pool, unlike many of its relatives, which can be rank growers. Although this plant is most at home in the shallows of a wildlife pool, it can be containerized easily. It makes a good low-growing spread of yellow flowers over a long season in a smaller pond, producing

semi-prostrate, reddish stems and dark green, lance-shaped leaves, 1–2.5cm (½–1in) long. The shallowly cup-shaped, bright yellow flowers, 2cm (¾in) in diameter, are borne in clusters in early summer.
Cultivation: Grow in full sun or partial shade.
Height: 60cm (2ft); *spread:* 1m (3ft).

Ranunculus lingua
Greater spearwort
This is a hardy, vigorous plant, with hollow, reddish stems. The long-stalked, heart-shaped leaves grow on the non-flowering shoots, and narrower, longer leaves with short stalks grow on the flowering shoots. The large yellow flowers are 2.5–5cm (1–2in) across. Its rather sappy growth means that it is easily blown over in exposed situations.
Cultivation: Grow in full sun in water up to 23cm (9in) deep.
Height: 1.5m (5ft); *spread:* 1.8m (6ft).

Sagittaria (Alismataceae)
A cosmopolitan genus, there are 20 species of aquatics found in a wide variety of habitats, but mainly in shallow water, on muddy shores and in marshes. They are often referred to as duck potatoes because the over-wintering tubers on the ends of their roots are often eaten by wildfowl. In deep water these plants produce only submerged, ribbon-like leaves, but when they are grown in the pond margins they produce their more characteristic arrow-shaped leaves.
Propagation: By division in spring.
Hardiness: Hardy to frost tender.

Sagittaria latifolia

Schoenoplectus lacustris subsp.
tabernaemontani 'Zebrinus'

Scrophularia auriculata 'Variegata'

Sagittaria latifolia
Duck potato, wapato
This is a hardy plant, which will tolerate a wide range of water depths. In shallow water it grows arrow-shaped leaves 10–30cm (4–12in) long and bears whorls of three-petalled white flowers in summer. Short branching tubers are produced on the tips of the roots.
Cultivation: Grow in full sun in water to 30cm (12in) deep.
Height: 45–90cm (18–36in); *spread:* 1m (3ft).

Sagittaria sagittifolia (syn. *S. japonica*)
Arrowhead
This hardy species is not quite as vigorous as *S. latifolia*. The arrow-shaped leaves, which grow to 20–25cm (8–10in), have long, acute basal lobes. The white flowers are borne on three angled stems in whorls of three with a purple blotch at the base of each petal.
Cultivation: Grow in full sun in water no deeper than 15cm (6in).
Height: 1m (3ft); *spread:* indefinite.

Sagittaria sagittifolia 'Flore Pleno'
This handsome, hardy, double form has round, double white flowers, about 2.5cm (1in) in diameter, arranged around a spike.
Cultivation: Grow in full sun in water no deeper than 5cm (2in) because flowering will be restricted in deeper water.
Height: 1m (3ft); *spread:* indefinite.

Saururus (Saururaceae)
Lizard's tail
The genus contains two shallow-water, clump-forming species from North America and east Asia. The common name refers to the distinctive pendulous flower spikes.
Propagation: By division in spring.
Hardiness: Hardy.

Saururus cernuus
American swamp lily
This is a rampant plant in shallow water. It has heart-shaped, bright green leaves and tiny, fragrant, white flowers held in a nodding, semi-pendulous spike, 10–15cm (4–6in) long in late summer.
Cultivation: Grow in water 10cm (4in) deep. It prefers full sun but will tolerate light shade.
Height: 30–60cm (1–2ft); *spread:* 30cm (1ft).

Schoenoplectus (Cyperaceae)
Bulrush
The 80 species in the genus are widely distributed in temperate and tropical areas, found in marshes and shallow water. Bulrushes have very long stems, which grow from a rampant stolon, and for this reason they need to be kept in a container in a small pool. They look best grown as a group at the side of a large wildlife pool.
Propagation: By division of the extensive rootstock during spring and summer.
Hardiness: Hardy.

Schoenoplectus lacustris subsp. *tabernaemontani* 'Albescens'
The erect, cylindrical stems have attractive cream banding which runs the length of the stem, making a bold display when they are seen against a dark background. The flowers are insignificant brown spikelets held on the tips of the long stems.

Cultivation: Grow in full sun (to encourage the colour of the stems) in water to 15cm (6in) deep. Cut out any all-green stems.
Height: 1.2–1.5m (4–5ft); *spread:* indefinite.

Schoenoplectus lacustris subsp. *tabernaemontani* 'Zebrinus'
Zebra rush
This variegated bulrush is very effective in groups around the edge of a large pond. This cultivar has horizontal cream stripes on the stems, which resemble porcupine quills. The inconspicuous flowers appear at the tips of the long leafless stems in the form of a brown spikelet.
Cultivation: Grow in full sun (to maintain the cream banding) in water 8–10cm (3–4in) deep. Cut out any all-green stems.
Height: 1–1.2m (3–4ft); *spread:* indefinite.

Scrophularia (Scrophulariaceae)
Figwort
Although there are almost 200 species in this widely distributed genus of temperate and subtropical plants, mainly from the northern hemisphere, only one species is used by the water gardener for planting in shallow water.
Propagation: By division in spring.
Hardiness: Hardy to half hardy.

Thalia dealbata

Scrophularia auriculata 'Variegata'
Water figwort
This is an evergreen, clump-forming, hardy perennial, with stiff square stems. The nettle-like leaves have creamy margins and light green centres; smaller leaves are almost entirely cream. Spikes of insignificant, greenish-purple flowers are held above the foliage and much appreciated by bees.
Cultivation: Grow in full sun in water no deeper than 8cm (3in).
Height: 1m (3ft); *spread:* 60cm (2ft).

Sparganium (Sparganiaceae)
Burr weed
There are 21 mainly temperate species in this genus. They are found throughout the northern hemisphere, where they are common on the edges of large lakes, forming clumps in association with reeds and reedmaces. They are valuable plants for waterfowl, which use them as nesting sites and winter food.
Propagation: By seed or by division in spring.
Hardiness: Hardy.

Sparganium erectum (syn. S. ramosum)
This species, which is native to Europe and Asia, has rhizomatous roots that have strong pointed tips and bear rosettes of long, sword-shaped leaves, which are triangular at the base. In summer erect, unbranched flower spikes bear densely packed round, greenish-brown flowerheads, which are followed by prickly brown fruit.
Cultivation: Grow in full sun in water to 45cm (18in) deep.
Height: 1.5m (5ft); *spread:* indefinite.

Thalia (Marantaceae)
The genus contains 12 swamp-loving species from tropical and subtropical America and Africa. One or two species make striking specimens for the waterside of tropical pools.
Propagation: Mainly by seed, but large clumps can be divided in spring.
Hardiness: Half hardy to frost tender.

Thalia dealbata
This architecturally striking plant is tender. It has long, thick, glaucous blue leaves dusted with a white powder. Carried high above the leaves are the unusual small violet flowers. In temperate areas it makes an excellent conservatory plant.
Cultivation: Grow in full sun in 30–45cm (12–18in) of water.
Height: 1.8–3m (6–10ft); *spread:* 1.8m (6ft).

Typha minima

Typha (Typhaceae)
Reedmace, cat's tail
The genus contains ten species of cosmopolitan marsh-loving plants. They should be introduced with caution, however, because most species are extremely invasive and are capable of puncturing pool liners with the needlelike tips of their extensive rhizomes. The brown, poker-like flower-heads make popular dried flowers.
Propagation: By division of the rootstock in spring.
Hardiness: Hardy.

Typha angustifolia
Lesser reedmace, narrow-leaved cat's tail
This hardy species has slender, dark green leaves. The characteristic brown flower spikes are held above the leaves, with the male and female flowers separated by a gap of about 2.5cm (1in).
Cultivation: Grow in full sun. They will tolerate a water depth of up to 45cm (18in).
Height: 1.5m (5ft); *spread:* indefinite.

Typha laxmannii (syn. T. stenophylla)
Graceful cat's tail
This species is more elegant and slightly less invasive than *T. angustifolia*. It has greyish-green, half-round leaves, which are grooved on one side.
Cultivation: Grow in full sun in water to 30cm (12in) deep.
Height: 1.2–1.5m (4–5ft); *spread:* indefinite.

Typha minima
This small species is suitable for even the smallest pool. The leaves are needlelike, and the dark brown flower spikes are round.
Cultivation: Grow in full sun in water 8–10cm (3–4in) deep.
Height: 30–45cm (12–18in); *spread:* 60cm (2ft).

Veronica (Scrophulariaceae)
Speedwell
The large variable genus contains about 250 species, mainly from the northern hemisphere, which include a few hardy marginals.
Propagation: By softwood cuttings from the young growth in summer.
Hardiness: Hardy to frost hardy.

Veronica beccabunga
Brooklime
This is a hardy species, bearing spikes of dark blue flowers with white centres and glossy, rounded, fleshy leaves, which grow from cylindrical, hollow stems. It is an excellent plant for covering muddy banks.
Cultivation: Grow in full sun in water no more than 8cm (3in) deep.
Height: 30cm (12in); *spread:* indefinite.

Zantedeschia (Araceae)
A genus of six tender South African species, these are marsh-loving plants with thick rhizomes and arrow-shaped leaves, often with white, transparent dots. Many hybrids have been developed as decorative container plants.
Propagation: By seed or division in spring.
Hardiness: Hardy to frost tender.

Zantedeschia aethiopica (syn. Calla aethiopica)
Arum lily
This is the familiar florist's arum lily which can also be grown in the water garden as a tender marginal aquatic. It makes a distinctive specimen plant, forming a clump of arrow-shaped, glossy green leaves. From late spring to midsummer it produces the striking, exotic-looking, white flowers with yellow centres.
Cultivation: Grow in full sun or partial shade. In temperate areas it requires protection from cold winds and frost; submerge the plants in 30cm (12in) of water in winter in order to protect them in cold areas.
Height: 60cm–1m (2–3ft); *spread:* 60cm (2ft).

Zantedeschia aethiopica 'Crowborough'
This cultivar is the hardiest of the arum lilies and for this reason it is highly recommended for growing in colder positions. It is a truly striking sight if it is planted in groups, particularly in the margins of an informal pool.
Cultivation: Grow in sun or partial shade in 15cm (6in) of water.
Height: 60cm (2ft); *spread:* 45cm (18in).

Zantedeschia aethiopica 'Green Goddess'
An interesting frost-hardy cultivar, this has white flowers, which are heavily flushed with green.
Cultivation: Grow in full sun in moist soil or shallow margins where the covering of water is no more than 2.5–5cm (1–2in).
Height: 70cm (28in); *spread:* 23cm (9in).

Veronica beccabunga

Zantedeschia aethiopica 'Crowborough'

MOISTURE-LOVING PLANTS

The water's surface forms only one part of the water garden, and beyond the actual margins of the pool where the soil becomes moist, but is not saturated, there is a huge canvas on which to compose a setting for the water. There is a wide range of plants that are ideally suited to this moist zone, ranging in size from trees to tiny carpeting plants. The art of planting this area is to make it appear as much a part of the water garden as the waterlilies. Whereas many marginals may survive in this drier regime, moisture-lovers cannot cross into the saturated soil where the lack of oxygen will kill the roots. With ample moisture, however, the plants will grow quickly, and restraint is necessary in the density of planting in the same way as for the shallow-water plants because they quickly become overgrown.

Achillea (Asteraceae)
Yarrow
The genus contains about 85 temperate species from Europe, western Asia and North America. Although most species prefer a drier soil, *A. ptarmica* thrives in the moist soil by the water's edge.
Propagation: By division.
Hardiness: Hardy.

Achillea ptarmica
Sneezewort
This invasive perennial has strong stems with narrow, toothed, lance-shaped, dark green leaves. The loose, white flower-heads, 2–10cm (¾–4in) across, appear from early to late summer. 'Unschuld' is also white.
Cultivation: Grow in full sun in moist, well-drained soil.
Height: 60–90cm (2–3ft); *spread:* 60cm (2ft).

Aconitum (Ranunculaceae)
Aconite, monkshood, helmet flower, wolfsbane
A genus of about 100 temperate species from Europe, Asia and North America, which are found mainly on grassland and scrub. Certain species look particularly beautiful when they are massed by the waterside where

Achillea ptarmica 'Unschuld'

their flowers become exceptionally large. It is important to note that all aconites are poisonous.
Propagation: By seed or by division.
Hardiness: Hardy.

Aconitum napellus
Helmet flower, turk's cap, friar's cap.
This erect, hardy perennial has rounded, deeply lobed, dark green leaves, with the lobes further divided. The navy blue flowers are borne in dense spikes in midsummer.
Cultivation: Grow in full sun in moist soil.
Height: 1.2m (4ft); *spread:* 30cm (12in).

Aconitum napellus

Ajuga (Lamiaceae)
Bugle
This is a genus of 40 temperate and subtropical perennial creeping plants, which thrive in the damp soil by streams and informal pools.
Propagation: By division or by separating root stems.
Hardiness: Hardy.

Ajuga reptans
This creeping perennial, which can become invasive, is a good ground-cover plant. It has dark green, oblong to spoon-shaped leaves, 5–8cm (2–3in) long. Dark blue flowers are held in short spikes, 15cm (6in) tall, in late spring and early summer. Several cultivars have colourful leaves.
Cultivation: Grow in any moist soil in partial shade because the foliage will scorch in full sun.
Height: 15–20cm (6–8in); *spread:* indefinite.

Alchemilla (Rosaceae)
Lady's mantle
This is a large genus of about 300 hardy temperate species from Europe, Asia and America. They have a wide variety of uses and are particularly attractive when ample moisture allows them to reach their full potential.
Propagation: By seed or by division of large clumps.
Hardiness: Hardy to frost hardy.

Alchemilla mollis
This hardy perennial has roundish, downy leaves, 10–13cm (4–5in) across. The tiny flowers are yellowish-green and held in feathery sprays in early summer. Deadhead after flowering to prevent self-sowing.
Cultivation: Grow in full sun or partial shade in rich, moist soil.
Height: 45cm (18in); *spread:* 75cm (30in).

Anagallis (Primulaceae)
Pimpernel
This is a widely distributed genus of 20 species of small herbs, found in bogs, meadows and dry sites around the Mediterranean and in western Europe. *A. tenella* is especially suitable for moist, almost boggy, sites.
Propagation: By seed.
Hardiness: Hardy to frost hardy.

Anagallis tenella
Bog pimpernel
This hardy perennial has creeping masses of small, light green, roundish leaves. Small, pink, scented, bell-shaped flowers appear in midsummer.
Cultivation: Grow in full sun in moist, well-drained soil.
Height: 5–10cm (2–4in); *spread:* 40cm (16in).

Alchemilla mollis

Anagallis tenella

Angelica (Apiaceae)

This is a genus of 50 temperate species from damp woodland, fens and stream banks in the northern hemisphere. They are generally large, architectural plants, which look well as specimens in an informal woodland water garden.
Propagation: By seed.
Hardiness: Hardy.

Angelica archangelica

Garden angelica, archangel
A statuesque addition to the water garden, this hardy perennial has large, deeply indented leaves, carried on thick stems. The small, cream-white flowers are clustered together in large, round umbels, 25cm (10in) across, on short ribbed flower stems.
Cultivation: Grow in full or partial shade in deep, rich soil.
Height: 1.8m (6ft); *spread:* 1.2m (4ft).

Arum (Araceae)

A genus of 26 species of tuberous perennials, flowering mainly in the spring, these plants are native to shaded habitats in southern Europe, northern Africa and western Asia.
Propagation: By seed in spring.
Hardiness: Hardy to half hardy.

Arum italicum

This hardy perennial has attractive, arrow-shaped, green leaves, marked with white veins and up to 35cm (14in) long, which appear from late winter until early summer. The flowers are greenish-white spathes, 15–40cm (6–16in) long, and they are followed by columns of vermilion berries on stout stalks.
Cultivation: Grow in partial shade in rich, well-drained soil.
Height: 30cm (12in); *spread:* 15cm (6in).

Astilboides tabularis

Arundo (Poaceae)

A genus of three reedy grasses from the warmer parts of the Old World. These decorative grasses carry large, feathery flower spikes and make distinctive specimen plants in containers in temperate areas so that they can be moved under cover in winter.
Propagation: By seed.
Hardiness: Half hardy.

Arundo donax

Giant reed
Although this magnificent plant can grow to 6m (20ft) in its natural habitat, it usually reaches only about 3m (10ft) in the colder parts of North America and Britain. It is grown for its attractive, bamboo-like foliage on thick, jointed stems and its large flower spikes, which are reddish at first, later turning white.
Cultivation: Grow in full sun, out of strong winds; protect in winter.
Height: 6m (20ft); *spread:* 1.5m (5ft).

Arundo donax var. *versicolor* (syn. *A. donax* 'Variegata')

This is smaller and less hardy than the species. The leaves are attractively striped with green and ivory-white.
Cultivation: Grow in full sun and give protection in winter.
Height: 1.8m (6ft); *spread:* 60cm (2ft).

Astrantia major subsp. *involucrata* 'Shaggy'

Astilbe (Saxifragaceae)

The genus contains about 12 temperate perennial species, originating from North America and S. E. Asia, and includes both tall and dwarf, handsome, herbaceous perennials. These make a colourful contribution to waterside planting. Their attractive foliage provides good undergrowth from which rise tapering, feathery spikes of white, crimson or pink flowers. The dry flower-heads are a rusty shade of brown, and provide an additional bonus in the autumn and winter if they are left on the plant.
Propagation: By division in early spring.
Hardiness: Hardy.

Astilbe × *arendsii*

This group contains many garden hybrids with a tremendous range of colours and foliage characteristics. They grow to 50–120cm (20–48in) tall. 'Elizabeth Bloom' is pale pink, while 'Fanal' has deep crimson flowers and dark green foliage.
Cultivation: Grow in sun or partial shade in moist, rich soil.
Height: 50–120cm (20–48in); *spread:* 20–90cm (8–36in).

Astilbe simplicifolia

This dwarf species from Japan bears short, attractively arched panicles of creamy coloured flowers above glossy foliage.
Cultivation: Grow in sun or partial shade in moist, rich soil.
Height and spread: 20cm (8in).

Astilboides (Saxifragaceae)

The single species in this genus is a moisture-loving perennial herb from woodland habitats in northern China. It thrives in shady, temperate gardens.
Propagation: By seed.
Hardiness: Hardy.

Astilboides tabularis (syn. *Rodgersia tabularis*)

This distinctive species has almost round, lotus-like, pale green leaves, borne on a central leaf stalk. The creamy white, clustered flowers are held above the leaves on strong stems.
Cultivation: Grow in shade in cool, moist soil and sheltered from wind.
Height: 1m (3ft); *spread:* 1.2m (4ft).

Astrantia (Apiaceae)

Hattie's pincushion, masterwort
The genus contains about 10 species of perennials, native to alpine woods and meadows of Europe and Asia.
Propagation: By seed or by division in spring.
Hardiness: Hardy.

Astrantia major

Greater masterwort
This European species bears five-lobed leaves in basal rosettes and erect umbels of small, five-petalled pink and green flowers, which are surrounded by bracts. *A. major* subsp. *involucrata* 'Shaggy' has white flowers and long, green-tipped bracts.
Cultivation: Grow in partial shade in rich, moist soil.
Height: 60cm (2ft); *spread:* 45cm (18in).

Arum italicum 'Pictum'

Astilbe 'Elizabeth Bloom'

Cardamine (Brassicaceae)

Bittercress
The genus contains 150 species of annuals and perennials, which mainly originate from the cool regions of the northern hemisphere. Some species in this genus become invasive weeds, so care must be taken.
Propagation: By seed.
Hardiness: Hardy.

Cardamine pratensis

Lady's smock, cuckoo flower, mayflower, meadow cress
The rosy-lilac flowers grow above cress-like leaves in late spring. It seeds itself easily when happy and makes an excellent plant for the fringes of the wildlife pool, where it can be successfully naturalized in long grass.
Cultivation: Grow in full or partial shade in rich soil.
Height: 30–50cm (12–20in); *spread:* 30cm (12in).

Cardamine pratensis 'Flore Pleno'

The double form is a more showy plant than the species. It has rosettes of cress-like leaves and masses of small, double, pale lilac flowers about 23–30cm (9–12in) tall. Being double flowered, it is unable to seed itself, but it spreads by the leaves taking root and developing new plantlets.
Cultivation: Grow in full or partial shade in rich soil.
Height: 20cm (8in); *spread:* 30cm (12in).

Cimicifuga (Ranunculaceae)

Bugbane, cohosh
The genus includes about 15 showy perennial species from Europe, central and eastern Asia and North America, where they are found in moist, shady grassland, woodland or scrub. The common name of bugbane owes its origin to the plant's traditional use to deter fleas.
Propagation: By seed.
Hardiness: Hardy.

Cimicifuga simplex

Flowering in late summer or early autumn, this clump-forming perennial has narrow spires of pure white, bottlebrush-like flowers. The plant has attractive, deeply divided leaves held on wiry stems, which, despite their fragile appearance, are extremely strong.
Cultivation: Grow in partial shade in fertile soil.
Height: 1.8m (6ft); *spread:* 60cm (2ft).

Cardamine pratensis

Cimicifuga simplex var. *simplex* 'Brunette'

This is a very striking cultivar which has purplish-black leaves and compact flower spikes. These grow to a length of 20cm (8in). This cultivar has purple-tinted, off-white flowers.
Cultivation: Grow in partial shade in fertile soil.
Height: 1.2m (4ft); *spread:* 60cm (2ft).

Crocosmia (Iridaceae)

Montbretia
The seven species of this genus are clump-forming, mainly hardy perennials, which are native to South Africa. They have long, narrow leaves, rather similar to those of *Iris*, and they make a very striking display in late summer when their mainly red or orange flowers appear.
Propagation: By seed or by dividing thick clumps in spring.
Hardiness: Hardy to frost hardy.

Crocosmia × *curtonus*

This forms a strong, upright clump of pleated mid-green leaves with bright tomato-red flowers nearly 5cm (2in) long on slightly arching, sparsely branched spikes in midsummer.
Cultivation: Grow in full sun or partial shade.
Height: 1–1.2m (3–4ft); *spread:* 15cm (6in).

Crocosmia 'Lucifer'

Another cultivar with upright flowers which are a bright tomato-red colour, 5cm (2in) long in bold, slightly arching spikes during midsummer.
Cultivation: Sun or partial shade.
Height: 1–1.2m (3–4ft); *spread:* 30cm (12in) or more.

Crocosmia 'Lucifer'

Crocosmia masoniorum

This species differs from the other crocosmias because its arching flower stems hold vermilion or orange flowers upright instead of facing forwards under the stem. The sword-shaped, dark green leaves turn a warm beige as they fade.
Cultivation: Grow in full sun or partial shade.
Height: 1m (3ft); *spread:* 8cm (3in).

Darmera (Saxifragaceae)

Formerly known as *Peltiphyllum*, this is a North American genus, containing a single species. It makes a versatile plant for the waterside, tolerating a wide range of conditions of varying degrees of moisture.
Propagation: By seed or by division in spring.
Hardiness: Hardy.

Darmera peltata (syn. *Peltiphyllum peltatum*)

Umbrella plant, Indian rhubarb
This hardy perennial will make a bold statement at the edge of a pool, where its large round leaves can be reflected in the water. In early spring, before the leaves appear, it produces small, starry, pink flowers, which are borne in rounded heads on slender, red-tinted stalks, 30–60cm (1–2ft) long. The leaves appear in mid-spring, after the frosts and, like the flowers, are held well above the ground on slender stalks. The common name derives from the shape of the leaves, which form large, deep green, heavily veined plates, deeply lobed and coarsely toothed, nearly 60cm (2ft) in diameter and turning beautiful shades of red in autumn. The roots form thick surface rhizomes, which are extremely useful for stabilizing the muddy banks of a pond.

Cimicifuga simplex

Darmera peltata

Cultivation: Grow in a sheltered position in muddy, almost saturated soil in full sun or partial shade. Do not grow where water covers the roots. *Height:* 1–1.8m (3–6ft); *spread:* 1m (3ft) or more.

Dodecatheon
(Primulaceae)
American cowslip
The genus contains 14 hardy perennial species from North America, ranging from damp valleys in the prairies to the Rocky Mountains. All the species closely resemble one another but vary in height. They become dormant in the summer after flowering and make good subjects for rocky slopes near a stream.
Propagation: By seed or divide large clumps in spring.
Hardiness: Hardy.

Dodecatheon meadia (syn. *D. pauciflorum*)
Shooting star
This species has distinctive rose-magenta, cyclamen-like flowers, 1–2cm (½–¾in) long, borne on strong stems above a basal rosette of oval, toothed, pale to mid-green leaves 25cm (10in) long. After fertilization the flowers point upwards, giving it the common name of shooting star.
Cultivation: Grow in full sun or partial shade in a moist, fertile soil.
Height: 60cm (2ft); *spread:* 25cm (10in).

Eupatorium (Asteraceae)
Hemp agrimony
The genus contains about 40 species of hardy perennials, annuals and sub-shrubs, mostly from America,

Dodecatheon meadia

Eupatorium purpureum

with some from the Old World. They are large, rather coarse, easily grown plants which are only suitable for large gardens in damp soil near extensive informal or wildlife pools.
Propagation: By division in spring.
Hardiness: Hardy to frost tender.

Eupatorium cannabinum
This tall, clump-forming, hardy perennial bears pink, purple or white flowers in terminal clusters in late summer and early autumn. The downy leaves are 13cm (5in) across with coarsely toothed lobes. It is prone to wilting in strong sun if there is inadequate moisture at the root.
Cultivation: Grow in partial shade.
Height: 60cm–1.5m (2–5ft); *spread:* 1.2m (4ft).

Eupatorium purpureum
Joe-pye weed
A clump-forming, hardy perennial, this resembles *E. cannabinum* but is larger and more brightly coloured, with flat flowerheads, sometimes reaching 30cm (1ft) across, of fluffy, mauve-pink, upturned flowers on dark purplish stalks.
Cultivation: Grow in partial shade.
Height: 2.2m (7ft); *spread:* 1m (3ft).

Filipendula (Rosaceae)
This small genus of about 10 species of hardy perennials, similar to *Spiraea* and found in the Himalayas, northern Asia, Europe and North America, prefer mostly moist places. Most are suitable for planting in a woodland garden or damp meadows near a wildlife pool.
Propagation: By seed.
Hardiness: Hardy.

Filipendula ulmaria

Filipendula ulmaria
Queen of the meadow, meadowsweet
This is a clump-forming perennial which is excellent for the wildlife garden. It produces creamy flowers in dense corymbs, to 25cm (10in) across, above strong, erect stems bearing pinnate leaves, 5–10cm (2–4in) across, which are downy on the underside.
Cultivation: Grow in full sun or partial shade.
Height: 1–1.5m (3–5ft); *spread:* 60cm (2ft).

Gentiana (Gentianaceae)
The large genus contains about 400 species of annual or perennial plants, which are widely distributed across Europe, Asia, North and South America and New Zealand. The more familiar blue-flowered gentians are excellent for growing in rock

gardens, provided that the soil is acidic. There is one species, however, *G. asclepiadea*, which prefers moist conditions in woodland, where it associates particularly well with grasses and ferns.
Propagation: By seed.
Hardiness: Hardy.

Gentiana asclepiadea
Willow gentian
This plant, which is native to Europe, is a reliable and graceful plant, with narrow, willow-like leaves and rich blue flowers, which are arranged in axillary clusters around the upper half of the stem.
Cultivation: Grow in deep moist soil and plenty of shade.
Height: 30–60cm (1–2ft); *spread:* 45cm (18in).

Geum (Rosaceae)
A genus of about 50 species of rhizomatous perennials, which are widely distributed throughout the world, especially in cold and temperate regions. They can be grown as border or rock plants, and some species are ideal in moist soil near an informal pool.
Propagation: By seed or by division in autumn or spring.
Hardiness: Hardy.

Geum rivale
Water avens
A lover of wet meadows and marshy places, water avens bears pendent, dull, purplish-pink flowers and strawberry-like leaves. The reddish-brown sepals are almost as long as the petals.
Cultivation: Grow in full sun.
Height: 25–30cm (10–12in); *spread:* 60cm (2ft).

Gentiana asclepiadea

Gunnera manicata

Gunnera (Gunneraceae)

A genus of 40–50 species of slightly tender perennials, which are widely distributed in the southern hemisphere. Some of them are gigantic plants, producing huge leaves, and they can be grown outside in temperate areas. Plenty of moisture and protection from wind is needed if they are to be seen at their best. Cover the crowns in winter with the dead leaves as soon as they are frosted.
Propagation: By seed.
Hardiness: Hardy to frost hardy.

Gunnera magellanica

This is a tiny, mat-forming herbaceous perennial. The dark green, rounded to kidney-shaped leaves grow to 6cm (2½in) across and are tinged bronze when young.
Cultivation: Grow in sun or partial shade.
Height: 8–15cm (3–6in); *spread:* 30cm (12in) or more.

Gunnera manicata (syn. *G. brasiliensis*)
Giant rhubarb
This is the largest species of *Gunnera*, with prickly stems 1.8m (6ft) tall and vast leaves, to 1.8m (6ft) across, that are harsh, bristly and deeply lobed. The curious flower spike is like a huge bottlebrush, 30cm–1m (1–3ft) tall, tinged with red. It grows from a very thick root covered in brown papery scales that look like fur. It is spectacular when reflected in water.
Cultivation: Grow in sun or partial shade.
Height: 2.4m (8ft); *spread:* 4m (13ft).

Hemerocallis (Hemerocallidaceae)
Daylily
This genus contains about 15 species of herbaceous perennials from eastern Asia, and they provide a colourful contribution to the sides of a water garden. The individual flowers last for only one day but are produced in a long succession. There are countless cultivars available, many of which are improved dwarf strains suitable for the smaller garden.
Propagation: By division in spring.
Hardiness: Hardy to frost hardy.

Hemerocallis cultivars

There are more than 30,000 named cultivars of *Hemerocallis*, many of which are derived from *H. fulva* and *H. multiflora*. They are mostly clump-forming plants, with arching, strap-shaped, dark green leaves, usually 75–120cm (30–48in) long, but many dwarfer forms are now being introduced. The flowers are borne on erect stems over a long period, mainly from late spring to late summer. The flowers range in colour from almost white, through yellow and orange to dark purple and deepest red-black. *H.* 'Wind Song' is a semi-evergreen cultivar with wide leaves and creamy-yellow almost round flowers, 15cm (6in) across, on sturdy stems in early and midsummer.
Cultivation: Grow in full sun.
Height: 62cm–1m (25–36in); *spread:* 45cm–1m (18–36in).

Heracleum (Apiaceae)
The genus contains about 60 species of large biennial or perennial plants from northern temperate regions and some tropical mountain regions. They should be avoided by those susceptible to skin allergies.
Propagation: By seed.
Hardiness: Hardy.

Heracleum mantegazzianum

Giant cow parsnip, giant hogweed
A good subject for the waterside, this plant has large, basal, divided leaves, 1m (3ft) wide, and wheel-like heads of white flowers on stout hollow stems.
Cultivation: Grow in sun or partial shade.
Height: 2.4–3m (8–10ft); *spread:* 1.8m (6ft).

Hosta (Hostaceae)
This genus contains about 70 species of hardy, clump-forming, handsome herbaceous perennials, which are mainly native to eastern Asia, especially Japan. From these species numerous cultivars have been developed, and the naming is often somewhat confused. Their foliage is especially attractive

Heracleum mantegazzianum

Hemerocallis 'Wind Song'

near the waterside, and although they can be grown in most soils, they are at their best in moist conditions.
Propagation: By division.
Hardiness: Hardy.

Hosta crispula

This has broadly lance- to heart-shaped leaves, wavy margined, 20–30cm (8–12in) long, tapering to twisted tips, and with irregular white margins. The flowers are lavender-white.
Cultivation: Grow in moist soil in full or partial shade.
Height: 80cm (32in); *spread:* 1m (3ft).

Hosta cultivars

H. 'Honeybells' grows to 75cm (30in) and spreads to 1.2m (4ft). It has pale-green, heart-shaped leaves, 28cm (11in) long, with strong vein markings, growing in an open mound shape. The bell-shaped flowers are white, occasionally lavender blue on stems reaching 1m (3ft) long in late summer. It should be grown in partial shade. 'Hadspen Blue' also prefers partial shade, and grows to 25cm (10in) high and spreads to 60cm (24in). This cultivar has thick, grey-blue, close-veined leaves, 13cm (5in) long. The bell-shaped, pale, grey-mauve flowers are held on purple-spotted flower spikes 35cm (14in) long. 'Sum and Substance', which can grow in sun or partial shade, grows to 75cm (30in) and spreads to 1.2m (4ft). This distinctive cultivar has heart-shaped glossy, yellow-green leaves, 50cm (20in)

Hosta sieboldiana

long, which become puckered when mature. Very pale lilac bell-shaped flowers are produced in midsummer on stems 1m (3ft) long.
Cultivation: Grow in moist soil in full or partial shade.

Hosta fortunei
A vigorous species, this has heart-shaped, matt, dark green, wavy edged leaves, about 20cm (8in) long. It has the bonus of striking, pale lilac flowers that are carried well above the foliage.
Cultivation: Grow in moist soil in full or partial shade.
Height and spread: 80cm (32in).

Hosta lancifolia
This hosta forms a dense mound of arching, long-pointed, shining dark green leaves, 10–18cm (4–7in) long, making overlapping mounds, from which arise large, deep lilac, trumpet-shaped flowers on tall, slender stalks.
Cultivation: Grow in moist soil in full or partial shade.
Height: 60cm (2ft); *spread:* 75cm (30in).

Hosta plantaginea
This is one of the choicest, plain-foliaged species. It has beautiful, glossy, bright green, arching, heart-shaped leaves, 15–28cm (6–11in) long. The trumpet-like, marble white flowers are produced late in the season and have a delicate, lily-like fragrance. Unusually, this species prefers a sunny position.
Cultivation: Grow in moist soil in sun.
Height: 60cm (2ft); *spread:* 1m (3ft).

Hosta sieboldiana
This species produces the most dramatic leaves of all the hostas. The large, distinctly pointed, cordate leaves may vary in depth of colouring, being grey-green, bluish or glaucous and reaching a length of 35cm (14in). In early summer bell-shaped, pale lilac-grey flowers, which fade to white, are borne on stems 1m (3ft) long.
Cultivation: Grow in moist soil in full or partial shade.
Height: 80cm (32in); *spread:* 1.2m (4ft).

Hosta undulata
This species has almost spirally twisted, pointed leaves, to 9cm (3½in) wide, with bold creamy-white variegation running lengthways down the leaf and dark green, undulating margins. Funnel-shaped mauve flowers are borne in early and midsummer.
Cultivation: Grow in moist soil in full or partial shade.
Height and spread: 45cm (18in).

Hosta ventricosa 'Variegata'
This variety has distinctive leaves which are irregularly margined with yellow and later turn creamy-white. Leafy flower stems, which grow to 80–100cm (32–40in) in height, bear tubular, bell-shaped, deep purple flowers in midsummer.
Cultivation: Grow in partial shade.
Height: 50cm (20in); *spread:* to 1m (3ft).

Inula
(Asteraceae/Compositae)
A genus of about 100 species of annuals, perennials and a few sub-shrubs found in temperate regions of Europe, Asia and America, these plants are characterized by their large, flat, daisy-like flower-heads. They make ideal plants for the wild garden.
Propagation: By division in autumn or spring.
Hardiness: Hardy to frost hardy.

Inula magnifica
This is a giant hardy perennial, which requires ample space to be appreciated. The enormous, broad, dock-like leaves have a rough matt texture, and they make a large mound at the base of the plant, becoming smaller as they climb the brown stems. At the tips of the stems, brown buds open to large, vivid deep yellow, fine-rayed daisies, 13–15cm (5–6in) across.
Cultivation: Grow in full sun.
Height: 1.8m (6ft); *spread:* 1m (3ft).

Inula magnifica

Iris (Iridaceae)
The genus contains about 300 species of herbaceous perennials from a wide range of habitats in the northern hemisphere. Irises are synonymous with water gardens, and a careful selection of forms will provide a lengthy flowering season. Three species suitable for the margins of a pool are described in the section on marginals.
Propagation: Those suitable for the moist areas near water are propagated by division.
Hardiness: Hardy to frost tender.

Iris chrysographes
A native of western China, this species has grassy leaves and flowers that are rich velvety purple with golden-yellow etched veins.
Cultivation: Grow in full sun.
Height and spread: 60cm (2ft).

Iris ensata (syn. *I. kaempferi*)
Japanese water iris
These clematis-flowered irises from Japan range in colour from white to shades of pink, lavender, blue, violet, yellow and crimson; some are plain and others have bold and elaborate markings on the petals. The leaves are 20–60cm (8–24in) long with a prominent midrib. They can flourish in shallow water during the summer but must not be waterlogged in the winter. They are the most exotic of all the irises, with their butterfly-like flowers, which are held horizontally, providing an unequalled show of colour.
Cultivation: Grow in full sun.
Height: 1m (3ft); *spread:* 30cm (1ft).

Iris fulva
Louisiana iris
Originating in the southern United States, these irises have strap-shaped, bright green leaves, arching at the tips. The slender, slightly zigzag stems bear from four to six copper or orange-red flowers, 6–7cm (2½–3in) across, in late spring.
Cultivation: Grow in full sun.
Height and spread: 60cm (2ft).

Iris sibirica
Siberian iris
Native to Europe and northern Asia, this iris has grass-like leaves, to 45cm (18in) long. Slender, branching heads of violet-blue flowers are produced in early summer, with the fall petals marked with an area of yellow or white veining in the centre. The narrow, shining, chestnut-brown seed-heads are an added attraction.
Cultivation: Grow in full sun.
Height: 1m (3ft); *spread:* indefinite.

Hosta ventricosa

Hosta ventricosa 'Variegata'

Iris sibirica

Leucojum aestivum

Lobelia cardinalis

Ligularia dentata 'Desdemona'

Leucojum (Amaryllidaceae)
Snowflake
The genus contains nine or ten species of bulbous plants originating from central Europe and the Mediterranean region. The green-tipped, white flowers resemble large snowdrops.
Propagation: By seed or by removing offsets from around the bulb once the leaves have died down.
Hardiness: Hardy to frost hardy.

Leucojum aestivum
Summer snowflake
This species looks spectacular when it is planted in large clumps by the waterside. It produces glossy, daffodil-like leaves of richest green and sturdy green stems, supporting bell-shaped white flowers with each outer petal tipped in green.
Cultivation: Grow in full sun.
Height: 30–60cm (1–2ft); *spread:* 8cm (3in).

Leucojum vernum
Spring snowflake
This delightful little spring-flowering species has strap-shaped, semi-erect, green basal leaves. Leafless stems bear one or two pendent, bell-shaped, fragrant flowers with six white petals tipped with green.
Cultivation: Grow in full sun.
Height: 20–30cm (8–12in); *spread:* 8cm (3in).

Ligularia (Asteraceae)
This is a large genus, containing about 180 species of herbaceous, moisture-loving perennials, which are native to the Old World, north of the tropics. They are imposing,

statuesque waterside plants, which can either be grown in striking groups or, alternatively, treated as specimen planting.
Propagation: By seed or by dividing in spring or after flowering.
Hardiness: Hardy.

Ligularia dentata 'Desdemona'
Rounded, brownish green leaves with a deep maroon-purple underside form a basal cluster below deep orange flower-heads.
Cultivation: Partial shade is better as the leaves are prone to wilting in strong sun.
Height and spread: to 1m (3ft).

Ligularia 'Gregynog Gold'
This is an excellent choice for the smaller water garden, where most of the ligularias would be too tall. This variety has handsome, richly veined, heart-shaped leaves, growing to 35cm (14in) long, and huge, conical spires of large, vivid orange-yellow flowers.
Cultivation: Grow in full sun or partial shade.
Height: 1–1.2m (3–4ft); *spread:* 1m (3ft).

Ligularia przewalskii (syn. *Senecio przewalskii*)
This species has very finely cut, dark green leaves, to 30cm (12in) long. The leaves resemble fingers and are borne on nearly black stems that bear a spire of small, yellow daisy-like flowers.
Cultivation: Grow in partial shade. It will wilt easily in bright light if the soil is not kept moist.
Height: 1.5–1.8 (5–6ft); *spread:* 1m (3ft).

Lobelia (Campanulaceae)
This genus of more than 350 species of annual and perennial plants is found in tropical and temperate regions, especially the Americas. The perennial species are elegant and brightly coloured waterside plants, which look stunning when planted in groups. Although ample moisture is required in the summer, they should not be too wet in the winter.
Propagation: By seed; take cuttings of *L. cardinalis* in summer.
Hardiness: Hardy to frost tender.

Lobelia cardinalis
Cardinal flower
This striking species is native to North America, and it is a clump-forming, rather short-lived, frost hardy rhizomatous perennial. The lance-shaped leaves make a basal rosette and may vary in colour from fresh green to red-bronze. Leafy stems support strong spikes of intensely vivid, scarlet-lipped flowers in late summer.
Cultivation: Grow in full sun.
Height: 1m (3ft); *spread:* 30cm (1ft).

Lobelia × *gerardii* 'Vedrariensis'
This is a reliable frost hardy perennial with basal rosettes of lance-shaped, dark green leaves, 10cm (4in) long, often with a reddish tinge. Stout stems bear racemes of long-lasting, rich violet flowers throughout the summer.
Cultivation: Grow in full sun.
Height: 1m (3ft); *spread:* 30cm (1ft).

Lobelia siphilitica
Blue cardinal flower
Native to the eastern United States, this clump-forming, hardy perennial bears erect stems with whorls of crinkly light green leaves on the lower part and blue, two-lipped flowers at the top.
Cultivation: Grow in partial or full shade.
Height: 60cm (2ft); *spread*: 30cm (1ft).

Lobelia × *speciosa*
This hybrid closely resembles *L. cardinalis* but is not so hardy. It has deeper and showier flowers and deep maroon leaves. There are numerous and beautiful cultivars, such as *L.* 'Queen Victoria' and *L.* 'Bees' Flame', both of which have dazzling, large, velvety, scarlet flowers and crimson-maroon leaves.
Cultivation: Grow in full sun or partial shade.
Height: 1m (3ft); *spread:* 50cm (20in).

Lychnis (Caryophyllaceae)
Catchfly, campion
The genus contains between 15 and 20 species of biennials and perennials, which are found in a wide range of habitats in northern temperate regions. One species make a charming waterside plant for the wildlife pool.
Propagation: By seed.
Hardiness: Hardy.

Lychnis flos-cuculi

Lychnis flos-cuculi
Ragged robin
Native to Europe, this species flowers in spring, bearing star-shaped, pale to bright purplish-pink flowers with deeply cut petals. The flowers are sparsely produced on loose stems.
Cultivation: Grow in full sun.
Height: 30–60cm (1–2ft); *spread:* 80cm (32in).

Lysimachia
(Primulaceae)
Loosestrife
A genus of 150 species of mostly herbaceous perennials, found through-out the world in temperate and subtropical regions. Larger species are suitable for moist mixed borders or bog gardens. Low-growing species provide ground cover in muddy soil.
Propagation: By seed or by division in spring or autumn.
Hardiness: Hardy to frost tender.

Lysimachia nummularia
Creeping Jenny
Originating in central Europe, this hardy creeping plant is useful for carpeting edges by the waterside. The small, rounded, green leaves hug the ground. In early summer bright yellow, cupped, upturned flowers, 2cm (¾in) across, are borne along the stems. The yellow-leaved cultivar, *L. nummularia* 'Aurea', is preferable to the green-leaved species.
Cultivation: Grow in full sun.
Height: 5cm (2in); *spread:* indefinite.

Lythrum (Lythraceae)
Loosestrife
There are about 38 species of hardy herbaceous plants and small shrubs in the genus. They are found in damp

Lythrum salicaria

places throughout the temperate regions and are ideal for mass planting in wild garden settings where there is plenty of moisture. They are extremely invasive, and the planting of some species is prohibited in many areas of the United States.
Propagation: By seed or by division in spring.
Hardiness: Hardy.

Lythrum salicaria
Purple loosestrife
This tall, leafy, clump-forming perennial has erect, stiff stems bearing lance-shaped, downy leaves, 10cm (4in) long. It produces tall, slender spires, 45cm (18in) long, of star-shaped, bright purple-red to purple-pink flowers from midsummer to early autumn.
Cultivation: Grow in full sun.
Height: 1.2m (4ft); *spread:* 45cm (18in) or more.

Lythrum salicaria 'Feuerkerze' (syn. *L. salicaria* 'Firecandle')
This is a slightly more compact cultivar, bearing intense rose-red flowers.
Cultivation: Grow in full sun.
Height: 1m (3ft); *spread:* 45cm (18in).

Macleaya (Papaveraceae)
Plume poppy
There are three species from China and Japan in this genus of large herbaceous plants with handsome leaves. They thrive in moist but well-drained soil.
Propagation: By seed or by division.
Hardiness: Hardy.

Macleaya cordata
A hardy perennial, this has grey to olive-green leaves with rounded, toothed lobes, which are white-downy

Macleaya cordata

Persicaria cuspidatum

beneath. Large, plume-like panicles of pendent buff-white flowers are borne on grey-green stems in midsummer.
Cultivation: Grow in full sun.
Height: 1.5–2.2m (5–7ft); *spread:* 1m (3ft).

Persicaria
(Polygonaceae)
This genus contains between 50 and 80 species of annual and perennial herbs, mainly from temperate regions around the world, which grow in the moist soils near pools and streams. They range in size from large, thicket-like canes to low-spreading, ground-cover plants.
Propagation: By division of the perennial species.
Hardiness: Hardy to half hardy.

Persicaria amplexicaulis (syn. *Polygonum amplexicaule*)
This hardy plant has a long-lasting display of spiky flowers from midsummer to autumn. It makes lush, leafy growth in moist soils, producing lance-shaped, mid-green leaves, 25cm (10in) long. The sprawling growth culminates in thin spikes of vivid crimson flowers.
Cultivation: Grow in full sun or partial shade.
Height and spread: 1.2m (4ft).

Persicaria bistorta (syn. *Polygonum bistorta*)
Snakeweed, bistort
This vigorous, hardy plant has clusters of basal leaves, 8–15cm (3–6in) long, that are oval, pointed and boldly veined. The flowers form erect, broad, pink spikes, 5–8cm (2–3in) long.
Cultivation: Grow in full sun.
Height: 80cm (32in); *spread:* 1m (3ft).

Persicaria bistorta 'Superba'

Persicaria bistorta 'Superba'
This hardy cultivar produces fat pokers of densely packed flowers of soft mauve-pink in midsummer above large, dock-like leaves.
Cultivation: Grow in full sun.
Height and spread: 1m (3ft).

Persicaria cuspidatum
Originating from Japan, Korea and China, this hardy, vigorous species grows on damp hillsides. It is ideal for a large garden where its spreading roots have ample room. It has several stems clothed with large, pale green, oval leaves, which hang over small chains of creamy green flowers.
Cultivation: Grow in sun or shade.
Height: 1.5–2.25m (5–7ft); *spread:* indefinite.

Petasites (Asteraceae)
Butterbur, sweet coltsfoot
The genus contains 14 to 15 species of moisture-loving perennials with invasive rhizomes from Europe, Asia and North America. The round leaves are effective but can be a nuisance once established.
Propagation: By division in spring and autumn.
Hardiness: Hardy to frost hardy.

Petasites fragrans

Petasites fragrans
Winter heliotrope
Native to Europe, this is one of the earliest flowering plants for the waterside, providing valuable early nectar for bees. From late winter to early spring the almond-scented clusters of starry, pale lilac flowers, which grow to 1cm (½in) across, are surrounded by large, rounded, light green leaves, 15–20cm (6–8in) in diameter. This is not reliably hardy, but the rhizome may survive below ground, even if the top growth is damaged by frost.
Cultivation: Grow in partial or full shade.
Height: 30cm (1ft); *spread:* 1.5m (5ft).

Phormium (Agavaceae)
Flax lily
The genus contains two species from New Zealand. They are exceptionally striking plants, providing strong architectural features in damp soil provided there is adequate drainage in winter. They make good plants for coastal gardens.
Propagation: By seed or by division in spring.
Hardiness: Borderline hardy.

Phormium tenax
New Zealand flax
This impressive plant has rigid, upright leaves, to 3m (10ft) long, which are dark green above and blue-green beneath. The stout flower stems grow above the foliage and support dull red, tubular flowers in a spike, which are followed by long-lasting, curved seed pods.
Cultivation: Grow in full sun.
Height: 3.6m (12ft); *spread:* 1.8m (6ft).

Primula (Primulaceae)
The large genus contains around 400 species, mainly from northern temperate regions. Many species are suited to the moist soil by streams and informal pools, where they provide a vivid display in late spring and early summer, particularly when they are massed into large groups.
Propagation: By seed as soon as ripe in late summer or by division in late summer or early autumn.
Hardiness: Unless specified, all those described here are hardy.

Primula alpicola
One of the many primulas from the Himalayas, this is native to Tibet. The toothed or scalloped elliptical leaves, 10cm (4in) long, form a rosette at the base of the plant. The pale yellow, white or violet, fragrant, tubular, drooping flowers are borne on mealy stems in umbels of 6–12 flowers.
Cultivation: Grow in partial shade.
Height: 15–50cm (6–20in); *spread:* 30cm (1ft).

Primula beesiana
This deciduous, sometimes evergreen, candelabra primula from China forms rosettes of leaves that die down in winter to basal buds or reduced rosettes. It has toothed, mid-green leaves with red midribs. White, mealy flower stems bear 2 to 8 whorls of yellow-eyed, reddish-pink flowers, 2cm (¾in) across.
Cultivation: Grow in partial shade.
Height: 23cm (9in); *spread:* 60cm (2ft).

Primula bulleyana
This Chinese candelabra primula is a rosette-forming species with toothed, mid-green, lance-shaped leaves,

which grow to 30cm (12in) in length. In early summer, stout stems bear 5 to 7 whorls of crimson flower buds which open to orange flowers.
Cultivation: Grow in partial shade.
Height and spread: 60cm (2ft).

Primula prolifera
This is a vigorous Chinese species. The spoon- to diamond-shaped basal leaves are finely toothed, deep green and to 35cm (14in) long. The candelabra flower spike bears from one to seven whorls of fragrant, white-mealy, pale to golden-yellow flowers, 2.5cm (1in) across.
Cultivation: Grow in partial shade.
Height: 1m (3ft); *spread:* 60cm (2ft).

Primula pulverulenta
Native to China, this is one of the most elegant candelabra primulas. The leaves are slightly smaller and more wrinkled than many of the other candelabra primulas, and the flowers are enhanced by the mealy farina on the flower stem. The tubular flowers are deep-red or red-purple, 2.5cm (1in) across, and are borne in early summer.
Cultivation: Grow in partial shade.
Height and spread: 60cm (2ft).

Primula rosea
Native to the Himalayas, this is one of the earliest to flower. The mid-green basal leaves, 20cm (8in) long, are lance-shaped, finely toothed and bronzed initially. They form rosettes and emerge after the flowers. The yellow-eyed, red-pink flowers, 2.5cm (1in) across, are produced in polyanthus-like umbels.
Cultivation: Grow in partial shade.
Height: 15–23cm (6–9in); *spread:* 20cm (8in).

Phormium tenax

Primula sikkimensis
Himalayan cowslip
The lance-shaped, pale green leaves, 30cm (1ft) long, are toothed, shiny and grow in basal rosettes. The white-mealy, funnel-shaped, yellow or cream flowers, 2.5cm (1in) across, are produced in umbels in late spring.
Cultivation: Grow in partial shade.
Height: 60cm–1m (2–3ft); *spread:* 60cm (2ft).

Primula vialii
The flowers of this frost hardy Chinese species resemble tiny red-hot pokers. The basal, rosette-forming leaves have toothed edges and are hairy and broadly lance-shaped, growing to 30cm (12in) long. Stiff, stout, white-mealy stems support dense flower spikes, 15cm (6in) long, of small, tubular, blue-violet flowers in midsummer.
Cultivation: Grow in partial shade.
Height and spread: 30cm (1ft).

Primula bulleyana

Primula beesiana

Ranunculus ficaria 'Brazen Hussy'

Rheum palmatum

Rodgersia pinnata

Senecio smithii

Ranunculus
(Ranunculaceae)

There are approximately 400 species of temperate and tropical moisture-loving and aquatic plants in this large, cosmopolitan genus. Of these, almost 40 can be grown in water.
Propagation: By division in spring and summer.
Hardiness: Hardy to half hardy.

Ranunculus ficaria 'Brazen Hussy'

This is a hardy cultivar of the lesser celandine which produces glossy, deep chocolate-brown leaves and shining, golden yellow flowers with a bronze reverse. The heart-shaped leaves, 2–5cm (¼–2in) across, appear in early spring and die down after flowering.
Cultivation: Grow in sun or partial shade.
Height: 5cm (2in); *spread:* 30cm (12in).

Rheum (Polygonaceae)

Originating in Siberia, the Himalayas and eastern Asia, this genus includes about 50 species of strong perennial herbs which have thick, woody rhizomes. They resemble giant rhubarbs and are a superb choice for specimen planting by the side of the pool.
Propagation: By seed or by division in early spring.
Hardiness: Hardy.

Rheum alexandrae

From western China, this species is much smaller than most other rheums. It has rosettes of attractively veined, dark green, glossy leaves, 20cm (8in) across, with heart-shaped bases. In early summer the yellow-green flowers appear in spikes that are 60cm (2ft) long, with the flowers partially obscured by creamy coloured bracts, which highlight the spike even more.
Cultivation: Grow in full sun or partial shade.
Height: 1m (3ft); *spread:* 60cm (2ft).

Rheum palmatum
Chinese rhubarb

Native to China and Tibet, this is the most often grown species. It has huge, apple-green, rounded, palmately lobed and coarsely toothed leaves, growing 1m (3ft) long and with red undersides. In early summer, stems 1.8 (6ft) high carry panicles of masses of tiny, star-shaped, creamy-green to deep-red flowers.
Cultivation: Grow in full sun or partial shade.
Height: 1.8–2.4m (6–8ft); *spread:* 1.8m (6ft).

Rodgersia (Saxifragaceae)

The genus of six species of handsome, erect, herbaceous perennials is native to China and Japan. The plants thrive in moist peaty soils if they are sheltered from wind; they do very well in the woodland margins.
Propagation: By seed or by division in early spring.
Hardiness: Hardy.

Rodgersia aesculifolia

This clump-forming Chinese species has leaves like those of the horse chestnut. They are 25cm (10in) long, with densely woolly, red-brown stalks and veins. The numerous small white or pink flowers are star shaped and are borne in large panicles, to 60cm (2ft) long, which resemble astilbes.
Cultivation: Grow in full or partial shade.
Height: 1.2–1.5m (4–5ft); *spread:* 1m (3ft).

Rodgersia pinnata

Another Chinese species, this has pinnate, crinkled leaves, which are glossy and dark green, 90cm (36in) long, and heavily veined. Reddish-green stems bear star-shaped, yellowish-white, pink or red flowers in panicles that are 30–70cm (12–28in) long.
Cultivation: Grow in full or partial shade.
Height: 1.2m (4ft); *spread:* 75cm (30in).

Schizostylis (Iridaceae)
Kaffir lily

The single species in this genus is a temperate, bulbous-like herbaceous plant from South Africa. It is rather similar to the gladiolus and is an excellent choice for near the water's edge. They flower late into the autumn and extend the colours of the water garden with various cultivars in shades of orange and pink.
Propagation: by seed or division in the spring.
Hardiness: Borderline hardy.

Schizostylis coccinea

The species has long, sheathing, sword-shaped leaves, 40cm (16in) long, with distinct midribs. The scarlet flowers are open, cup-shaped, 2cm (¾in) across, and are held on spikes in the autumn.
Cultivation: Grow in full sun.
Height: 60cm (2ft); *spread:* 30cm (1ft).

Senecio
(Asteraceae)

The huge genus contains about 1,000 species, which are found throughout the world, mainly in mountain or temperate regions. Only one of these species is suitable for the moist soil of the informal temperate water garden, where it requires plenty of space to show off its handsome leaves and flowers.
Propagation: By division.
Hardiness: Hardy to frost tender.

Senecio smithii

Native to southern Chile and the Falkland Islands, this hardy herbaceous perennial has spear-shaped, coarsely serrated, dark green, leathery leaves, about 45cm (18in) long and 23cm (9in) across. The densely clustered flower-heads are composed of several yellow-eyed white daisies, each 2.5cm (1in) across.
Cultivation: Grow in full sun or partial shade.
Height: 1.2–1.5m (4–5ft); *spread:* 1m (3ft).

Trollius (Ranunculaceae)
Globeflower

There are about 30 species of hardy herbaceous perennials in this genus from Europe, Asia and North America. Compact in growth, they love moist soils. The profuse flowers of many species look like double buttercups.
Propagation: By seed or by division as soon as new growth begins or in autumn.
Hardiness: Hardy.

Trollius × cultorum cultivars

These cultivars have glossy basal leaves, 18cm (7in) long, which are divided into segments. Bowl-shaped flowers, 2.5–6cm (1–2½in) across, are borne from mid-spring to midsummer in various shades of orange and yellow.
Cultivation: Grow in full sun or partial shade.
Height: 1m (3ft); *spread:* 45cm (18in).

Trollius europaeus

Native to Europe, this species has deeply divided leaves, 13cm (5in) long, and toothed lobes. The erect stems bear smaller leaves and spherical, lemon-yellow flowers, 5cm (2in) across, in early and midsummer.
Cultivation: Grow in full sun or partial shade.
Height: 60cm (2ft); *spread:* 45cm (18in).

Trollius × cultorum cultivar

FERNS

These plants excel in cool, shady places in moist soil near water. Many styles of garden are linked to different types of plant, and the wooded, shady Japanese-type garden makes great use of these subtle plants. Colour is replaced by form, texture and shape, with the fronds offering a huge variation of interest. There are many situations in the Western garden where it would be more sensible to site a pool in shade rather than in the sunniest spot, and a shaded pool surrounded by ferns is the epitome of peace and calm and can be easier to maintain than a pool in full sun.

The following selection includes the most easily grown ferns and those that are most widely available commercially.

Adiantum (Adiantaceae)
Maidenhair fern

The genus contains more than 200 species, which are widely distributed in temperate and tropical areas and which are reasonably adaptable to many soils, although they prefer moist, humus-rich soils with low to medium levels of light.
Propagation: By sowing spores or by division in spring.
Hardiness: Few species are totally hardy unless their rhizomes are covered adequately with a humus-rich mulch in severe winters.

Adiantum aleuticum
Aleutian maidenhair fern, northern maidenhair fern

A deciduous or semi-evergreen species from North America and E. Asia, this fern has short rhizomes which support pale to mid-green, kidney-shaped fronds, 20–30cm (8–12in) long, with numerous segments, black stalks and midribs.
Cultivation: Grow in shade in moist but well-drained soil.
Height and spread: 45cm (18in).

Asplenium (Aspleniaceae)
Spleenwort

This is a large genus of about 700 widely distributed, mainly tropical and subtropical ferns. Many species produce "bird's nest" type leaf arrangements, and many are epiphytic.
Propagation: By sowing spores or by dividing in early spring.
Hardiness: Hardy to frost tender.

Asplenium scolopendrium (syn. *Phyllitis scolopendrium, Scolopendrium vulgare*)
Hart's tongue fern

This is one of the few temperate species native to Europe. It is a hardy terrestrial fern, with irregular shuttle-cock-like crowns of undulating, strap-like, leathery, glossy, bright green fronds, 40cm (16in) or longer, which are heart-shaped at the bases. The ideal planting spot for these plants is the shaded vertical faces of rocky outcrops near waterfalls or streams.
Cultivation: Grow in partial shade in well-drained, rich soil. Avoid full sun.
Height: 45–70cm (18–28in); *spread:* 60cm (2ft).

Athyrium (Woodsiaceae)
The genus includes nearly 200 species of deciduous terrestrial ferns from widely diverse parts of the world, although all prefer moist woodland.
Propagation: By sowing spores as soon as ripe or by dividing in spring.
Hardiness: Hardy to frost tender.

Athyrium filix-femina
Lady fern

This hardy deciduous fern, which is native to Europe, North America and Asia, is one of the most attractive hardy ferns. It has elegant, arching fronds, which are pinnate, lance-shaped and light green. They look like shuttlecocks that splay out towards the edge and each frond grows to 1m (3ft) long.
Cultivation: Grow in moist, neutral to acid soil. It prefers brighter light than most ferns as long as it is filtered.
Height: 1.2m (4ft); *spread:* 60cm–1m (2–3ft).

Adiantum aleuticum

Dryopteris erythrosora

Blechnum (Blechnaceae)
Hard fern

This is a widely distributed genus of about 200 mainly evergreen terrestrial ferns, which are found in sheltered, acid conditions mostly in the southern hemisphere. Some of the tender species develop quite distinctive "trunks".
Propagation: By sowing spores in late summer or by division in spring.
Hardiness: Hardy to frost tender.

Blechnum spicant
Hard fern, deer fern

From northern temperate regions, this hardy evergreen fern makes a strong clump. It produces two types of frond: slender fertile fronds, 30cm–1m (1–3ft) long, which mass together in the centre of the clump, and sterile, deep green, shining fronds that spread flat and are about 45cm (18in) long.
Cultivation: Grow in humus-rich soil in partial or full shade.
Height: 20–50cm (8–20in); *spread:* 60cm (2ft) or more.

Dryopteris (Dryopteridaceae)
Buckler fern, wood fern

A large genus, containing between 150 and 200 species of terrestrial ferns, these are found mainly in the temperate regions of the northern hemisphere. Mostly deciduous, they will remain almost evergreen in mild winters.
Propagation: By spores as soon as ripe or by dividing older specimens in spring.
Hardiness: Hardy to half hardy.

Asplenium scolopendrium

Matteuccia struthiopteris

Onoclea sensibilis

Osmunda regalis

Dryopteris erythrosora
Japanese shield fern, copper shield fern
Native to Japan and China, this beautiful, frost to half hardy fern produces young fronds, 25–60cm (10–24in) long, of glossy copper and pink, which mature to a rich glossy green. The fronds develop scarlet spore capsules on the undersides.
Cultivation: Grow in shelter and partial shade.
Height: 60cm (2ft); *spread:* 38cm (15in).

Matteuccia (Woodsiaceae)
This a genus of four species of deciduous, terrestrial ferns, common in deciduous woodlands of Europe, east Asia and North America. They are characterized by having two types of frond: the fertile fronds grow erect in the centre while the flatter, sterile ones grow around them. They need moisture all year round.
Propagation: By sowing spores as soon as ripe or by dividing established clumps in spring.
Hardiness: Hardy.

Matteuccia struthiopteris
Ostrich-plume fern, shuttlecock fern
This attractive and graceful hardy fern has lance-shaped, erect, divided fronds, each of which grows to 1.2m (4ft). These are surrounded by shorter, flatter fronds, 30cm (12in) long. Small shuttlecocks can be produced about 10cm (4in) away from the main crown on the spreading rhizomatous roots.
Cultivation: Grow in partial or dappled shade.
Height: 1.7m (5½ft); *spread:* 1m (3ft).

Onoclea (Woodsiaceae)
The genus contains a single species of deciduous hardy, terrestrial ferns from temperate regions of east Asia and North America.
Propagation: By sowing the spores as soon as they are ripe or by dividing established clumps in spring.
Hardiness: Hardy.

Onoclea sensibilis
Sensitive fern
This fern can quickly clothe large areas of moist soil with dense carpets of arching, divided, triangular or lance-shaped fronds, each to about 60cm (2ft) long. The fronds may be pinkish bronze in the spring.
Cultivation: Grow in light dappled shade; the fronds will burn if they are exposed to strong midday sun.
Height: 60cm (2ft); *spread:* indefinite.

Osmunda (Osmundaceae)
Flowering fern
The genus includes 12 species of hardy, deciduous, terrestrial ferns which are found everywhere except Australasia.
Propagation: By spores sown as soon as ripe or by dividing established clumps in spring or autumn.
Hardiness: Hardy.

Osmunda regalis
Royal fern
One of the finest ferns for the waterside, this species has sterile fronds, to 1.2m–1.5m (4–5ft) long, which are a delicate pale green tinted with coppery brown when young. They are particularly beautiful when they unfurl and provide a double bonus in the autumn when they develop a deep russet colour before the frosts. Erect pale brown fertile fronds are very conspicuous in the centre of the clump.
Cultivation: Grow in partial shade and cover the rootstock in the winter with a humus-rich mulch.
Height: 1.8 (6ft); *spread:* 4m (13ft).

Polypodium (Polypodiaceae)
This is a large genus of about 75 cosmopolitan ferns, most of which are evergreen, with leathery fronds and rhizomes close to ground level. These ferns are suitable for the sides of streams where the humidity is high but the surface roots are not waterlogged.
Propagation: By sowing spores when ripe or by division in spring.
Hardiness: Hardy to frost tender.

Polypodium vulgare
Common polpody
A hardy evergreen fern, from temperate regions, this species is a colonizer of damp places where there is adequate drainage. If left undisturbed, it will form large clumps of long, deep green, deeply cut fronds, 8cm (3in) wide, which look particularly fine in a wild garden. The surface rhizomes are thickly matted with hairy brown scales.
Cultivation: Grow in sun or dappled shade with shelter from wind.
Height: 30cm (1ft); *spread:* indefinite.

Polystichum (Dryopteridaceae)
The genus contains nearly 200 species of terrestrial ferns, usually remaining evergreen, from a wide cosmopolitan distribution. They enjoy moist, well-shaded and well-drained conditions.
Propagation: By sowing spores when ripe or by division in spring.
Hardiness: Hardy to frost tender.

Polystichum setiferum
Soft shield fern, hedge fern, English hedge fern
Native to Europe, this is one of the most tolerant of the hardy evergreen ferns, surviving in sun or shade and in moist or dry soil. When grown in moist, shady spots it assumes its true elegance, with softly textured, dull green, lance-shaped, pinnate fronds, 30cm–1.2m (1–4ft) long. The stems are partly encased in soft brown scales, which creep up the frond. The fronds of *P. setiferum* Divisilobum Group are covered in white scales.
Cultivation: Grow in partial shade.
Height: 1.2m (4ft); *spread:* 1m (3ft).

Polystichum setiferum Divisilobum Group

Polypodium vulgare

ORNAMENTAL GRASSES

With the immediate margins of a pond being dominated by the grass-like foliage of reeds, rushes and sedges, the foliage of true grasses makes a natural transition to the drier soils away from the pool possible. Although some of the ornamental grasses prefer a drier soil, there are several species that need ample moisture to attain their full stature and flower potential. Although they are easy to grow, requiring no more than cutting down hard each spring, they have been a much neglected group of plants for the water garden, but with the advent of a more natural approach to planting schemes they are becoming increasingly popular again. There are grasses for every situation in the garden, including stream sides and rocky banks. Some have such impressive, tall flowers that it is difficult to resist planting them where their reflections can be seen in the water.

The following selection includes some of the main genera that prefer slightly moister conditions.

Calamagrostis (Poaceae)

Reed grass

This genus contains about 250 species of perennial, tufted grasses, tolerant of all but the poorest of soil conditions.
Propagation: By division in spring.
Hardiness: Hardy.

Calamagrostis × *acutiflora* 'Stricta'

Feather reed grass

Its elegant inflorescence, architectural form and long-lasting character make this an extremely useful grass. It is an erect, clump-forming plant, which has slightly glossy, narrow, dark green leaves and shiny, green, straight stems. The stems bear slender panicles, which open to reveal subtle purple tints. After flowering the heads close up and become slender again, changing colour to a deep beige. The heads are held throughout winter. *C.* × *acutiflora* 'Overdam' is smaller at 1.2m (4ft), with leaves with pale yellow margins and stripes which fade with age, while the purple flower-heads become greyish pink as the summer advances.
Cultivation: Grow in full sun or partial shade.
Height: 1.5m (5ft); *spread:* 60cm–1.2m (2–4ft).

Carex oshimensis 'Evergold'

Deschampsia cespitosa

Hakonechloa macra 'Alboaurea'

Carex (Cyperaceae)

Sedge

This genus contains about 1,000 species, which are distributed throughout the world in temperate and tropical areas. Sedges are very versatile and can be used in nearly every part of the garden. Some species are also described in the section on marginal plants, but the one that is described here prefers much more oxygen around its roots than many of the other sedges.
Propagation: By division.
Hardiness: Hardy to frost tender.

Carex oshimensis 'Evergold' (syn. *C.* 'Evergold')

This hardy clump-forming cultivar provides a splash of colour for the pond margins where there is good drainage. It produces fountain-like tussocks of dark green leaves, each with a wide, creamy-yellow central stripe. The brown flower spikes are borne on stems 15cm (6in) long in mid- and late spring.
Cultivation: Grow in full sun or partial shade.
Height: 30cm (12in); *spread:* 35cm (14in).

Deschampsia (Poaceae)

Hair grass

There are about 50 species of hardy, tufted grasses in the genus. They are found in the cooler parts of the northern hemisphere, and they look exceptionally attractive when they are grouped beside water where the light, airy and wispy panicles are caught by the sun.
Propagation: By division in spring.
Hardiness: Hardy.

Deschampsia cespitosa

Tufted hair grass

This delicate ornamental grass forms dense tufts of narrow, rough-edged, arching, dark green leaves, which send up numerous, erect, slender stems, from which hang dainty, open panicles of tiny, greenish-purple flowers. These have the added advantage of turning to brownish-yellow spikelets that last into the winter.
Cultivation: Grow in full sun or partial shade.
Height: 1m (3ft); *spread:* 60cm (2ft).

Hakonechloa (Poaceae)

The genus contains a single species of deciduous, clump-forming, perennial mountain grasses. The species, *H. macra*, is native to Japan, where it prefers the cool shade of woodland margins and moist, but well-drained soil.
Propagation: By division in spring.
Hardiness: Hardy.

Hakonechloa macra 'Alboaurea'

This hardy grass makes a lovely specimen or group plant in Japanese-style water gardens, where it forms a rounded cushion of tapering foliage. The leaves are variegated with yellow and green stripes, and turn russet in the autumn. Small flowers are borne in summer and early autumn. It thrives in moisture-retentive soil and is suitable for growing in a container.
Cultivation: Grow in partial shade for the best variegation.
Height and spread: To 45cm (18in).

Calamagrostis × *acutiflora* 'Overdam'

Miscanthus (Poaceae)

There are between 17 and 20 species in the genus of perennial grasses, which occur from Africa to Asia in moist meadows and marshland. The leaves are reed-like but the full beauty lies in the flower-heads of spikelets above the leaves in late summer.
Propagation: By division.
Hardiness: Hardy to frost hardy.

Miscanthus sinensis

Native to Japan and China, this hardy vigorous clump-forming grass has flat, long, blue-green leaves, to 1.2m (4ft) long. The autumn flowers form pyramidal spikes about 40cm (16in) long of silky, hairy, pale grey spikelets tinted maroon or purple-brown.
Cultivation: Grow in well-drained soil in full sun.
Height: 4m (13ft); *spread:* 1.2m (4ft).

Miscanthus sinensis 'Kleine Fontäne'

This hardy cultivar has a narrow, vertical habit of green leaves and thick stems which hold on to the fluffy flower-heads well into the winter.
Cultivation: Grow in full sun.
Height: 1.2m (4ft); *spread:* 60cm (2ft).

Miscanthus sinensis 'Zebrinus'

Zebra grass
This frost hardy cultivar has creamy-white or pale-yellow horizontal banding on arching leaves.
Cultivation: Grow in well-drained soil in full sun.
Height: 1.2m (4ft); *spread:* 1m (3ft).

Molinia (Poaceae)

The genus contains two or three species of densely tufted perennial grasses from Europe and Asia. They have tight or compressed narrow

Miscanthus sinensis 'Kleine Fontäne'

Molinia caerulea

Panicum virgatum

spikes, which sometimes open in autumn to form lovely loose panicles.
Propagation: By division in spring.
Hardiness: Hardy.

Molinia caerulea

Purple moor grass
This grass is a native of European moorlands. It has upright stems topped with tight, purplish flower-heads in late summer which last into the autumn. The foliage is green, with good yellow autumn colour.
Cultivation: Grow in full sun or partial shade and moist soil.
Height: 1.2m (4ft); *spread:* 60cm (2ft).

Panicum (Poaceae)

Crab grass
This widespread genus contains about 470 species of annual, perennial, evergreen and deciduous grasses. They are valued for their light, airy inflorescences, which are panicles with narrow, or more often open, branches.
Propagation: By seed or by division.
Hardiness: Hardy to half hardy.

Pennisetum alopecuroides

Spartina pectinata 'Aureomarginata'

Panicum virgatum

Switch grass
This is a narrowly upright, deciduous, hardy perennial with clumps of glaucous, mid-green stems. These bear flat, upright leaves, 60cm (2ft) long, which turn yellow in autumn. The weeping panicles of tiny, purple-green spikelets reach 50cm (20in) in length and appear in autumn.
Cultivation: Grow in full sun.
Height: 1m (3ft); *spread:* 75cm (30in).

Pennisetum (Poaceae)

There are about 80 species of annual and perennial grasses in this genus. They are of mainly tropical origin, but a few species are hardy in temperate regions. They are grown for their feathery, spike-like panicles.
Propagation: By seed or by division in spring or autumn.
Hardiness: Hardy to frost tender.

Pennisetum alopecuroides (syn. *P. compressum*)

Fountain grass
Native to eastern Asia to western Australia, this frost hardy evergreen perennial species produces delightful purple or yellow-green, bottlebrush-like flower spikes, 20cm (8in) long, in autumn. The leaves are deep green, pointed and 30–60cm (1–2ft) long.
Cultivation: Grow in full sun.
Height: 1m (3ft); *spread:* 60cm–1.2m (2–4ft).

Phalaris (Poaceae)

The genus contains about 15 species of temperate perennial and annual grasses from southern Europe and temperate regions of America. They originate from a range of habitats, from dry scrub to moist areas by pools and lakes. They do well in gardens, but can be invasive.

Propagation: By division in spring or autumn.
Hardiness: Hardy to frost hardy.

Phalaris arundinacea var. *picta*

Gardener's garters
This erect, hardy perennial grass has flat, narrow, short-pointed, white-striped leaves. In early and midsummer, it bears narrow spikes of pale green flowers, 18cm (7in) long, which fade to buff with age. It is also invasive. 'Feesey' is an improved form of gardener's garters (*P. arundinacea* var. *picta*). It has pink flushes at the base of the stems and light green leaves with broad white stripes. The flower spikes also have a purplish tinge. It is not quite so invasive as the species.
Cultivation: Grow in full sun or partial shade.
Height: 1m (3ft); *spread:* indefinite.

Spartina (Poaceae)

Marsh grass, cord grass
This genus contains about 15 species of tall, perennial grasses, which are native to wet areas of America, Africa and Europe, especially in the subtropical and temperate zones. Only one species is grown in the ornamental water garden, where its flowers associate well with reeds.
Propagation: By division.
Hardiness: Hardy to frost tender.

Spartina pectinata 'Aureomarginata'

This hardy form spreads rapidly by rhizomes. It has strong upright to arching stems, and the leaves have bright yellow variegated margins. The creamy flowers open in mid- to late summer in stiff panicles.
Cultivation: Grow in full sun.
Height: 2.2m (7ft); *spread:* indefinite.

TREES AND SHRUBS

A water garden surrounded purely with herbaceous plants lacks a framework in winter, when both the aquatics and the surrounding plants die back, and brown, dead foliage predominates. The value of the woody growth of trees and shrubs comes into its own at this time of year, when stems, silhouettes and evergreen foliage take on a new dimension when they are reflected in the clear water. Dwarf conifers planted at the side of a watercourse running through rocks complete the setting for a stream at a time when shapes become as important as colour. The following plants are just a few of the trees and shrubs that could be used to create a setting for water. They are tolerant of a wide range of soils and locations.

Abies (Pinaceae)
Silver fir
The genus contains about 50 species of evergreen conifers from Europe, North Africa, Asia and North America. Unlike spruces, which have pendulous cones, those of fir trees are erect. There is a wide range of sizes and shapes, but those described here are ideal for a rocky bank near water.
Propagation: By seed.
Hardiness: Hardy.

Abies cephalonica 'Meyer's Dwarf'
This low, spreading, mounded conifer has short leaves, 9mm–1cm (⅜–½in) long, which are arranged radially around the shoots.
Cultivation: Grow in full sun.
Height: 50cm (20in); *spread:* 1–3m (3–10ft) in time.

Abies koreana 'Silberlocke'
The dimensions indicated are those the tree might be expected to achieve in 10–15 years. This slow-growing, dwarf form of the Korean fir has needlelike leaves, which tend to twist above the fawn-coloured shoots revealing the silver undersides. The lateral shoots are effective when hanging over a small stream.
Cultivation: Grow in full sun.
Height: 1.5–1.8m (5–6ft); *spread:* 1.2m (4ft).

Abies procera 'Glauca Prostrata'
Although *A. procera* is the stately, noble fir seen in large plantations, this cultivar has a shrubby, rather prostrate habit. Its great attraction is the glaucous bright blue foliage.
Cultivation: Grow in full sun.
Height: 90cm–1.2m (3–4ft) in 10–15 years; *spread:* 1.2–1.5m (4–5ft).

Acer (Aceraceae)
Maple
The large genus contains about 150 species of evergreen and deciduous trees and shrubs from Europe, North Africa, Asia and North and Central America. They vary in size from huge

Abies cephalonica 'Meyer's Dwarf'

trees to small, elegant shrubs, which are incredibly effective when they are reflected in water.
Propagation: By seed.
Hardiness: Hardy to frost tender.

Acer palmatum
Japanese maple
This hardy maple is very familiar in the ornamental garden. It is more likely that one of the cultivars will be grown than the species. The cultivars are much smaller and have interesting variations of the palmate leaves, which turn vivid colours in autumn. *A. palmatum* var. *dissectum*

has finely cut leaves that turn gold in autumn.
Cultivation: Grow in partial shade. All Japanese maples prefer a moist but well-drained soil and a position that is sheltered from wind.
Height: 7.6m (25ft); *spread:* 10m (30ft).

Acer palmatum f. *atropurpureum*
This impressive and popular Japanese maple has deeply lobed, red-purple leaves, which turn shades of brilliant red in autumn.
Cultivation: Grow in partial shade.
Height: 3m (10ft); *spread:* 4m (13ft).

Acer palmatum var. *dissectum*

Alnus incana 'Aurea'

Acer palmatum 'Ôsakazuki'
This is one of the best cultivars for autumn colour. It has large, deeply lobed leaves, 10–13cm (4–5in) long, which turn a brilliant red in autumn.
Cultivation: Grow in partial shade.
Height and spread: 6m (20ft).

Alnus (Betulaceae)
Alder
The genus contains about 35 deciduous trees and shrubs, widely distributed in temperate areas of the northern hemisphere, which tolerate extremely wet soils. Male and female catkins appear on the same tree: the male catkins are cylindrical and 5–15cm (2–6in) long, the female flowers are shorter, woody, and resemble conifer cones.
Propagation: By seed.
Hardiness: Hardy.

Alnus glutinosa
Common alder, European alder, black alder
This hardy species originated in Europe, western Asia and North Africa and is now naturalized in eastern North America. It is a rather slender tree with a central trunk and small, horizontal branches. The broad, dark green, pear-shaped leaves, coarsely toothed and 5–10cm (2–4in) long, are sticky on the upper surface.
Cultivation: Grow in full sun.
Height: 24m (80ft); *spread:* 10m (30ft).

Alnus incana 'Aurea'
This tree is an attractive specimen, with yellow leaves, 10cm (4in) long, which turn pale green in summer, and orange shoots and catkins in winter.
Cultivation: Grow in full sun.
Height: 10m (30ft); *spread:* 4.5m (15ft).

Andromeda (Ericaceae)
The two species in this genus are low-growing, wiry-stemmed evergreen shrubs, found in acid peat bogs in cooler regions of the northern hemisphere. Ideal for a shady streamside.
Propagation: By softwood cuttings in midsummer.
Hardiness: Hardy.

Andromeda polifolia

Betula utilis var. *jacquemontii*

Andromeda polifolia
Bog rosemary
This semi-erect, hardy shrub has pointed, oblong, leathery, dark green leaves, 1–4cm (½–1½in) long. Slender flower stalks carry white or pale pink flowers, 4cm (1½in) across, in spring and early summer.
Cultivation: Grow in full sun or partial shade.
Height: 40cm (16in); *spread:* 60cm (2ft).

Betula (Betulaceae)
Birch
The genus contains about 60 species of deciduous trees which originate from the northern temperate and Arctic regions. They are graceful trees, often with pendulous branches, carrying neat, small leaves and long, swinging catkins in spring. They prefer moist, sandy soil, but many species are adaptable to a variety of soil conditions.
Propagation: By seed.
Hardiness: Hardy.

Betula nigra
River birch, red birch
This North American species forms a graceful pyramidal shape. It is noted for its reddish-brown bark, which takes on a ribboned look as it ages and becomes ragged. The diamond-shaped, glossy, dark green leaves are 8cm (3in) long and turn yellow in autumn.
Cultivation: Grow in full sun.
Height: 15–24m (50–80ft); *spread:* 12m (40ft).

Betula papyrifera
Paper birch
This conical tree has white bark, which peels in thin layers and is pale orange-brown in colour when it is

newly exposed. The oval, dark green leaves grow to 10cm (4in) long and turn yellow to orange in autumn.
Cultivation: Grow in full sun.
Height: 30m (100ft); *spread:* 10m (30ft).

Betula pendula
Siver birch, white birch, common birch
This elegant tree, which is native to Europe and Asia, has silvery, peeling bark that eventually becomes dark and rough at the base. The neat, dainty leaves are 6cm (2½in) long and are carried on pendulous branches.
Cultivation: Grow in full sun.
Height: 18m (60ft); *spread:* to 10m (30ft).

Betula utilis
Himalayan birch
This tree, which is native to China and the Himalayas, has copper-brown or pinkish, peeling bark. The dark green leaves are 13cm (5in) long and turn yellow in autumn. *B. utilis* var. *jacquemontii* has white bark.
Cultivation: Grow in full sun.
Height: 18m (60ft); *spread:* to 10m (30ft).

Cedrus (Pinaceae)
Cedar
The genus contains four species of evergreen coniferous trees, which are native to the Himalayas and Mediterranean littoral. Although they grow to majestic specimen trees, which are too large for the average garden, there are some excellent, small, slow-growing cultivars, which clothe large rock areas and give added interest throughout the year to a watercourse.
Propagation: By seed.
Hardiness: Hardy.

Cedrus deodara 'Feelin' Blue'
The dimensions indicated are those the tree might be expected to achieve in 10–15 years. This is one of the few slow-growing, dwarf cedars with bluish-grey foliage. It hugs the ground and is an excellent specimen at the water's edge.
Cultivation: Grow in well-drained soil in full sun.
Height: 60cm (2ft); *spread:* 1.8m (6ft).

Cedrus deodara 'Golden Horizon'
This is a low-growing cultivar which can be easily kept in check by the judicious removal of leading branches in the spring. It has yellowish or yellowish green foliage when grown in full sun but this becomes a duller blue-green if grown in shade. It is much brighter when grown in full sun.
Cultivation: Grow in well-drained soil.
Height: 1.8m (6ft); *spread:* 3m (10ft).

Chamaecyparis (Cupressaceae)
Cypress, false cypress
The seven or eight species in the genus are evergreen coniferous trees from Taiwan, Japan and North America. They are a common garden conifer, often used for hedging or lawn specimens. There are several dwarf forms available for the sides of rocky watercourses, and the following species is a particularly attractive, slow-growing specimen.
Propagation: By seed.
Hardiness: Hardy.

Chamaecyparis obtusa 'Nana Gracilis'
This attractive conifer will take many years to reach the dimensions noted below. It has a very dense, pyramidal habit with rich green foliage, which has a slightly curly appearance.
Cultivation: Grow in full sun.
Height: 3m (10ft); *spread:* 1.2m (4ft).

Cornus (Cornaceae)
Dogwood, cornel
The genus contains about 45 species of mainly deciduous trees and shrubs, distributed widely over temperate parts of the northern hemisphere. Many of the shrubs thrive in wet situations, where their coloured stems are reflected in the water. The species grown for their stem colour should be cut back hard in spring to encourage the strong growth of the new stems.
Propagation: By seed or by hardwood cuttings.
Hardiness: Hardy to frost hardy.

Cornus alba
Red-barked dogwood
This hardy, rampant, deciduous species from Siberia and northern China has stems that become blood-red in winter. It bears oval, dark green leaves, 10cm (4in) long, which turn red or orange in autumn. White flowers are borne in flat cymes, about 5cm (2in) across, in late spring and early summer, and develop into white, blue-tinged oval fruit. 'Spaethii' is a superb form with the most attractive variegated leaves, which are green with yellow margins.
Cultivation: Grow in full sun.
Height and spread: 3m (10ft).

Chamaecyparis obtusa 'Nana Gracilis'

Cornus mas

Metasequoia glyptostroboides

Cornus mas
Cornelian cherry
This hardy deciduous species from Europe and west Asia has dark green leaves, 10cm (4in) long, which turn purplish red in autumn. In later winter, before the leaves appear, yellow flowers are produced in umbels, up to 2cm (¾in) across. Bright red, edible fruits are produced in late summer.
Cultivation: Grow in full sun.
Height and spread: 4.5m (15ft).

Cornus sanguinea 'Winter Beauty'
This hardy cultivar is not as vigorous as many of the *C. alba* and *C. sanguinea* cultivars, but has bright orange and yellow winter shoots.
Cultivation: Grow in full sun.
Height: 3m (10ft); *spread:* 2.4m (8ft).

Cornus stolonifera
Red osier dogwood
This hardy species has dark-red stems in winter. It is a vigorous, suckering shrub, with oval, dark green leaves, about 13cm (5in) long, which turn red or orange in autumn. The white flowers are borne in flat cymes, 5cm (2in) across, in late spring and early summer and are followed by white fruit, often tinged blue.
Cultivation: Grow in full sun or partial shade.
Height: 1.8m (6ft); *spread:* 4m (13ft).

Cornus stolonifera 'Flaviramea'
This hardy dogwood has yellow stems, which need regular pruning to encourage the coloration in the shoots. If left unpruned, terminal clusters of whitish-cream berries are produced in autumn.

Cultivation: Grow in full sun or partial shade.
Height: 1.2m (4ft); *spread:* 4m (13ft).

Metasequoia
(Taxodiaceae)
The genus contains a single species of deciduous conifer, discovered in the 1940s in China. Tolerant of water-logged soils, it quickly becomes established as a narrow specimen tree.
Propagation: By seed.
Hardiness: Hardy.

Metasequoia glyptostroboides
Dawn redwood, water larch
This is a moisture-loving, fast-growing tree with an attractive, reddish, fibrous bark, which becomes fluted with age. Growing in a narrow conical habit, it briefly assumes attractive autumn colours when its small larch-like, soft green leaves, about 1cm (½in) long, turn yellow and orange before falling.
Cultivation: Grow in full sun.
Height: 30–35m (100–115ft); *spread:* 4.5m (15ft).

Picea (Pinaceae)
Spruce
The genus includes 30–40 species of coniferous, evergreen trees, occurring in cool temperate regions of the northern hemisphere. Many are grown for timber, but there are some excellent specimen trees, which look lovely used as a background to a large pool and planted to be reflected in the water. There are also a number of small cultivars, which are suitable for planting on rock banks by streams.
Propagation: By seed.
Hardiness: Hardy to frost hardy. (Those described here are hardy.)

Picea breweriana
Brewer's spruce
This is a slow-growing, columnar tree with level branches and pendulous side branches. Blunt-ended flat leaves are deep green above and whitish beneath, 2.5–4cm (1–1½in) long, and there are pendulous cones, 8–14cm (3–5½in) long. The drooping tips to the shoots make this a most elegant specimen tree.
Cultivation: Grow in full sun.
Height: 10–15m (30–50ft); *spread:* 3–4m (10–13ft).

Picea glauca var. albertiana 'Alberta Globe'
This is very similar to *P. albertiana* 'Conica' when small and they are difficult to tell apart. As it matures, it develops a more flattened, globose, bush shape, rather than the more typical cone shape.
Cultivation: Grow in full sun.
Height: 1.5m (5ft); *spread:* 1m (3ft).

Picea glauca var. albertiana 'Conica'
This garden gem is a neat, cone-shaped conifer growing to a dwarf bushy shape. It is a first-class rockery plant, reaching 75 by 30cm (30 by 12in) in ten years, but which can be kept tight by annual trimming.
Cultivation: Grow in full sun.
Height: 1.8–6m (6–20ft); *spread:* 1–2.4m (3–8ft).

Pinus (Pinaceae)
Pine
The large genus contains about 120 species of evergreen conifers, which are widely distributed in the northern hemisphere. Pines are versatile plants, being used in forestry and as windbreaks and specimen trees, while some dwarf species make a strong impact in a rock garden. They are distinguished by having needlelike leaves, which are clasped at the base in twos, threes or fives.
Propagation: By seed.
Hardiness: Hardy to frost hardy. (Those described here are hardy.)

Pinus mugo
Dwarf mountain pine
A spreading, almost shrubby pine, this has well-spaced pairs of dark to mid-green leaves, 3–8cm (1¼–3in) long. It looks good among rocks.
Cultivation: Grow in full sun.
Height: 3.4m (11ft); *spread:* 4.5m (15ft).

Pinus mugo 'Corley's Mat'
The mountain pine has produced several seedlings of which this cultivar is one of the better forms. It has a tighter habit than the species, forming a compact, rounded bun of short needles suitable for rock gardens.
Cultivation: Grow in full sun.
Height: Up to 60cm (2ft); *spread:* to 1.2m (4ft).

Pinus sylvestris 'Watereri'
This dwarf form of the common Scots pine is a dense specimen, with an upright habit and needles, 5–8cm (2–3in) long, held in pairs.
Cultivation: Grow in full sun.
Height: 4m (13ft); *spread:* 7m (23ft).

Salix (Salicaceae)
The genus contains around 300 species of trees and shrubs from the cooler parts of the temperate northern hemisphere. Several species thrive in wet or moist soil, and can be used as specimen plants or as group plantings for winter bark colour.
Propagation: By softwood cuttings in summer or hardwood cuttings in autumn.
Hardiness: Hardy.

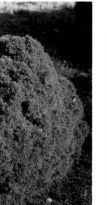

Picea glauca albertiana 'Alberta Globe'

Pinus mugo 'Corley's Mat'

Salix alba 'Chermesina'

Salix integra 'Hakuro-nishiki'

Salix alba 'Chermesina'
Scarlet willow
This cultivar of the more common *S. alba* (white willow) provides a blaze of colour in winter with its brilliant display of scarlet-orange branches. It is particularly effective when prevented from growing into a tree and pruned hard each spring to ensure there is a regular supply of young bushy branches near the ground.
Cultivation: Grow in full sun.
Height: 18–24m (60–80ft); *spread:* 10m (30ft).

Salix alba var. *sericea* (syn. *S. alba* f. *argentea*)
Silver willow
The common name derives from the silvery grey leaves. This is a smaller, less vigorous form than *S. alba*.
Cultivation: Grow in full sun.
Height: 15m (50ft); *spread:* 8m (26ft).

Salix alba subsp. *vitellina* 'Britzensis'
This cultivar is grown more for its orange-red bark than as a tree. It is very similar to the cultivar *S. alba* 'Chermesina', under which name it is sometimes sold. It is best cut hard back each spring rather than allowed to grow into a full-sized tree.
Cultivation: Grow in full sun.
Height: 18m (60ft); *spread:* 8m (26ft).

Salix babylonica var. *pekinensis* 'Tortuosa' (syn. *S. matsudana* 'Tortuosa')
Corkscrew willow, contorted willow
This is a cultivar of a species that is native to northern China and Korea. It is one of the most striking and easily identified of the willows because of the remarkable corkscrew arrangement of the branches and leaves, which are also twisted.
Cultivation: Grow in full sun.
Height: 12–15m (40–50ft); *spread:* 8m (26ft).

Salix caprea
Goat willow, pussy willow
This common, spreading, deciduous tree from Europe and Asia has golden catkins, which appear in spring. The broad leaves are oblong and downy at first, woolly beneath and grey-green in colour. This tree is suitable only for large-scale planting in natural areas, but for garden use there is a grafted weeping tree called *S. caprea* 'Kilmarnock', which grows to 1.5–1.8m (5–6ft) high and is much better suited to waterside planting.
Cultivation: Grow in full sun.
Height: 6–10m (20–30ft); *spread:* 6m (20ft).

Salix daphnoides
Violet willow
This tree, which is native to Europe, bears shoots that are downy at first, then become purple with a waxy bloom. The leaves are oval to lance shaped, smooth and shiny, 12cm (5in) long. This is ideal for a wildlife pond.
Cultivation: Grow in full sun.
Height: 10–12m (30–40ft); *spread:* to 6m (20ft).

Salix exigua
Coyote willow
Native to North America, this upright, thicket-forming, suckering shrub has narrow, grey-green leaves, which grow to about 10cm (4in) in length, and will do well on sandy soils.
Cultivation: Grow in full sun.
Height: 4m (13ft); *spread:* 4.5m (15ft).

Salix gracilistyla 'Melanostachys'
A spreading, bushy shrub, this has arching shoots, which are silky and hairy when young, and finely toothed and grey-green when mature. It has the most distinctive catkins, which are black with brick-red anthers.
Cultivation: Grow in full sun.
Height: 3m (10ft); *spread:* 4m (13ft).

Salix integra 'Hakuro-nishiki'
This willow is actually a shrub, which is usually sold grafted onto a clear stem to create a round-headed, miniature tree. The leaves, variegated with pink and cream, keep a good colour well into summer.
Cultivation: Grow in full sun.
Height: 1.5m (5ft); *spread:* 1m (3ft).

Salix lanata
Woolly willow
This shrubby species is native to northern Europe. The buds and young branches are covered with soft, grey hairs. It looks beautiful when it is allowed to form grey mounds at the waterside.
Cultivation: Grow in full sun.
Height: 90cm (3ft); *spread:* to 1.5m (5ft).

Taxodium (Taxodiaceae)
Bald cypress
The three species in this genus are ornamental, pyramid-shaped, deciduous conifers, which are native to the southeastern United States and Mexico. They are semi-aquatic in their native habitat but are also capable of thriving in ordinary soils. They are generally too large for the small to average-size garden.
Propagation: By seed.
Hardiness: Hardy.

Taxodium distichum
Swamp cypress
This species has a narrow pyramidal habit. The soft, deciduous, flat leaves are short, only 2.5cm (1in) long, yellowish-green in colour and turn brown in autumn in two ranks. Buttressed roots, known as "knees", can appear in shallow water. For garden use it has been largely superseded by the smaller *Metasequoia glyptostroboides* (dawn redwood).
Cultivation: Grow in full sun.
Height: 30–37m (100–120ft); *spread:* 6–8.5m (20–28ft).

Vaccinium (Ericaceae)
Bilberry, blueberry, cranberry
There are about 450 species of deciduous and evergreen shrubs and some small trees in this genus. Some species are grown for their edible fruits, and the more ornamental species are ideal for an acid soil along a shady waterside.
Propagation: By seed or by softwood cuttings.
Hardiness: Hardy to frost hardy.

Vaccinium macrocarpon
Cranberry
This is a hardy, prostrate, mat-forming evergreen shrub. The oblong leaves are shiny, dark green, 2.5cm (1in) long, and turn bronze in the winter. Bell-shaped, pink flowers, 1cm (½in) across, are produced singly in the summer and are followed by edible, spherical, red berries.
Cultivation: Grow in sun or partial shade.
Height: 15cm (6in); *spread:* indefinite.

Taxodium distichum

ALPINES

To complete the range of plants required to make a water garden with an associated rock feature, this section includes some scrambling plants that can be grown in dry soil along the edges of streams, rock pools and small pools that have been made with preformed units. The soil at the sides of these features can be dry, particularly if the feature is built into a mound of soil. Despite the normal association with moisture-loving plants along these edges, these would not do well if planted in a dry soil, and it is far better to use alpines that are capable of thriving in these conditions.

Antennaria (Asteraceae)
Cat's ears
The genus contains about 45 species of evergreen and semi-evergreen, mat-forming perennials, widely distributed in the northern hemisphere. These accommodating ground-cover plants are excellent for crevices or between paving.
Propagation: By seed.
Hardiness: Hardy.

Antennaria dioica
This useful carpeting plant has tufts of grey leaves. The leaves are covered with white hairs on the underside. In summer small fluffy, rose-pink flowers are produced.
Cultivation: Grow in full sun.
Height: 5cm (2in); *spread:* 45cm (18in).

Arenaria (Caryophyllaceae)
Sandwort
This is a genus of about 160 species of annuals and low-growing perennials, some of which are evergreen, from northern regions of the northern hemisphere. They hug the ground and make excellent plants for screes and rock crevices, where they soon spread over the rock faces.
Propagation: By seed.
Hardiness: Hardy.

Arenaria balearica
Corsican sandwort
A useful, small, prostrate, evergreen, mat-forming perennial, this has minute, shiny, light green leaves. These green carpets break into a sheet of clear white, star-like flowers in late spring.
Cultivation: Grow in partial shade.
Height: 1cm (½in); *spread:* 30cm (1ft).

Aurinia (Brassicaceae)
This genus comprises seven species of clump-forming biennials or evergreens from Europe, Russia and Turkey, where they grow in rocky, mountainous areas. They are robust growing plants, frequently used to clothe dry walls and large rock banks.
Propagation: By seed or by softwood cuttings.
Hardiness: Hardy.

Aurinia saxatilis (syn. *Alyssum saxatile*)
Gold dust
This is a reliable, mound-forming, evergreen perennial. The grey-green, hairy, toothed leaves grow in rosettes, and in late spring and early summer the plants are covered with bright yellow, four-petalled flowers.
Cultivation: Grow in full sun.
Height: 20cm (8in); *spread:* 30cm (12in).

Campanula (Campanulaceae)
The large genus contains 300 annuals, biennials and perennials, distributed widely throughout temperate regions of the northern hemisphere, in habitats ranging from meadows and woodland to rocky slopes. Many species are suitable for rock and scree gardens and form cushions of spreading, tight, green leaves.
Propagation: By seed or softwood cuttings.
Hardiness: Hardy to frost tender. (Those described here are hardy.)

Campanula carpatica
This widely grown herbaceous bellflower from the Carpathian mountains forms small tufts with bright green, oval, sharply toothed leaves. The upright, bell-shaped flowers, 2.5–4cm (1–1½in) across, are violet, purple, blue or white and appear in summer and autumn.
Cultivation: Grow in sun or partial shade. They are at their best in well-drained soil.
Height and spread: 20–30cm (8–12in).

Campanula portenshlagiana (syn. *C. muralis*)
Dalmatian bellflower
This is an old favourite in the garden. It is a perennial, semi-trailing evergreen, which has kidney-shaped, glossy, mid-green leaves. In midsummer sumptuous, tubular to funnel-shaped, violet to deep purple flowers are borne in profusion.
Cultivation: Grow in sun or partial shade. They are at their best in well-drained soil.
Height: 15cm (6in); *spread:* 50cm (20in).

Campanula poscharskyana
This vigorous, trailing perennial spreads by underground runners. It is a good selection for bolder parts of a rock garden, producing a glorious tangle of long, slender branches which bear downy, mid-green leaves. From midsummer to autumn, constellations of pretty, star-shaped, pale lavender flowers appear.
Cultivation: Grow in sun or partial shade.
Height: 15cm (6in); *spread:* 60cm (2ft).

Cerastium (Caryophyllaceae)
The genus of about 100 species of annuals and carpet-forming tufted perennials is widely distributed in temperate zones of Europe and North America. The species recommended here is very vigorous and a classic spreader for the most difficult situations where it seldom fails.
Propagation: By seed or by softwood cuttings.
Hardiness: Hardy.

Cerastium tomentosum
Snow-in-summer
This is a rampant, seemingly indestructible, mat-forming perennial, which will give the most astonishing display of gleaming white blooms under the most adverse conditions. There are woolly, silvery-white leaves, and in late spring and summer a profusion of star-like white flowers appears.
Cultivation: Grow in full sun in any soil.
Height: 5–8cm (2–3in); *spread:* indefinite.

Campanula portenschlagiana

Antennaria dioica

Campanula carpatica

Convolvulus
(Convolvulaceae)

This is a large genus containing 250 species of climbing and scrambling annuals and perennials and some evergreen sub-shrubs and perennials. They originate from a diverse range of habitats in subtropical and temperate areas. The scrambling and bushy forms make good, quick covering plants for the hard edges of preformed units.

Propagation: By division in spring.
Hardiness: Hardy to half hardy.

Convolvulus sabatius (syn. *C. mauritanicus*)

This is a slender-stemmed, trailing, half hardy perennial with mid-green leaves. From summer to early autumn it bears clusters of funnel-shaped, pale to deep lavender-blue flowers.
Cultivation: Grow in full sun. It loves a gritty well-drained soil on a bank.
Height: 15cm (6in); *spread:* 50cm (20in).

Diascia (Scrophulariaceae)

There are 50 species of annuals and semi-evergreen, suckering perennials in the genus, which are found in mountain regions of southern Africa. They have become popular for their long flowering season, when mainly pinkish-red flowers are produced on bushy plants, which quickly cover difficult areas.
Propagation: By seed or by softwood cuttings.
Hardiness: Borderline hardy.

Diascia rigescens

This is an excellent plant for well-drained soils, where it will give a profusion of flowers the whole summer long. It is a trailing perennial with stiff, branching stems and mainly stalkless, toothed, heart-shaped leaves. The mid- to deep salmon-pink flowers, with short, incurved spurs, are produced on tall dense spikes.
D. rigescens 'Variegata' is an attractive cultivar with creamy, variegated leaves.
Cultivation: Grow in full sun. Deadhead to extend the flowering season.
Height: 20cm (8in); *spread:* 50cm (20in).

Erigeron (Asteraceae)
Fleabane

This genus of about 200 species of annuals, biennials and perennials has a wide distribution, especially in North America where the plants are found in dry grassland and mountainous areas. They have become popular in coastal gardens on sandy soil for their ability to resist drought.
Propagation: By seed or by division in spring.
Hardiness: Hardy.

Erigeron karvinskianus (syn. *E. mucronatus*)

An easily grown little charmer, this species is very suitable for crevices in walls and paving. Carpeting and with a rhizomatous root, this vigorous spreading perennial has grey-green, hairy leaves on lax, branching stems. In summer masses of yellow-centred, daisy-like flowerheads are produced, opening white and gradually fading through pink and purple.
Cultivation: Grow in full or partial shade in well-drained soil.
Height: 15–30cm (6–12in); *spread:* 1m (3ft).

Cerastium tomentosum

Convolvulus sabatius

Geranium (Geraniaceae)
Cranesbill

There are about 300 species of annuals, biennials and herbaceous perennials in the genus, widely distributed in all temperate regions except very damp habitats. They should not be confused with pelargoniums, whose common name is geranium. The trailing, mat-forming and spreading species are superb for rock gardens near a stream or as ground cover in partial shade.
Propagation: By seed or by division.
Hardiness: Hardy to half hardy. (Those described here are hardy.)

Geranium cinereum 'Ballerina'

This dwarf evergreen perennial forms rosettes of grey, deeply lobed leaves, 5cm (2in) across. Short-stalked, upward-facing, cup-shaped purplish red flowers, 2.5cm (1in) across, with dark red veins and dark eyes, appear in late spring and early summer.
Cultivation: Grow in full sun.
Height: 15cm (6in); *spread:* 30cm (12in).

Geranium orientalitibeticum (syn. *G. stapfianum* var. *roseum*)

This is a delightful dwarf perennial with underground, tuberous runners. The marbled dark and pale green leaves are deeply cut with toothed divisions. In summer cup-shaped, pink to deep purplish pink flowers with white centres are produced.
Cultivation: Grow in sun or partial shade.
Height: 30cm (12in); *spread:* 1m (3ft) or more.

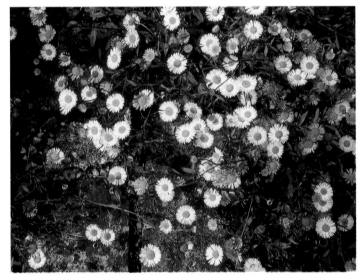

Erigeron karvinskianus

Geranium cinereum 'Ballerina'

Helianthemum
(Cistaceae)

Rock rose, sun rose

The genus contains just over 100 species of evergreen or semi-evergreen shrubs from North and South America, Asia, Europe and North Africa, where they occur in alpine meadows and open scrub. The sun or rock roses are an asset to any garden because they produce flowers for a very long period in summer. They are superb in a rock garden setting, where they can bake in a well-drained soil and show off their range of colourful flowers.

Propagation: By seed or by softwood cuttings.

Hardiness: Hardy to frost hardy.

Helianthemum 'Rhodanthe Carneum' (syn. *H.* 'Wisley Pink')

This hardy cultivar is a vigorous, fast-growing, spreading, evergreen shrub. It has grey leaves and delicate, saucer-shaped, pale pink flowers with yellow-orange centres, which appear in profusion.

Cultivation: Grow in full sun. Cut back after flowering to keep neat and dense.

Height: 30cm (12in); *spread:* 45cm (18in).

Helianthemum 'The Bride'

This hardy cultivar has large white flowers and grey foliage.

Cultivation: Grow in full sun.

Height: 23cm (9in); *spread:* 25cm (10in).

Iberis (Brassicaceae)

Candytuft

The genus contains about 40 species of annuals, perennials and evergreen sub-shrubs from the Mediterranean countries, where they are found in well-drained, open sites. They are an excellent choice for spreading over the sides of preformed stream units and the sides of waterfalls.

Propagation: By seed or by softwood cuttings.

Hardiness: Hardy to frost tender.

Iberis crenata

From central Spain, this tough, erect hardy annual has straight, branching stems and narrow leaves, which are finely toothed. In spring and early summer, it produces a dense flower-head of white flowers that are deeply notched.

Cultivation: Grow in full sun.

Height and spread: 30cm (12in).

Helianthemum 'Rhodanthe Carneum'

Helianthemum 'The Bride'

Iberis crenata

Linum (Linaceae)

A genus of 200 species of evergreen and deciduous annuals and biennials from dry, grassy slopes of the northern hemisphere. They have colourful funnel to saucer-shaped flowers and many are suited to rock gardens where they flower for long periods.

Propagation: By seed or semi-ripewood cuttings in summer.

Hardiness: Hardy to frost hardy.

Linum flavum 'Compactum'

This woody, hardy perennial has an upright habit. The leaves are spoon-shaped and dark-green, growing to 2–4cm (¾–1½in) long. The upward-facing, funnel-shaped, golden yellow flowers, 2.5cm (1in) across, appear on the tips of the many branched stems in summer when they open in the sunshine.

Cultivation: Do best in full sun on light, well-drained soils. Protect from winter wet.

Height and spread: 15cm (6in).

Lithodora
(Boraginaceae)

The seven species in the genus are low-growing, spreading or erect evergreen shrubs and sub-shrubs. They originate from southwestern Europe to southern Greece, Turkey and Algeria, where they are found growing in scrub and thickets. These plants introduce the loveliest shade of blue into the rock garden by the waterside.

Propagation: By semi-ripewood cuttings.

Hardiness: Hardy to frost hardy.

Lithodora diffusa 'Heavenly Blue'

This delightful, prostrate, spreading, frost hardy evergreen shrub has deep green, pointed, hairy leaves. In summer it bears masses of open funnel-shaped, azure blue flowers.

Cultivation: Grow in full sun in acid, humus-rich soil.

Height: 15–30cm (6–12in); *spread:* 45cm (18in).

Parahebe
(Scrophulariaceae)

There are 30 species in the genus. They are evergreen or semi-evergreen sub-shrubs and perennials, mainly from Australia and New Zealand, occurring in dry stony habitats and screes. Their mat-forming, semi-prostrate habit makes them suitable for gravel gardens or rock gardens.

Propagation: By seed or by semi-ripewood cuttings.

Hardiness: Frost hardy.

Parahebe catarractae

This charming, frost hardy evergreen sub-shrub has oval, sharply toothed, dark green leaves. The young leaves are tinged with purple. Sprays of saucer-shaped white flowers, heavily shaded and veined with purplish-pink, are produced in profusion in the summer.

Cultivation: Grow in full sun.

Height and spread: 30cm (1ft).

Phlox (Polemoniaceae)

A genus of nearly 70 species of evergreen or herbaceous, low-growing or mat-forming perennials mainly found in North America. The mat and cushion-forming species

Linum flavum 'Compactum'

Pratia pedunculata

Saxifraga cochlearis

Sedum spurium 'Variegatum'

originate in dry, rocky habitats and are therefore suited to growing in rock gardens.
Propagation: By softwood cuttings from non-flowering stems of the cushion-forming types in spring or removing rooted pieces of the trailing forms in early autumn.
Hardiness: Hardy to half hardy.

Phlox subulata
Moss phlox
This dense, evergreen, hardy perennial forms cushions or mats of narrow, bright green leaves, 5mm–2cm (¼–¾in) long. The flowers can be purple, red, lilac, pink or white, 1–2.5cm (½–1in) across, appearing in a star-like formation of petals in spring and early summer.
Cultivation: Grow in full sun.
Height: 5–15cm (2–6in); *spread:* to 50cm (20in).

Phlox subulata 'Emerald Cushion Blue'
This hardy cultivar of the moss phlox has lilac flowers and hugs the ground in dense mats.
Cultivation: Grow in full sun.
Height: No higher than 5cm (2in); *spread:* to 60cm (24in).

Pratia (Campanulaceae)
The genus contains about 20 species of prostrate, spreading evergreen perennials which originate from Africa, Asia, Australia, New Zealand and South America, where they are found growing in damp, shady habitats. They are superb plants for growing in the crevices between rocks with a shady aspect or for forming deep green "grouting" between paving stones, and they like the dampness produced by a nearby watercourse or pool.
Propagation: By division.
Hardiness: Hardy to frost hardy.

Pratia pedunculata
A ground cover for moist conditions, this vigorous, invasive, ground-hugging, hardy perennial has small, rounded leaves and is covered with star-shaped, pale to mid-blue flowers over a long period in summer.
Cultivation: Grow in partial or deep shade.
Height: 1cm (½in); *spread:* indefinite.

Saxifraga (Saxifragaceae)
This is a large genus of more than 400 species of mat or cushion-forming, evergreen or deciduous perennials from a wide distribution in the northern hemisphere, where they are found in mountainous regions. They have a wide variation in habit and leaf form and are widely grown in rock gardens, where they appreciate well-drained soil.
Propagation: By seed or by separating offsets from parent rosettes.
Hardiness: Hardy.

Saxifraga cochlearis
This plant forms a dense cushion of spoon-shaped, mid-green leaves, 4cm (1½in) long, with lime-encrusted margins. In early summer, flower-heads, 6–10cm (2½–4in) long, of white flowers, sometimes red-spotted, rise above a cushion of dense rosettes.
Cultivation: Grow in full sun.
Height: 20cm (8in); *spread:* 15cm (6in).

Saxifraga 'Tumbling Waters'
This is a slow-growing, mat-forming evergreen perennial. It grows in tight rosettes of narrow, lime-encrusted, silvery leaves. When mature, after several years, dense, arching conical heads of small, open cup-shaped, white flowers are produced, after which the main rosette dies and the small offsets grow on.
Cultivation: Grow in full sun.
Height: 60cm (2ft); *spread:* 20–30cm (8–12in).

Sedum (Crassulaceae)
Stonecrop
This large genus contains around 400 species. It is a diverse group of plants, many of which are succulent. They originate from the northern hemisphere, where they are found growing in mountainous and arid regions. These are ideal plants for withstanding difficult conditions such as drought and strong sunshine, and some of the alpine types have a creeping, scrambling habit, which will cover rock edges.
Propagation: By seed or by softwood cuttings.
Hardiness: Hardy to frost tender.

Sedum acre
Common stonecrop, biting stonecrop
This evergreen, mat-forming, hardy perennial has dense, spreading shoots covered in minute, fleshy, triangular, pale green leaves and flat-topped heads of tiny, star-shaped yellow-green flowers.
Cultivation: Grow in full sun.
Height: 5cm (2in); *spread:* 60cm (2ft) or more.

Sedum spathulifolium
This mat-forming, hardy perennial has rosettes of spoon-shaped, fleshy, brittle green or silver leaves, often tinted with bronze and purple. Sprays of tiny, star-shaped, bright yellow flowers appear in summer.
Cultivation: Grow in full sun or light shade.
Height: 5cm (2in); *spread:* indefinite.

Sedum spurium 'Variegatum'
This vigorous, mat-forming, frost hardy evergreen perennial has branching red stems and variegated leaves, 2.5cm (1in) long. Star-shaped, pink, purple or white flowers, 2cm (¾in) across, are produced in rounded flowerheads, 4cm (1.5in) across in late summer.
Cultivation: Grow in full sun.
Height: 10cm (4in); *spread:* to 60cm (2ft).

Veronica
(Scrophulariaceae)
Speedwell, brooklime
This genus contains about 250 species, growing in diverse habitats, mainly in Europe. Some are cushion- or mat-forming species and can be used to soften unsightly edges.
Propagation: By seed or by division in autumn.
Hardiness: Hardy to frost hardy.

Veronica prostrata
Prostrate speedwell
This mat-forming, hardy species has bright to mid-green, oval and toothed leaves. In early summer, it produces erect spikes of small, saucer-shaped flowers of a most brilliant blue.
Cultivation: Grow in fairly poor, well-drained soil in full sun.
Height: 15cm (6in); *spread:* 40cm (16in).

Veronica prostrata

For many water gardeners, a selection of ornamental fish is the main reason for having water. Fish provide great

FISH AND OTHER FAUNA

interest with their graceful movement and colour, while at the same time keeping pests and midge larvae from building up. For a wildlife pool, fish should not be considered a priority as they eat many of the invertebrates that make up a wildlife community.

OPPOSITE: **A stream is alive with insects, birds and submerged life, making complete the pleasure of a wildlife-friendly feature.**

A BALANCED ECOSYSTEM

Examine a drop of pool water under a microscope and you will be amazed at the life on display. These tiny organisms are the basis of a clear, healthy and balanced pool. A diverse mix of organisms in the right proportions helps to prevent the growth of algae and provides the basis of a food chain that supports larger animals that bring so much added interest and pleasure.

THE FOOD CHAIN

Pond water hides a never-ending struggle for life. Fungi, worms, bacteria, nematodes and snails feed on organic debris, while further up the food chain, and preying on these tiny organisms, are the larvae of dragonflies, water beetles and crayfish. These are, in turn, eaten by fish, frogs, newts and salamanders. This intriguing web of life has a final layer of predation in the form of herons, kingfishers and, in tropical waters, alligators. The chain of feeding depends on size; for example, small fish fry are eaten by beetles, which die and become food for the worms. Maintaining the cycle in a natural wetland habitat should be the main goal in the sensitive management of an informal garden pool. Many gardeners will happily leave nature to develop a balance, but a man-made pool has not evolved naturally and so is prone to periodic upsets, particularly if the volume of water is very small.

BELOW: **The depth of the main part of this pool is over 1m (3ft). This will prevent marginal plants from taking over the pond, and destroying its natural balance.**

GREEN WATER AND ALGAE

A dramatic symptom of an imbalance in the pool's micro-organisms is green water, which is caused by excess algae. The algae are minute, single-celled organisms that thrive in sunlight, nutrient-rich water and warmth. Although they are a source of food to some members of the food chain, they are unlikely to be eaten in sufficient quantity in a small pool, and without competition they become dominant. They usually make their presence felt in a newly installed pool where there is an abundance of mineral salts and no competition from plants for the available nutrients. As soon as plants develop, they compete with the algae for food, and the shade from their leaves denies the algae the sunlight that is essential for their growth. The regular introduction of tapwater, which is rich in the chemicals on which the algae feed, also upsets this balance, and wherever possible rainwater should be used for any topping up.

The other type of algae that can become a nightmare to water gardeners is known as blanketweed, a filamentous algae that, unlike the free-floating, single-celled algae, attach themselves to higher plants or other objects. Blanketweed – *Spirogyra*, to give it its botanical name – gathers together in great masses, which are clearly visible in the water because it resembles green cotton wool. In spring these masses rise to the surface, buoyed up by the bubbles of oxygen – and a useful reminder of the value of all green plants as oxygenators.

OTHER AQUATIC FAUNA

One of the fascinations of a pool is the way insects seem to be able to walk over the surface of the water. There is an invisible elastic skin, the meniscus, supporting small creatures above and below it. A group of insects, including the pond skater and whirligig beetle, feed on the dead and dying insects that fall onto the surface of the water, but they are the least well adapted to aquatic life as they seldom need to go under the water. The larvae and pupae of gnats and mosquitoes, on the other hand, can suspend themselves under the film when they surface to take in air.

Away from the surface of clear water, aquatic leaves are a home to larvae, caterpillars and snails, which can become pests of ornamental plants by eating holes in

A CROSS-SECTION OF POND LIFE

Some of the more common inhabitants of the garden pool which
go towards forming a balanced ecosystem.

Dragonfly

Pond skater

Frog

Frog spawn

Water boatman

Great diving beetle

Great pond snail

Caddis-fly larva

Dragonfly nymph

the leaves. Preying on all of these are several carnivo-
rous animals, such as the great diving beetle, the water
boatman, the water scorpion and nymphs of dragonflies and damselflies. In the mud at the pool bottom
are a number of specialized creatures that can survive
in the deoxygenated conditions. The most common of
these are the red bloodworm larvae of midges and, in
larger pools, mussels, which dig their fleshy feet into
the mud, taking in large quantities of water through
a siphon tube, extracting oxygen and plankton and
passing out the spent water through another tube.

The array of visitors to the pool, in the form of
birds, grass snakes, frogs and water voles, is one of
the reasons that gardeners develop an informal water
garden to encourage wildlife. However, we must
return to the open water, where, in contrast to the
microscopic life, are the largest of the permanent pool
dwellers, the fish.

LEFT: **Lush ferns by
the side of this shady
stream provide good
cover for birds,
snakes, amphibians
and mammals.**

STOCKING THE POOL

As we have seen, the biological balance of a pool is susceptible to upset in a small, artificial pool. The addition of large fish in too great a number can also upset this balance. In natural pools, the fish will have developed in the community, and their feeding habits will be in tune with the foodstuffs around them. Such fish are often bottom dwellers, not highly coloured, and in small pools or shallow streams they are generally small.

HOW MANY FISH?

The impact on the pool of several large fish is far reaching. Apart from the physical disturbance to the soil around the roots in container plants, their mouthparts will be large enough to devour many of the lower forms of pool life that have hitherto contributed to the balance of the food chain. Fish should not, therefore, be added to a pool on impulse. Rather, the choice of species, their size, and the number that the pool will sustain in a healthy environment must be carefully considered. The maximum number that a pool will sustain is based on the surface area of the pool that is free from vegetation and the size of the fish. Volume of water is not used as a criterion in stocking because a very deep pool with only a small surface area does not absorb atmospheric oxygen as well as a shallow pool with a large surface area. Depth is, of course, important

BELOW: **The colour and movement of fish bring life to this well-designed pool.**

LEFT: **The markings and colours of koi are very important to keen koi collectors.**

in providing protection in the winter and a stable temperature in the summer, but it is a secondary factor in determining stocking levels.

A good guideline to use in a still pool is not to exceed 5cm of body length of fish to 900 square centimetres (2in to 1 square foot) of surface area. Taken literally, this could become a choice of two or three very large fish or several smaller ones, but it is strongly recommended that you go for the latter option, that is, several smaller fish. You should also bear in mind that little fish will grow and that the calculation made when the fish were small may be inaccurate in two or three years' time.

The guideline is also based on the dimensions of a still pool. As soon as you introduce a watercourse or have a fountain playing constantly in summer, the oxygen levels are increased and the pool will support slightly larger numbers. If biological filtration is introduced as well, the number of fish can be increased even more.

The type of fish is also a factor in stocking levels, not only because of their ultimate size but also because of their habits, which make volume as well as surface area significant. Koi, for instance, have different requirements from goldfish, and, given their ultimate size,

they need a volume of water greater than 10,000 litres (2642 gallons) and a minimum area of 20 square metres (215 square feet). Again, if a filtration system is used, these figures can be reduced and if the fish are only small and removed to another pool when they get very large, the ultimate volume and size are not as important.

BELOW: **These goldfish and koi, which are on sale in an aquatic centre, are clamouring for food from all and sundry.**

TYPES OF FISH

There is a wide range of fish available to the gardener, but before buying it is important to consider not only the ultimate size of the fish in relation to the size of the pool, but also the type of fish in relation to the type of water feature you have. Koi, for example, will not only look out of place in a natural pool, but they might also have a deleterious effect on the food chain in such a pool. In a natural pool, where the aim is to provide a habitat for a wide range of plants and wildlife, less glamorous species will be a much more appropriate choice. In a smaller, formal pool, however, decorative and eye-catching goldfish can be introduced to enhance the overall appearance of the pool, and in such a pool the balance of plant life and animal life can be more easily controlled to accommodate the fish, making it more appropriate for exotic introductions.

BELOW: **The mixed colourings and patterns of these fish form an interesting mosaic against the dark water.**

GOLDFISH

The suitability of goldfish for ornamental pools was recognized centuries ago in China, where they were kept as pets during the Sung dynasty, which reigned from 960 to 1279. Breeding really got under way in Japan at the beginning of the 18th century, and since then several variants of the common goldfish have become available. With the more recent introduction of koi, however, the goldfish has become much undervalued, but it is one of the most adaptable of all pool fish, capable of living in total harmony with other species of fish and not causing upset to the plant life.

Goldfish can live for about 20 years and achieve a maximum length of 35cm (14in), weighing up to just over a kilogram (2¼lb). They are omnivorous, and they can tolerate high levels of acidity or alkalinity in

the water and much lower oxygen levels than most other ornamental fish. In addition, they can tolerate a wider range of temperature levels, although the optimum temperature is 22–25°C (72–77°F). Goldfish will breed easily, maturing when they are three or four years old. They prefer still, fairly shallow water, which is heavily planted. When they are very young they are almost transparent, turning brown and then the more familiar orange colour when they are about six months old.

COMET GOLDFISH

An attractive variant on the standard goldfish is the comet goldfish, which has a long body, growing to 38cm (15in), and extensive, graceful fins and tail. The comet has resulted from painstaking selections by breeders in the United States. Similar in shape to goldfish, these fish are extremely tolerant of a wide range of temperatures and can even survive in temperatures as low as 0°C (32°F). They feed at all levels in the water but need more space than the common goldfish. They are available in a variety of markings, from white to black and from gold to vermilion. Feeding with a high-protein flake brings out the red colouring.

SHUBUNKIN

The other hardy goldfish variant is the shubunkin, which is similar to the comet and available in a range of colours. The popular varieties feature mottling of black, red, purple, blue and brown under pearly scales. Extensively bred in Japan since the early years of the 20th century, the blue colorations are highly prized. They feed at all levels and will grow to 38cm (15in).

ORANDA AND BLACK MOORS

The oranda is similar to the fantail but has a more compact body, a longer tail and fins and an intriguing cap-like addition to the head. This is a delicate fish and should not be kept outdoors in winter in temperate climates.

The black moor, a black fantail, either fascinates or repels, with its extended goggle-like eyes. It is an egg-shaped fish, with a velvety-black body and long fins and tail. Black moors grow to about 12cm (4½in) long, and they feed at all levels. They should be kept indoors in winter. They belong to a large group of exotic varieties, including lionheads, celestials and red telescopes, which are mainly the province of the specialist fish-keeper in warm climates. Even in

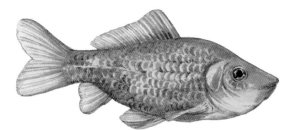

Common goldfish

Comet goldfish

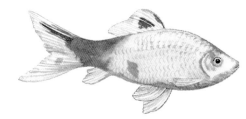

Shubunkin

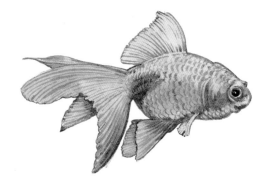

Oranda

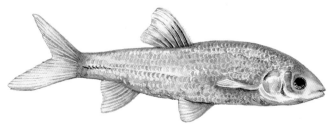

Golden orfe

Fantail

Koi

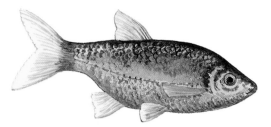

Golden rudd

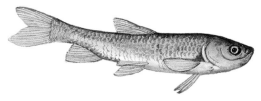

Grass carp

Minnow

Stickleback

the summer months in a temperate climate, their appendages and bulky, flowing fins make them vulnerable to predators.

GOLDEN ORFE

The golden orfe are a favourite hardy fish for pools. When viewed from above, their sleek bodies are not unlike those of a trout, and they dart quickly around the pool in shoals. For this reason, it is important that you should introduce at least four of this species if this is your choice. They do, however, need space to move quickly so they are not the most suitable fish for a very small pool. They are a surface-swimming fish, which require plenty of oxygen, and they are among the first to suffer on warm nights in summer when oxygen levels are low.

Golden orfe are golden-yellow on top with silver-white undersides. They grow to 30–50cm (12–20in) in length and live for about 15 years. They are very effective at keeping down mosquito larvae, often leaping out of the water at high speed.

FANTAIL AND CALICO FANTAIL

Less hardy but beautiful fish for warmer climates are the fantails and the calico fantails. They have rather egg-shaped bodies and seldom exceed 9cm (3½in) in length. They have long, double tails. Extremely sedate swimmers, the fantail and calico fantail can be identified by their colouring. The fantail is a golden-orange with black-and-white splashes; the calico is a multicoloured form with patches of black, blue, red, white and gold. If the water temperature falls below 15°C (59°F) these fish should be moved indoors.

KOI

A visit to the fish department of an aquatic centre will quickly reveal what has become the most popular fish in recent years. This position in the popularity stakes must go to koi, which is the Japanese word for carp. As collectors' fish, they have a bewildering classification system related to their markings, and the fancy koi are strictly known as Nishikigoi or brocaded koi. Most enthusiasts are happy to refer to them as koi, however.

This is a fish that needs a special pool if you are going to become an enthusiast for the species, rather than an enthusiast for the water garden, because the two are not always compatible. Regrettably, people's appetites are whetted by the enormous specimens they see on display at aquatic centres, where the fish have highly coloured patterns and may even take food from the visitor's hand.

Small koi might seem an appealing buy for the pool, but you should remember that these fish can grow very large and a small pool will quickly become unsuitable for them. Being carp, they are bottom-feeders and their huge mouths blow and suck around the plant roots and oxygenators, causing the water to become cloudy and the plants to be dislodged. Ideally, koi should be kept in a pool that is specially designed to meet their particular requirements – they need high, vertical side walls, a bottom drain and a filtration system in their pool.

GOLDEN RUDD

If you have an informal or wildlife pool, you might want to consider keeping golden rudd, which are ideal candidates for the conditions in this type of pool. Similar in shape to the orfe but slightly fatter, these fish are covered with rather large and coarse silvery scales. They can reach 25cm (10in) in length and can be recognized by the reddish colour of the fins. Surface-feeders and tolerant of a wide range of temperatures, golden rudd will happily breed in a pool provided there is ample vegetation.

GRASS CARP

These fish, which are mostly imported from China, have become more widely available in recent years. They have voracious appetites for soft green vegetation, such as duckweed, and, if food is short, even for blanketweed, and they should, therefore, be introduced only if soft vegetation needs to be kept under control. They are silver-grey in colour, and their wide mouths are adapted to feeding on plants. They will grow quickly to 60cm (2ft) in length, so they need a large pool. They are middle- to bottom-feeders and will thrive in temperatures of 0–20°C (32–68°F).

MINNOWS AND STICKLEBACKS

In contrast to the grass carp, these fish do not require much space, and they are ideal for small wildlife pools. Minnows grow to 8–15cm (3–6in) and prefer clear, shallow, well-oxygenated water. Male fish develop a red coloration in the mating season. Sticklebacks are about the same size and, like minnows, prefer shallow water. Do not introduce more than two couples into a small pool because they become territorial and protective of their young.

LEFT: **The patternings and markings on fish is one of the reasons that they are so popular among pool owners.**

BELOW: **Feeding fish is one of the pleasures of keeping them. These koi are waiting in keen anticipation.**

BUYING FISH

Because so many ornamental fish are imported, they can be very weak after transportation and a period in quarantine. It is sensible to search for a reliable supplier, who will have sorted out weak and damaged fish before placing his stock in display tanks for sale. A supplier who provides hygienic conditions for fish at this stage can do much to help reduce the incidence of diseases.

CHOOSING A HEALTHY FISH

The best time to buy fish is in late spring and summer, when the water temperature will be above 10°C (50°F). Try to buy in groups of six, as several fish seem to be less nervous than a single fish. Before buying, examine the fish carefully for damaged or missing scales because exposed tissue is vulnerable to infection. The larger the fish, the more likely it is that some scales will be missing because bigger fish are more aggressive in display tanks, and can damage themselves more easily.

Choose a fish that is lively. The dorsal fin should be erect, and the eyes bright. If the body shape seems slightly bent, this could be a sign of damage to the nervous system. Reject any fish that appears to be scraping itself against the bottom of the tank; this is an indication of a scale disorder. The more highly coloured the fish, the more likely it is that it has been only recently imported. If the tanks are under cover the colours will be more subdued, but the fish will be becoming more acclimatized to the quarantine conditions and therefore less vulnerable to infection.

Resist the urge to select large fish; instead, choose smaller ones, ideally 8–13cm (3–5in) long. At this size, they are not only cheaper, but will become acclimatized to new conditions more easily than larger fish.

A good supplier will place the fish in a small amount of water in a strong polythene (polyethylene) bag. Before sealing, pure oxygen will be pumped into the bag, and as long as the bag is not opened this will provide oxygen for at least 24 hours, depending on the number of fish. In warm weather get the fish home as quickly as possible because the temperature in the bag will rise very quickly. Place the bag inside a cardboard box with a lid so that light can be excluded during the journey. Keep the boxes in the boot of the car, as sunlight streaming through the windows onto the box will heat up the water. Do not lift the bag out of the box to examine the fish: this will cause unnecessary distress to the fish and possibly damage the fins.

Avoid introducing the fish to the pool immediately because the drop in temperature in the large volume of water in the pool would be a terrible shock to the fish. Instead, gently place the sealed bag on the surface of the pool and allow it to float there for a while so that the temperature inside the bag gradually matches the pool temperature. This will take about two hours.

Only then should you think about releasing the fish. Cut the neck of the bag and let in some of the pool water, then carefully let the fish escape. They will swim to the bottom, and if there is any cover in the pool they will hide. In a day or two the fish will become more inquisitive and a small amount of food can be given.

BELOW: **If handling is necessary, try to balance and secure the fish between the head and body with both hands.**

BELOW RIGHT: **After the journey from the supplier, immerse the bag in the pool for two hours to allow the temperature of the water to reach the same level as the pool before freeing the fish.**

FEEDING FISH

LEFT: **Floating pelleted food allows you to see if the fish are using up the food quickly.**

In a large, well-established pool that is amply stocked with plants and in which the number of fish does not exceed the recommended stocking rate by too much, there should be little need to give any supplementary feed. In smaller pools, however, it is important for you to provide extra food, and, to minimize pollution, the food should be carefully chosen and given in limited amounts.

WHEN TO FEED

The most important times to provide a food supplement are spring and autumn. Spring feeding boosts the fish after the winter period when they do not eat, and an autumn feed helps to build them up for winter. The water temperature plays an important part in a fish's need for food. If the water temperature is below 8°C (46°F), there is no need to feed; at this temperature the fish go into a semi-lethargic state and consume nothing. There are often mild intervals in the winter when the water temperature hovers around and sometimes exceeds this level and the fish become active. Resist the temptation to feed them as the food will remain undigested in the gut as soon as the temperature drops again.

As the temperature warms up in spring, begin feeding once a day at the same time and in the same place. Commercial preparations of suitable food have improved dramatically, particularly floating types that let you see if the food is being eaten. A high-protein food, such as floating pellets or flakes, is ideal. Give no more food than the fish can consume within five minutes. Overfeeding is not only wasteful, it will have a detrimental effect on the water chemistry, as the decomposing uneaten food will accumulate and pollute the water. Feeding little and often is generally a better approach as summer advances, and occasional treats, such as live water fleas (*Daphnia*), will be useful if the fish are breeding. Live food is often difficult to obtain, however, and supplements such as frozen shredded shrimp, dried flies and ants' eggs are often more easily obtained. Even food that is marketed principally for koi is suitable for other species if they are large enough. As the weather cools down again in autumn, gradually reduce the amount of food and use a wheatgerm pellet or flake in the cooler water.

If you have a small pool, missing feeding for a day or two will not be a problem, but arrange for a friend to feed the fish if you are to be away for a week or two.

FISH PROBLEMS

Dragonfly

Dragonfly larva
attacking a fish

Damselfly

Damselfly
larva

Great diving beetle

The majority of fish will survive and flourish happily for many years. Provided you have chosen the right type of fish and your pool is not overstocked, the fish should survive and even, in time, breed. From time to time, however, even in a well-balanced and well-maintained pool, the fish may suffer from a variety of problems, including diseases and pests.

FISH DISEASES AND OTHER PROBLEMS

Diseases are often introduced into a pool with a new fish, and this is why it is important to obtain your fish from a good supplier. Fish that are under stress because of poor environmental conditions – such as insufficient volume of water, pollution, overcrowding, lack of oxygen and insufficient or poor food – are susceptible to infection.

No matter how careful you are, however, it is almost inevitable that your fish will, at some point, be affected by disease, and the following disorders are the most common. Where practicable, home treatments are indicated. If you are in any doubt, seek the advice of the vet and do not make matters worse by incorrect handling. If you use a proprietary treatment, make sure that it is diluted with clean water as indicated by the manufacturer.

Dropsy This bacterial disease causes swollen bellies, lethargy, bristling scales and sunken or staring eyes. If the attack is very acute the fish will die rapidly, but it is often sick for several weeks before it dies. The bacteria are present in all expanses of water, and a healthy fish will produce enough antibodies to fight infection. Consult a fish specialist if you suspect this disease.

Bacteria can also be responsible for ulcers, which are easier to identify and can only be treated if they are caught very early on.

Fungal infections The most common fungus is referred to as "cotton wool fungus" or "cotton wool disease". Fungi grow on the damaged skin of weak fish and, if left untreated, the fungus is invaded by toxins and the fish dies. There is also a disease known as fin rot or tail rot, which attacks more decorative types of goldfish with long fins. The diseased area becomes ragged or bloodshot.

Both these ailments can be treated by a proprietary treatment, administered by placing the fish into a separate tank. Sea salt is sometimes recommended as an effective remedy. Small quantities of sea salt are added to the water to a level of 10g per litre (¼oz per 2 pints). When the fungus is cured, start to replace the saltwater with fresh water. Working at two-hourly intervals and using fresh water at room temperature, change one-third of the water, then one-half and then another half.

Loss of balance Occasionally a fish may be swimming on its side or suspended upside-down. Constipation through eating too much dried food of the wrong type may be the cause, but more often it is a problem of the swim bladder, the fish's balancing mechanism. The kindest answer is to kill the fish by a sharp tap on the head.

Parasites Fish seen rubbing themselves on the bottom of the pool is a sign of parasitic infection. In severe cases, the fish may secrete a grey mucus, become listless and clamp its fins close to its body. Treat individually with a proprietary treatment in a quarantine tank.

White spot The early stages of fungus infection should not be confused with this disease, which is caused by a tiny parasite. Be careful, too, not to confuse the spots with white pimples that occur on the gill plates of male fish during the mating season. The symptoms of white spot are tiny, clearly defined white spots on the body and fins. In order to ease the irritation that the spots cause, the infected fish will be seen scraping themselves on the bottom or sides of the pool. Treatment tends to be effective only if the infection is caught early. Try the proprietary treatments that can be added to the pool as a whole before resorting to one of the specialist treatments for individual fish in isolation.

A DISEASED FISH

Fish can succumb to a number of unpleasant diseases, some of which are shown here.

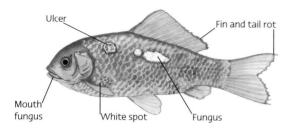

Ulcer

Fin and tail rot

Mouth fungus

White spot

Fungus

FISH PESTS

Ornamental fish are prone to attack from pests and predators from both outside and within the pool. Dense planting of strong species will deter most cats, and an overlapping paved edge will provide a hiding place for fish. More serious are birds like kingfishers and herons.

Herons The heron is a fish's most serious enemy, even in relatively built-up areas, and control against them is difficult. A standard recommendation is to surround the pool with two inconspicuous horizontal wires, one at a height of about 45cm (18in) and the other 75–90cm (30–36in), held on closely spaced canes to keep the wires taut. As the heron walks towards the pool, it should be alarmed as it reaches the water and fly off. There is a range of proprietary guards on the market, the best of which relies on a similar line held under tension. When it is touched, it releases a catch that explodes a cap to startle the bird. Decoy herons are often tried, but their guile tends to overcome all but the most skilful of defences.

Great diving beetle This is a real menace to fish fry and small species of fish. The adult beetle has a dark brown body with a distinctive gold or yellow edge and

reaches a length of 5cm (2in). It lives for nearly three years, mostly in the water. It flies only at night and survives underwater by storing oxygen in its wing cases. It preys on newts, tadpoles and small fish and is difficult to eradicate. Try to catch it in a net immediately.

Dragonfly and damselfly larvae These larvae have a scorpion-like outline and a "mask", which shoots out to catch passing fish. The green to brown nymphs can live for up to five years on the pool bottom, during which time they devour a large number of small fish with the lobster-like claws on the "mask", which they use to pull the victim into the mouthparts. The only method of control is to remove the larvae by hand, a job so unpleasant that it is seldom practised.

Water boatmen Few people realize that this insect can be an aggressive predator of small fish. Although only 10–15mm (about ½in) long, it can kill a small fish by injecting poison through its piercing mouthparts. Netting is the only effective method of control.

Whirligig beetle Another frequently seen inhabitant of the summer pool is the whirligig beetle, which can be seen in groups of 20 or more at a time. The black, oval beetles are only 3–5mm (⅛–¼in) long, and although they are air-breathing insects, they spend nearly half their lives in water. They do this by creating an air bubble to breathe as they dive for food on the pool bottom. They are too small to inflict damage on adult fish, but are a pest for fish fry. To control, net off from the surface of the water.

Water scorpion This pest lives in shallow water from which they seldom move. They are about 2.5cm (1in) long, and, being poor swimmers they remain motionless. The snorkel-like spine at the tip of the body enables them to breathe from the surface. It will grab small fish with its pincer-like legs, while the sharp mouthparts pierce the fish and kill it. Apart from removal by hand, hygiene in the small pool is the only method of control.

Leeches, lice and anchor worms These predatory creatures attach themselves to the side fins or gills. They are large enough to see with the naked eye and can be removed with tweezers. Proprietary antiseptics should always be used to disinfect small wounds after removal. There are other chemical treatments if you find yourself unable to perform these surgical tasks with tweezers.

Water boatman

Water scorpion

Whirligig beetle

Clockwise from left: Anchor worm, leech and louse

Heron

OPPOSITE: **Cotton wool fungus on the tail of a minnow.**

LEFT: **Cotton or fishing line above the water deters herons.**

An ample supply of water leads to extensive plant growth both under the water and in the shallow margins.

CARE AND MAINTENANCE

This growth dies down in winter in temperate climates and leads to a build up of rotting vegetation. Regular maintenance is thus vital in a well-stocked pool to keep a healthy balance and to prevent it becoming a reservoir of pea-green water.

OPPOSITE: **Autumn leaves on the surface of a pond create fleeting compositions, but should not be allowed to build up.**

STRUCTURAL REPAIRS

In summer evaporation will probably cause a drop in the level of the water in the pool of about 1cm (½in) a week, and in very hot weather the water loss may be even greater. There are, however, other reasons for a drop in the water level, and if your pool seems to be losing water all year round, it might be because it is damaged. The main problem with a leak is locating it. Normally, the water level will remain just below the damage, so this line becomes the starting point for detailed examination.

REPAIRING A CONCRETE POOL

Concrete pools develop hair-line cracks over the years, as the earth surrounding the pool moves slightly. A crack may extend in any direction, so it is advisable to drain the water away well below the suspect area so that the surface of the concrete can dry out thoroughly. Clean the damaged area with a wire brush or scrubbing bush and wash it thoroughly. When the surface has dried again use a thin stone chisel in order to widen and deepen the crack slightly, by tapping gently along the length of the crack. Thoroughly brush out the enlarged crack and the immediate surrounding area with a wire brush. Then fill the crack with new mortar, using a small flat-pointed trowel. Allow the mortar to dry for 48 hours and then apply a proprietary sealant.

With old concrete pools this is only likely to be a temporary improvement, and a fresh crack may occur quite soon afterwards. It is often more sensible to line the whole concrete pool with a flexible liner, which is both a long-lasting and an effective remedy and is likely to be far less costly than it may first appear, particularly when the time and trouble involved in repairing the concrete are taken into account.

REPAIRING PREFORMED POOLS

A preformed unit can succumb to irregular ground pressure around the pool by developing cracks. Fibreglass units can be repaired by using the repair kits that are sold for patching holes or cracks in motor vehicles and that contain a piece of matting, which has a mesh structure to bond the repair better. Roughen the damaged area with sandpaper and clean it thoroughly. Then apply the fibreglass matting repair to cover an area that is greater in all directions than the damaged area. Follow the instructions given with the repair kit and allow a minimum of 24 hours for the compound to dry.

REPAIRING FLEXIBLE LINERS

Modern, high-quality, flexible liners are far less prone to leaks than old concrete pools and the old-style flexible liners. Suppliers of liners also sell repair kits that make the job of patching a flexible liner quite straightforward. Black double-sided adhesive water-proof tape will be adequate for small punctures or tears in the liner. The damaged area must be thoroughly

---

FIXING A CONCRETE POOL

Hair-line cracks in concrete pools can be repaired by filling with new mortar.

1 Clean the damaged area with a wire brush and wash thoroughly. Use a stone chisel to enlarge the crack.

2 Brush out the enlarged crack thoroughly with the wire brush and fill in with fresh mortar, using a small, flat-pointed trowel.

3 Allow the fresh mortar to dry for 48 hours and then apply a proprietary sealant.

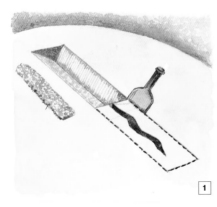

cleaned and dried: wipe it with a soft cloth dampened with spirit. Apply the tape over the hole and remove the protective cover on the tape, allowing the surface to become tacky. A patch from a spare piece of liner should then be pressed on to the tape. Make sure that the edges are well firmed. Wait at least 12 hours before refilling the pool.

If there is a watercourse or waterfall the leak may not be in the reservoir main pool but in the stream system itself. Check this by turning off the pump when the bottom pool is quite full and wait a day to see if there is any drop in the level. If the water level remains constant the leak is likely to be in the watercourse, and each individual waterfall and stream section will have to be dried out and cleaned to identify the position of the leak.

REPAIRING CLAY-LINED POOLS

Penetration by the roots of trees is the most common reason for a leak in a clay-lined pool. The shallower parts of the sides may also be suspect if the clay has been allowed to dry out in a prolonged hot spell when the water level might have dropped significantly.

The powdered form of bentonite comes into its own as a repair material for a clay lining. Finding the right place to apply it poses much the same problem as locating the leak in a flexible liner or concrete pool. Tracers such as vegetable dyes can be used to indicate the position of the leak, for there will be a higher concentration of the dye at the point of the leak if the pool is emptied. If soil covered the clay lining, it will have been eroded by the leak and could be a good clue to finding the place where the water has been leaking away. Once you have located the leak, apply an ample covering, about 8–10cm (3–4in), of bentonite powder over the suspect point and the area immediately surrounding it. Cover this with an additional 23–30cm (9–12in) of soil before reintroducing the water.

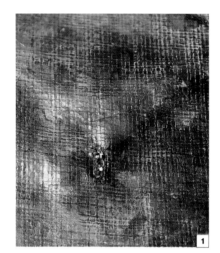
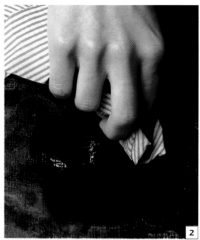

MENDING A FLEXIBLE LINER

Most modern liners are less prone to leaking than earlier makes. If a leak does occur, it is easy to repair.

1 Damage to liners, such as holes that have reached this size, will soon drain a small pond. Finer tears may need the liner lifting to the light to see the tear clearly.

2 Clean the damaged area very carefully with a cloth that has been dampened first with methylated spirits.

3 Use black, double-sided, adhesive waterproof tape to stick a small piece of liner over the tear.

FIXING A PREFORMED UNIT

Preformed units that are made from fibreglass can be easily repaired using a repair kit which is similar to that sold for patching holes or cracks in cars. The patch is made from a very thin, meshed material.

1 Clean the damaged area with a cloth that has been dampened with methylated spirits.

2 Using a large paintbrush, paint over the crack with adhesive.

3 Glue the patch over the crack and seal with a proprietary sealant.

WATER QUALITY

The colour of the water is a very good indicator of its quality. The most common problem is green water, which is associated with an excess of tiny algae feeding on mineral salts. Do not use tap water when topping up the pool because this contains high levels of salts. Collect rainwater in a butt and use this for topping up.

Water that takes on other shades, however, may be suffering from some of the less common disorders. Brown water is most often caused by the constant disturbance of the pond bottom by fish which churn up the mud and cause myriads of fine particles to be held in suspension in the water. This can be remedied by the use of pond treatments called flocculators which cause all the tiny particles to clump together and sink

to the bottom. There is little point in doing this if the fish constantly disturb the mud, so a complete clean out to remove all the organic matter on the bottom will be necessary. Alternatively, the fish can be removed or the species of fish changed. Koi will churn up the bottom and if the fish are big, the problem gets worse. If bottom mud is likely to be a permanent feature, use surface swimming fish like orfe to reduce the problem.

Very dark water or black water is mainly a sign of excess rotting vegetation on the pond bottom. Where oxygenators have not been trimmed back enough or yellow and brown waterlily leaves have not been removed, they build up and decay on the bottom. Where this is excessive the water gradually becomes

darker and blackens, and this is not possible to control by chemicals. If the matter cannot be removed, then partial water changes are the only alternative. This means changing no more than approximately one-third of the pool volume about every six weeks to reduce the concentration of brackish water in the pond.

Milky water is also a sign of some rotting organism on the bottom. The pond may be otherwise quite clean and the milkiness appears only in the summer when the water warms up. More often than not in a small pool this is caused by a dead animal, such as a frog, toad or even a rodent which may have fallen in.

Sometimes oily patches float about on the surface during the summer. This is caused by waterlily leaves dying and rotting on the surface. Remove any dying leaves as soon as they appear and then lay newspaper on the water surface to absorb the oil.

LEFT: **Algae and blanketweed can soon build up on the intake of pumps. Clean strainers and inlet holes regularly.**

BELOW: **At the first signs of autumn leaf fall, suspend a fine plastic net over the pond surface to prevent leaves sinking into the water.**

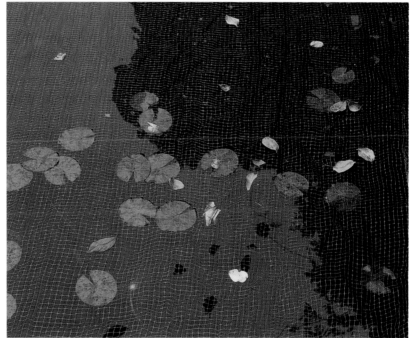

LEFT: **An overflow pipe connected from a rainwater butt to the pool is a useful way of reducing the need to use mains water when topping up.**

PLANT CONTROL

An aquatic environment is one of rapid and extensive growth, resulting in time in an overgrown pond surface if no control is practised. The main task in maintaining ponds is undoubtedly the constant cutting back of excess vegetation. In a small pond this is not too much of a burden, but in larger ponds where there is a natural bottom of mud, this is a time-consuming process. There are several submerged oxygenators like *Myriophyllum* (milfoil), which, if allowed to grow unchecked, would completely swamp a small pond in no time. Similarly there are marginals capable of forming rafts of floating roots into the deeper water, and over a number of years such ponds lose the water surface completely.

Fortunately the domestic ornamental pond makes use of aquatic containers to restrain growth, it normally has a lined bottom rather than mud, and there is the opportunity to choose the species in the pond rather than it becoming naturalized with rampant indigenous species.

Late spring can be a difficult time to keep down blanketweed as the waterlily leaves have not yet fully grown and cut down light. Consequently the clear water surface receives high intensity spring sunshine, and as the water warms up so the blanketweed capitalizes

on the conditions. Reduce as much of the growth as possible by hand using a split cane or a proprietary device with wire coils on the end of a long shank. Even if the blanketweed is to be treated chemically, it is best to remove as much as possible first as its rapid death can lead to a shortage of oxygen in the water when large masses decompose.

TOP RIGHT: **Numerous tiny creatures live in blanketweed, and the removed weed should be left at the side for a while until the creatures can escape and return to the water.**

RIGHT: **To clear water of blanketweed, insert a cane into the water and twist it to wind the weed around it, rather like candyfloss.**

As the summer progresses the submerged oxygenators, which enjoy the warmer water, try to reach the sunlight and can spread quickly across the water surface. As they have such poor root systems, they can be removed by tools such as wire rakes which catch the stems. In smaller ponds where this would be too severe they can be simply cut back with shears.

The free-floating plants on small ponds are much easier to remove and you will find that a large net will be adequate for the job. Floaters such as the water soldier (*Stratiotes*) are more of a problem in that they sink partially during part of their life cycle and are therefore more difficult to reach and net out in the deeper water.

ABOVE: **Oxygenators and floaters can soon take over small ponds. Keep removing excess growth with a net.**

ABOVE LEFT: **Duckweed or other floaters can be useful initially in preventing green water, but they soon spread and need constant thinning.**

LEFT: **When oxygenating plants become congested, lift out clumps and tear them apart, returning about a half to two-thirds to the water.**

FAR LEFT: **Remove duckweed before it has a chance to spread. You will need to check for it on a regular basis.**

CLEANING OUT THE POOL

RIGHT: **Waterlily** leaves thrusting in dense clusters above the water surface are a sure sign that the plant needs lifting and dividing.

Even if you follow a regular maintanance programme, the pool will need to be completely cleaned out every few years, depending on its style, size and site. There will, inevitably, be an accumulation of mulm on the pool bottom, submerged plants and waterlilies become overgrown, and marginals will benefit from being divided and given a new start. The process of cleaning out the pool will, however, mean that the balance of life achieved over the years is going to be severely disrupted, and everything should be done to renew the harmony that was achieved.

The timing of the operation is the first important decision. If it is tackled too early in the spring, there is a risk of harming overwintering amphibians or young hatching offspring that are not old enough to fend for themselves. If it is tackled too late in the autumn, plants and creatures may not have time to recover before winter. Cleaning out a pool in midwinter would cause a great deal of damage by disturbing hibernating creatures.

THE POOL CLEAN-OUT

A pool needs to be cleaned out every few years in addition to following your normal maintenance programme. The best time to carry out this task is mid- to late summer. The following points should serve as a helpful step-by-step sequence for completely overhauling your pond:

- Start pumping out the water, filling a temporary pool for any fish
- Begin to net any fish before there is too much disturbance to the pool
- Remove containers of marginals from the shelves. They will not need immersing in the temporary pool provided they are not out of the water for more than two or three days
- Net out the remaining fish as the water gets shallower and before the mud gets too disturbed on the bottom. Start the aerator in the temporary pool and place a net over the top

- Lift out the containers from the bottom of the pool. These can be extremely heavy and may need sliding out over the edge; take care that you do not damage the flexible liner when you are doing this. If you have waterlilies or other deep-water aquatics, cover the leaves with wet newspaper while they are left standing at the side of the pool. Remove healthy young growth of the oxygenators and submerge in containers at the side
- As soon as it is difficult for the pump to operate, bale out the remaining water and mud. Keep about half a bucket of mud to reintroduce a small amount of microscopic life into the clean pool
- Rinse and brush the sides. Check for any possible damage to the liner and, if necessary, reinforce with patches of repair tape

- Divide and repot the waterlilies, using fresh aquatic compost (soil mix)
- Begin to refill the pool as soon as possible in order to return the fish, waterlilies and freshly planted cuttings of the oxygenators back into the pool.
- Return the fish, some of the old mud and the old pool water from the temporary pool
- Divide and repot the marginals and replace them on the marginal shelves
- Do not fill the pool to the very top until the new leaves from the waterlilies reach the surface; alternatively, place some temporary bricks under the containers until the plants are growing again, when the bricks can be removed
- Scatter ample floating-leaved plants on the surface of the pool in order to create shade for a few weeks when the balance of the pool will be returning to normal

This leaves mid- to late summer as the time when least damage will be done, and it allows plants to become re-established before the onset of winter.

The main problem with carrying out the work in summer will be the temporary care of the fish during what might be a hot spell. Adequate measures for their temporary housing should be planned well in advance, and every effort must be made to maintain adequate oxygen levels, even if this means using a small aerating block in the short-term accommodation. Depending on the size and quantity of the fish, children's paddling pools make good temporary housing, and a net placed across the top will prevent a cat or heron from exploiting the vulnerable fish and the fish from leaping out in fear. If possible, choose an overcast day: this is a hot and smelly job, and there will be less stress to plants and fish if it is cool.

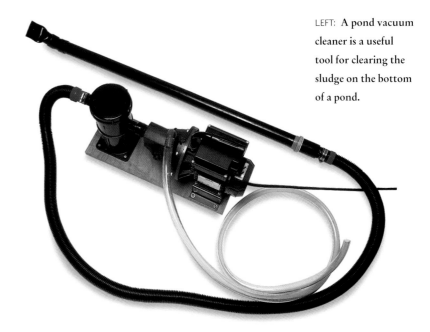

LEFT: **A pond vacuum cleaner is a useful tool for clearing the sludge on the bottom of a pond.**

PROTECTING POND PUMPS

If you leave a pump in your pond over winter, ice may damage it, so store it in a dry place, rather than simply take it out of the pond and leave it where moisture can enter.

1 Remove submersible pumps from the water before penetrating frosts cause the water to freeze deeply.

2 Clean the pump before you put it away. It will probably be covered with algae which can be scrubbed off.

3 Remove the filter and either replace it or clean it. Follow the instructions provided by the manufacturer.

4 Make sure all the water is drained from the pump. If your pump is an external one, make sure the system is drained.

5 Read the manufacturer's instructions, and carry out any other servicing that is necessary before storing the pump in a dry place. It may be necesssary to send it away for a service, in which case do it now instead of waiting until spring.

CALENDAR OF CARE

It would be misleading to suggest that introducing a pool into the garden is an easy option, but the ever-changing delights of the pool and its plants combined with the wildlife both within the water and attracted to it make any extra work more than worth it. Once your pool is built and the plants are established, the work needed to keep it looking its best soon becomes routine, and the main seasonal tasks are summarized here.

SPRING

• If an electric heater has been kept in the pool for the winter, it can be removed now and the filter started up if it was turned off for the winter.
• Any brown stems left on marginal and moisture-loving plants for winter attraction or protection for shy creatures can be cut back. Ornamental grasses should be pruned to just above the new green shoots.
• Plant any new moisture-loving plants or alpines.
• Herons are at their hungriest in spring, so take the necessary precautions to protect fish.
• Start feeding the fish again, offering small quantities of a high-protein food as soon as the watertemperature climbs above 10°C (50°F). Check the fish for any disorders to which they may have succumbed in winter.
• Clean off algae from paved or wooden surfaces.
• Protect sensitive plants, such as skunk cabbage (*Lysichiton*); by placing horticultural fleece over the flowers if late frosts are forecast. The young growth of plants, such as giant rhubarb (*Gunnera manicata*), should have a protective covering of dead leaves until all danger of frosts has passed.
• Cut back the shoots of coppiced waterside shrubs, such as dogwoods (*Cornus*) and the coloured-stemmed willow (*Salix*).
• The young growth of tender marginals such as *Mimulus* and *Lobelia*, which has been protected by thick organic mulches, will be sprouting. Lift the plants and divide them or take cuttings of the young shoots and root them in a frost-free greenhouse.
• Strong spring sunshine could spark off algal growth in shallow pools where the surface is clear until the waterlily leaves begin to grow. This should correct itself as the surface leaves develop.

SUMMER

• Now is a good time to propagate any plants that have become overgrown or if extra plants are needed.
• Everything should be in full growth, particularly the oxygenators. Keep cutting these back so that the submerged shoots do not spread to the surface and become overgrown.
• Pests such as blackfly or thrips on waterlily leaves can be jetted off with a strong hose.
• Some sappy marginals, such as marsh marigolds (*Caltha palustris*), develop mildew in early summer.

BELOW: **In spring, prune shrubs, such as dogwood (*Cornus*), which grow by the side of the water.**

BELOW RIGHT: **Summer is a good time to propagate any plants that have become overgrown or if you need more plants for a pond.**

Cut off affected leaves completely; they will soon grow again.

• Fish are very active now, but do not be tempted to overfeed. Feed little and often, and never with more than they can eat in five minutes.

• Slow-release pellets or sachets of fertilizer are sold for aquatics, particularly waterlilies. Push these just under the surface of the compost (soil mix).

• The meshes on submersible pumps will clog quickly if there is any blanketweed near the pump. Check regularly to keep this clear because it reduces the efficiency of the pump.

• If there are fish in the pool, keep the pump running for watercourses or fountains on hot nights to help maintain oxygen levels. If there is no pump, spray the surface of the water with a hosepipe.

• Remove blanketweed so that it does not develop into thick mats, which can entangle small fish.

• Tender floating plants, such as water hyacinth (*Eichhornia*) and water lettuce (*Pistia*), can be introduced to add interest.

AUTUMN

• Thin out and cut back the oxygenators because this growth will rot in the water over winter causing deoxygenation and pollution.

• If the weather continues to be warm, fish should be offered a high-fibre food such as wheatgerm pellets until the water temperature drops to 10°C (50°F).

• Protect frost-tender marginals by providing a heavy, organic mulch over the crowns. As the first frosts blacken large-leaved plants such as *Rheum* and *Gunnera*, lay the plants' own blackened leaves and other dead leaves over the crowns of the plants to protect them for the winter.

• Net the surface of the pool to prevent autumn leaves from blowing into the water.

• Remove tender floating plants and store them indoors in a frost-free place on compost (soil mix) that is kept saturated.

WINTER

• If the winter is severe ice can be a problem if it covers the pool for prolonged periods. Methane gas, which is given off by decomposing vegetation, forms under the surface of the ice instead of being released to the atmosphere, and, because it is unable to escape, the methane is reabsorbed by the water, which becomes toxic to the fish. Use an electric

heater to keep a small circle of the pool's surface free of ice. Alternatively, place a hot pan on the ice until it melts a hole and repeat this daily until the ice thaws. Never break the ice by smashing through with a hammer, as this causes shock waves in the water that can damage the torpid fish.

• The expansion of thick ice can damage the sides of the pool. A pool with vertical side walls is more likely to be damaged than one with sloping sides. Placing objects such as spongy balls or pieces of wood in the water helps to absorb the pressure.

• If the pump is still operating a watercourse, lift it from the bottom so that it circulates colder water near the surface and does not disturb the beneficial layer of warmer water at the bottom of the pool.

• If spells of mild weather trigger activity by the fish do not be tempted to feed them.

• Brush snow off the ice to allow light into the pool.

• If there are long periods of drying winds that cause the level of the pool to drop it is as important to top up in these periods as it is in the summer.

• Net off any stray leaves that fall in the pool in gales.

• The dwarfer forms of waterlily may be damaged by severe cold in shallow pools. Remove them to a frost-free container full of water until the weather improves.

ABOVE: **Ice forming on the surface should not be allowed to persist for long periods without an air hole if fish are present.**

SUPPLIERS

UNITED KINGDOM

General distributors of a wide range of water garden products

Blagden Water Gardens
Bath Road
Upper Langford
North Somerset BS18 7DN
Tel: 01934 853531

Bradshaws
Nicolson Link
Clifton Moor
York YO1 1SS
Tel: 01904 691169

Heissner UK Ltd.
Regency Business Centre
Queens Road
Kenilworth
Warwickshire CV8 1JQ
Tel: 01926 851166
Fax: 01926 851151
email: heissner@regency
businesscentre.co.uk

Hozelock Cyprio Ltd.
Waterslade House
Haddenham
Aylesbury
Buckinghamshire HP17 8JD
Tel: 01844 291881

Lotus Water Garden Products
P.O. Box 36
Junction Street
Burnley
Lancashire BB12 ONA
Tel: 01282 420771

Oase (UK) Ltd.
3 Telford Gate
Whittle Road
West Portway Industrial Estate
Andover
Hampshire SP10 3SF
Tel: 01264 333225

Stapeley Water Gardens Ltd.
London Road
Stapeley
Nantwich
Cheshire
CW5 7LH
Tel: 01270 623868

Trident Water Garden Products
Carlton Road
Folehill
Coventry CV6 7FL
Tel: 024 7663 8802

Specialist Suppliers

Civil Engineering Developments Ltd.
728 London Road
West Thurrock
Grays
Essex RM16 1LU
Tel: 01708 867237
Rock supplier

Interpret
Interpret House
Vincent Lane
Dorking
Surrey RH4 3YX
Tel: 01306 881033
Fish foods and medicines

Pinks Hill Landscape Merchants
Broad Street
Wood Street Village
Guildford
Surrey
Tel: 01483 571620
Rock supplier

Rein Ltd.
Clifton Hall
Ashbourne
Derbyshire DE6 2GL
Tel: 01335 342265
Reinforced fibres for mortar

Tetra
Lambert Court
Chestnut Avenue
Eastleigh
Hampshire SO53 3ZQ
Tel: 023 8064 3339
Fish foods and medicines

Volclay Limited
Leonard House
Scotts Quay
Birkenhead
Merseyside L41 1FB
Tel: 0151 638 0967
Clay liners

Wychwood Waterlily and Carp Farm
Farnham Road
Odiham
Hook
Hampshire RG29 1HS
Tel: 0256 702800
Fish supplier

UNITED STATES

General distributors of a wide range of water garden products

Hyannis Country Garden
380 West Main Street
Hyannis, MA 02601
www.gardengoods.com

M&S Ponds and Supplies
14053 Midland Road
Poway, CA 92064
Tel: (858) 679-8729
Fax: (858) 679-5804

North American Rock Garden Society
P.O. Box 67
Millwood, NY 10546
www.hubris.net/nargs.org

Speciality Suppliers

Garden Rock Covers
P.O. Box 1133
Friday Harbor, WA98250
www.gardenrockcovers.com

Select Stone Inc.
P.O. Box 6403
Bozeman, MT 59771
Tel: (406) 582-1000
Fax: (406) 582-1069
www.selectstone.com

Sticks and Stones Farm
197 Huntingtown Road
Newtown, CT 06470
www.sticksandstonesfarm.com

CANADA

Aquascape Ontario
9295 Colborne Street Ext
Chatham
ON N7M 5J4
Tel: (888) 547-POND
Fax: (519) 352-1357

Aquatics & Co.
Box 445
Pickering, ON N7M 5J4
Tel: (905) 668-5326
Fax: (905) 668-4518
www.aquaticsco.com

Burns Water Gardens
RR2, 2419 Van Luven Road
Baltimore, ON K0K 1C0
Tel: (905) 372-2737
Fax: (905) 372-8625
www.eagle.ca/-wtrgdn

Picov's Water Garden Centre
and Fisheries
380 Kingston Road East
Ajax, ON L1S 4S7
Tel: (905) 686-2151
Fax: (905) 686-2183
www.picovs.com

Water Arts Inc.
4158 Dundas Street West
Etoklcoke, ON M8X 1X3
Tel: (416) 239-5345
Fax: (416) 237-1098

AUSTRALIA

Classic Garden Products
18 Baretta Road
Wangara, WA 6065
Tel: (61) 8 9409 6101

Diamond Valley Garden Centre
170 Yan Yea Road
Plenty Vic 3090
Tel: (61) 3 9432 5113

Ponds & Pumps
6 Parkview Drive
Archerfield Qld 4107
Tel: (61) 7 3276 7666

Universal Rocks
39 Stanley Street
Peakhurst NSW 2210
Tel: (61) 2 9533 7400

Waterproofing Technologies
Level 1, 210 Homer Street
Earlwood, NSW 2206
Tel: (61) 2 9558 2161
Pond liners

INDEX

ACKNOWLEDGEMENTS

All the pictures in this book were taken by Peter Anderson with the exception of the following:

KEY   l = left r = right t = top b = bottom c = centre
Jonathan Buckley: 17 (Chelsea 2000); 69b; 71t; 85b (Chelsea 2000); 162 (Chelsea 2000); 208t; 201br; 214 (all); 215 (all); 220t; 220br; 221bl and br; 222tl and tr; 223tl; 223tc; 223b; 252 (Chelsea 2000). **Sarah Cuttle:** 43br; 95; 102 (designer: Simon Harman); 108 (Hampton Court 2000); 120 (Longstock Water Gardens); 155; 174l; 183bl; 187bl; 189tl; 195b; 197bl; 201bl; 206br; 248br (Hampton Court 2000); 250; 254 (Tatton Park Flower Show 2000). **Simon McBride:** 221tr; 251. **Jo Whitworth:** 15; 37tr; 50; 51b; 55bl; 94; 112r.

The publishers would like to thank the following picture agencies and photographers for kindly allowing their images to be reproduced in this book:

Heather Angel: 236br. **A–Z Botanical Collection:** 8 (Adrian Thomas); 93tr (P. Etchells) **BBC Natural History Unit Picture Library:** 184r (Jeff Foott); 192b (Doug Wechsler); 220bl (Duncan McEwan). **Jonathan Buckley:** 8 (Glen Chantry, Essex); 195tl (Great Dixter, East Sussex); 203tr (Upper Mill Cottage, Kent); 203bl (Great Dixter, East Sussex); 205bl (Beth Chatto Gardens, Essex); 207tr (Great Dixter, East Sussex); 209br (Susan Sharkey's garden, Brentford); 211tc (Great Dixter, East Sussex). **Elizabeth Whiting Associates:** 20l; 21b. **FLPA:** 177l and r (Anthony Wharton); 229b (Linda Lewis). **Garden Exposures Picture Library:** photography copyright Andrea Jones 32t; 56b (designer: Christopher Bradley-Hole, Chelsea 2000); 58 (James Davidson Lighting Design); 74 (Chelsea 2000). **The Garden Picture Library:** 10 (Ron Sutherland); 20t (Geoff Dawn); 25tr (John Glover); 32b (Ron Sutherland); 33 (Vaughn Fleming); 37l (Sunniva Harte); 42 (Eric Crichton); 43t (Lamontagne); 43bl (John Glover); 48 (Ron Sutherland); 57b (Ron Sutherland); 60 (Ron Sutherland); 65t (Ron Sutherland); 67t (Ron Sutherland); 67b (Bob Challinor); 68 (Ron Sutherland); 69t (Gary Rogers); 71b (JS Sira); 72 (John Glover); 75t (Howard Rice); 76 (Tim Griffith); 77t (John Glover); 77c (Martine Mouchy); 78 (Mayer/Le Scanff); 80 (Marie O'Hara); 85t (Marie O'Hara); 86 (Bob

Challinor); 87 (JS Sira); 90 (Christi Carter); 106 (Ron Sutherland); 112tl (David Askham); 112b (John Glover); 122t (Juliet Greene); 122b (Michael Paul); 124 (Christi Carter); 148t (Ron Sutherland); 148b (Ron Sutherland); 150 (Mayer/Le Scanff); 184l (Howard Rice); 185bl (Vaughn Fleming); 185br (Howard Rice); 193tl (Jerry Pavia); 193tr (Eric Crichton); 193b (Howard Rice); 195tr (Jerry Pavia); 198tl (Geoff Dawn); 198b (Jerry Pavia); 199b (Eric Crichton); 200tl (Sunniva Harte); 200b (Ron Sutherland); 202tl (Brian Carter); 202tr (Eric Crichton); 202br (John Glover); 203tl (JS Sira); 204bl (John Glover); 205tr (John Glover); 205bl (JS Sira); 205br (Sunniva Harte); 206bl (John Glover); 208b (Jacqui Hurst); 209bl (Mark Bolton); 210tl (Philippe Bonduel); 210tr (Neil Holmes); 211tr (Marijke Heuff); 216br (Didier Willery); 217tl (John Glover); 219tl (John Glover); 221tl (JS Sira); 228 (Ron Sutherland); 230 (Bob Challinor); 233b (Juliet Greene); 238 (Michael Paul); 249 (Didier Willery). **Garden & Wildlife Matters:** 14t and b; 16t and b; 25br; 77b; 84l; 88; 118; 121b. **S & O Mathews:** 20b; 53t; 91bl; 92; 121t. **Peter McHoy:** 103tl; 109 (all). **NHPA:** 176l and r (Stephen Dalton); 180bl (Martin Garwood); 182br (Martin Garwood); 183 (Hellio & Van Ingen). **Hugh Palmer:** 6; 52bl; 82. **Photos Horticultural:** 59; 142 (Lambeth Horticultural Society); 146 (MJK/The Bonsai Nursery, Cornwall).

The publishers would like to give special thanks to Heissner UK for lending the majority of materials and equipment featured in this book. Heissner can be contacted at The New Regency Business Centre, Common Lane Industrial Estate, Kenilworth, Warwickshire CV8 2EL (tel: 01926 851166).

The publishers would also like to thank the following garden owners for kindly allowing their gardens to be photographed:
Mr. and Mrs. D. Anderson, Suffolk; Mr. and Mrs. R. Baxter, Suffolk; Mrs. G. Calder, Suffolk; Mr. and Mrs. A. Cooper, Suffolk; Docton Mill, Devon; Mrs. B. Gillot, Suffolk; Tim Gittins, Yorkshire; Mr. and Mrs. J. Hale, Suffolk; Marwood Hill, Devon; Mill Water Gardens, Hampshire; Mrs. J. Piercy, Suffolk; Pinks Hill Landscape Merchants, Guildford; Mr and Mrs P. Robinson, Suffolk; Rosemary Rogers, Yorkshire; Rowden Nurseries, Devon; The Royal Botanic Gardens, Kew; Mr. and Mrs. P. Savage, Suffolk; Mr. and Mrs. R. Wilton, Suffolk.